THE SOCIAL PSYCHOLOGY
OF AGGRESSION

To Justin

The Social Psychology of Aggression

Barbara Krahé
University of Potsdam

Published in 2001 by Psychology Press Ltd
27 Church Road, Hove, East Sussex, BN3 2FA

www.psypress.co.uk

Simultaneously published in the USA and Canada
by Taylor & Francis Inc
325 Chestnut Street, Suite 800, Philadelphia, PA 19106

Psychology Press is part of the Taylor & Francis Group

British Library Cataloguing in Publication Data
A catalogue record for this book is available from the British Library

Library of Congress Cataloging-in-Publication Data
Krahé, Barbara.
    The social psychology of aggression / Barbara Krahé.
        p. cm. — (Social psychology, ISSN 1368-4574)
    Includes bibliographical references and index.
    ISBN 0-86377-775-9 – 0-86377-776-7 (pbk.)
        1. Aggressiveness. I. Title. II. Social psychology (Philadelphia, Pa.)

    HM1116.K37 2001
    302.5'4—dc21   00-046028

    ISBN 0-86377-775-9 (hbk) 0-86377-776-7 (pbk)
    ISSN 1368-4574 (Social Psychology: A Modular Course)

Cover design by Joyce Chester
Cover illustration: *Violence*, used with permission from dpa
Typeset in Palatino by Mayhew Typesetting, Rhayader, Powys
Printed and bound in the UK by TJ International Ltd, Padstow, Cornwall

Contents

Preface

Writing this book has been both a challenge and a pleasure: a challenge, because of the sheer volume of new and exciting research on the various aspects of aggression that needed to be considered; a pleasure because it provided an opportunity to look beyond the confines of my immediate research interests and "exploit" the excellent work of other specialised researchers. The richness and quality of the material that I encountered dealing with all the different issues of the fascinating, albeit depressing, subject of aggression gave a new boost to my enthusiasm for social psychology. It also raised my confidence that social psychological research has a real contribution to offer to the solution of pressing social problems, both by explaining their causes and origins and by highlighting avenues for prevention. I hope that at least some of that enthusiasm and confidence comes across to the readers and will eventually be shared by them.

In completing this book, I have received valuable support and encouragement from a number of colleagues and friends. I am indebted to Hans-Werner Bierhoff, Jeff Bryson, and Brad Bushman for their constructive feedback on the manuscript, which greatly helped to improve its clarity and precision. I would like to thank Evelyn Fischer, Steffen Bieneck, Ingrid Möller, and Sabine Quandte for their help in preparing the final manuscript. Thanks are also due to Rachel Brazil and Mandy Collison at Psychology Press for the competence with which they steered the book to its final stage and appearance. I am particularly grateful to Barbara Lloyd for many stimulating meetings and discussions in a pleasant environment and to Jannet King for providing much-appreciated breaks and conversations during the phase of solitary confinement necessary to complete the book in time. Finally, special thanks go to my husband Peter for his continuous support and encouragement and to my children Charlotte and Justin for all those hours of "silent reading time".

Introduction

On Brighton's Palace Pier, one of the many amusement piers which are greatly popular in seaside resorts all along the British coast, visitors can enjoy in a leisurely way an entertainment device called the *Real Puncher*. This ingeniously designed machine enables them to work out their aggressive impulses in a carefully designed sequence of events.

Just take a moment to picture yourself in front of the *Real Puncher*, having inserted a £1 coin (this would have done in March 2000; rates may well have gone up since).

First, you are asked to position yourself in front of the machine so that a picture of your face can be taken by a mounted camera. This picture is then digitalised and displayed on a large colour screen.

As soon as your digitalised portrait appears, you are asked to don two large boxing gloves and punch your photographed face as hard as you can by slamming on a pad. Please note the special instructions on how to deliver the blow without injuring your fists and wrists!

The effects of the punch to your face are graphically displayed on the screen and, in case you haven't taken it in properly, accompanied by a message of success printed in large letters underneath: DEFORMED!

Special thrill is to be gained from the game if played in the two-player mode, in which case the portraits of both players are digitalised and the "partners" can take turns deforming each other's faces.

What does this piece of equipment for an amusement arcade have to do in the introduction of a book on aggression research? When I first encountered the *Real Puncher* in the early planning stages of this volume, it struck me that it nicely, if inadvertently, illustrates a variety of aspects involved in the social psychological study of aggression. First, it simulates a behaviour that is intended to inflict harm or injury on a person and thus meets a core criterion in the definition of aggressive behaviour. Second, it reflects the extent to which aggression is part and parcel of our daily lives in that the deformation—albeit in a virtual reality—of one's own and others' facial features is presented as an acceptable and enjoyable leisure activity. In so doing, it touches upon the controversial issue of fictitious aggression in the media and its effects on viewers' aggressive tendencies. By providing an opportunity for "real action", it even surpasses media depictions of aggression that confine the viewer to the passive role of recipient. Furthermore, its entertainment value is predicated on the assumption that the release of destructive impulses through the act of punching is a pleasurable experience for which people are willing to pay. Finally, the fact that the *Real Puncher* is accessible to the general public of all age groups reflects a consensus, at least among the regulating authorities, that no harmful effects result from releasing destructive impulses in this way—provided the warnings are observed about protecting wrists and fists. Looming behind these last two aspects is the notion of *catharsis* inherent in both psychoanalytic thinking and common-sense discourse, which regards the imaginary or "innocuous" release of destructive energy as an effective way of controlling aggression. As we shall see, however, this view is fundamentally challenged by social cognitive models of aggressive behaviour.

These are but some of the aspects addressed by social psychological research on aggression to be presented in this volume. Given the complexity of human aggression, it is self-evident that no single psychological discipline can offer a comprehensive understanding of its manifestations, causes and consequences. Therefore, it is important to stress at the outset the issues that are at the focus of a *social* psychological perspective on aggression as well as to mention those aspects that fall primarily into the realm of other fields.

From a social psychological point of view, aggression is conceptualised as a particular form of social behaviour that is both shaped by an individual's social world and has effects on that social world and its inhabitants. Therefore, in terms of looking at *manifestations* of aggression, the focus will be on aggressive behaviour occurring in social relationships between individuals and/or groups. This means that other forms of aggression, such as self-destructive behaviour, psychopathological forms of aggression or destructive behaviour against material objects, will not be given special consideration. Similarly, in terms of *explaining* the occurrence of aggressive behaviour, the focus will be on social factors, such as socialisation experiences, situational context variables and social information processing and their interactions with individual dispositions. Other causal influences, such as hormonal and neurophysiological processes, are given less weight, not because they are deemed less relevant but because they focus on non-social determinants of aggression. They are, however, given comprehensive coverage in other recent reviews (e.g., Bond, Lader, & Da Silveira, 1997; Renfrew, 1997). Finally, our examination of the *consequences* of aggression will also be concentrated on the social functioning of both victims and perpetrators in the context of their interpersonal relationships, excluding such issues as the forensic or psychiatric treatment of aggressive offenders and clinical help for target persons of aggressive behaviour in coping with their victimisation.

Moreover, it seems appropriate at this point to try and locate the present volume in the current landscape of the literature on aggression. For those who look for a comprehensive and in-depth coverage of social psychological aggression research, excellent volumes are available with which the present volume neither can, nor aspires to, compete (Baron & Richardson, 1994; Berkowitz, 1993; Geen & Donnerstein, 1998; Tedeschi & Felson, 1994). On the other hand, readers looking for a summary of the main issues and findings of aggression research will find a pertinent chapter in every textbook of social psychology. The present volume is designed to take an intermediate position between these two levels of specificity. Its aim is to provide an up-to-date and critical overview of aggression research from a social psychological perspective to inform readers about the central concepts, issues, and findings in the study of aggression. Moreover, it is intended to create a knowledge base from which more specialised literature dealing with complex issues and research programmes can be approached (e.g., Feshbach & Zagrodzka, 1997; Huesmann, 1994; Potegal & Knutson, 1994). Because of the availability of several excellent earlier volumes, one priority of the present volume is to concentrate on the most recent research not covered by these previous sources. As the reader will notice, a large proportion of studies quoted in this book were published in the second half of the 1990s and thus represent the current state of social psychological knowledge on aggression, its causes, and its consequences.

The topics addressed in this volume reflect the fact that progress in aggression research has been stimulated by two distinct but complementary sources. On the one hand, there has been a long-standing theoretical interest in how to conceptualise, explain, and predict the occurrence of aggression as a particular form of (anti)social behaviour. On the other hand, applied psychologists and practitioners in a wide range of fields have become increasingly concerned about the damaging effects of aggression on individuals, groups, and society at large. They have been looking to psychology in general and social psychology in particular for guidance in the search for a systematic understanding of the incidence and determinants of aggressive behaviour as well as for the development of successful intervention strategies. The challenge to psychology of providing a sound and systematic knowledge base for tackling the problems of aggression and violence has recently been picked up by the two major professional organisations in psychology. It has stimulated the development of a "behavioral science research plan for violence" as part of the *Human Capital Initiative* launched by the American Psychological Society (1997) and also features prominently in the *Decade of Behavior* campaign initiated by the American Psychological Association (Azar, 1998). These initiatives are built on the conviction that

> basic research should be aimed at obtaining a better understanding of the causes of violent behavior. [. . .] Applied prevention research should be directed at developing the tools to prevent and treat violent behavior within the framework of knowledge on causation provided by basic research. (American Psychological Society, 1997, p. 5)

The dual role of social psychological aggression research as a basic and an applied discipline is reflected in the organisation of the present volume: In the first five chapters, basic issues of definition, measurement, and explanation will be discussed that are of general significance to the understanding of aggressive behaviour irrespective of its specific manifestations. In *Chapter 1*, issues of defining and measuring aggression will be discussed to provide a platform for presenting research findings based on different conceptualisations and methodologies. The advantages and limitations of studying aggression in the artificially created settings of the psychological laboratory or in the realistic contexts of naturally occurring situations play an important part in this discussion. *Chapter 2* presents an overview of theories explaining aggressive behaviour, dividing them into approaches that stress the biological foundations of aggressive behaviour and those that explain aggression as the result of psychological processes. It will become clear that there is a considerable diversity of views on the causes of individuals' aggressive response tendencies and the processes that lead to aggressive behaviour.

Chapter 3 is concerned with the development of individual differences in aggressive behaviour and the stability of such differences in aggression over the lifespan. These issues are important because common-sense discourse is quick to point to adverse social conditions, such as poverty, media influences, or poor parent–child relationships, as explanations of aggression and violence without paying sufficient attention to the fact that not all individuals exposed to these adverse conditions show the same response to them. Furthermore, gender will be discussed as another variable associated with stable individual differences in aggression. Traditionally, the working hypothesis underlying this line of research has been that men are more aggressive than women. This has led to a focus on male aggression and an almost total neglect of women's aggressive behaviour. There are signs, however, of an increasing interest in female aggression, stimulated in part by a perceived increase in female participation in domestic violence and by a growing number of girls involved in juvenile delinquency.

In *Chapter 4*, situational factors will be discussed that are assumed to facilitate aggression. The discussion includes the role of aggressive cues enhancing the salience of aggression as a potential response, the disinhibiting effects of alcohol, and the role of living conditions, such as spatial density and high temperature. Throughout this chapter, it will be shown that no matter how powerful situational factors are as determinants of behaviour, they do not affect individuals in a uniform way. Therefore, for a proper assessment of the determinants of aggression, the impact of situational factors needs to be considered in interaction with individual difference variables.

Both short-term and long-term factors enhancing the probability of aggressive behaviour are addressed in *Chapter 5*, which is devoted to the effects of violent media contents on viewers' aggressive tendencies. This chapter picks up an issue that has attracted intense controversy, particularly in public debate and in confrontation between social scientists and the media industry. Two aspects will be at the focus of the analysis: (a) a discussion of the evidence addressing the general question of whether exposure to aggressive media contents leads to increased aggression in viewers, in particular children and adolescents; and (b) an examination of the role of pornography as a causal factor in aggression generally and sexual aggression in particular.

In sum, the first five chapters provide a review of issues that belong to the standard repertoire of any introductory text on aggression. They are indispensable for providing a comprehensive picture of the state of knowledge in aggression research and for establishing an understanding of basic concepts and processes against which to look at specific forms of aggressive behaviour. Examining these manifestations of aggressive behaviour in different social domains, which—with the possible exception of sexual aggression—go largely unmentioned in the textbook literature, will be the objective of the second part of the book.

The next three chapters are devoted to specific manifestations of aggression in society. Despite common underlying mechanisms in the manifestation of aggression in a variety of contexts (such as the imitation of aggressive role models), more specific explanations are required to understand different forms of aggressive behaviour. Thus, the dynamics of intergroup behaviour are essential to understand gang violence, and sexual aggression cannot be properly understood without taking gender socialisation and prevailing sex role stereotypes into account.

In *Chapter 6*, different forms of aggression will be examined that take place in the public sphere and, unfortunately, are part and parcel of everyday life: bullying at school and at the workplace, aggression motivated by ethnic prejudice and political interests, and aggression arising out of confrontations between hostile groups, such as football hooliganism or gang fighting. In addition, this chapter will review evidence on homicide as the most extreme form of aggression.

Chapter 7 deals with aggression in a domestic context and covers issues such as child abuse, spouse battering, and elder abuse. Unlike aggression in the public domain, these forms of aggressive behaviour occur in the confined sphere of the home, making it easier for perpetrators to conceal their aggression and more difficult for their victims to attract attention to their plight. At the same time, they are particularly traumatising because they involve a breach of trust by the very people the victims love and depend on.

The same holds true for sexual aggression, which is the topic of *Chapter 8*. The majority of sexual assaults take place between individuals who know each other, often in the context of dating relationships. We will review a rapidly growing body of evidence that has established the widespread prevalence of sexual aggression in different populations. Moreover, research will be presented that examined causal explanations of male sexual aggression, and identified risk markers of female sexual victimisation in the form of behavioural patterns and biographical variables associated with an increased risk of victimisation. Finally, the chapter will discuss evidence on the consequences of sexual assault for the victim and briefly explore a new and controversial issue on the agenda of sexual aggression research: women's sexual aggression against men.

The last chapter, *Chapter 9*, will be devoted to strategies aimed at controlling and preventing aggressive behaviour. Given the scope of aggression and violence, stopping individuals and groups from acting aggressively towards others is a daunting task and, as annual crime statistics reveal, success has so far been limited. First, proposals for controlling aggression will be reviewed that refer to general principles of intervention potentially applicable to many forms of aggressive behaviour. In terms of general strategies, the review will include measures targeting the individual aggressor in an attempt to change his/her emotions, cognitions, and behaviour. Moreover, we will look at societal-level interventions, in particular with respect to the deterrent function of capital punishment and the potential effectiveness of tighter gun control legislation. The perspective will then shift to measures custom tailored to deal with specific forms of aggression, such as bullying and gang violence, domestic violence, and sexual aggression. It is evident that this chapter in particular will have to look beyond the boundaries of social psychological research to include relevant contributions from sociology, criminology, and other related fields.

In conclusion, the present volume aspires to present an up-to-date account of current social psychological knowledge on aggression. It will address the prevalence, causes, and consequences of aggressive behaviour in its numerous manifestations and illustrate strategies for prevention and intervention. It will become clear in the course of the book that not all the conclusions generated and supported by this research will be gladly accepted outside the academic debate. This is true, for example, for evidence on the detrimental effects of media violence or on the positive effects of tightening gun control legislation, neither of which has been, or will be, translated into policy responses without strong opposition from the respective interest groups involved. In addition to accumulating knowledge about the different facets of aggression, psychological aggression research is therefore faced with the challenge of promulgating this knowledge beyond the scientific community to influence both policy makers and public opinion.

Concepts and measures of aggression 1

The purpose of this chapter is to address two fundamental issues to set the stage for the discussion of social psychological research on aggression in the chapters to follow. First, the meaning of our key concept, i.e., aggression, must be defined to delineate the phenomena falling within the boundaries of this construct. It is important to establish a consensus about the basic criteria for deciding whether or not a given behaviour should be classified as aggressive, and to have a typology of different forms of aggression for coming to grips with the multiplicity of forms in which aggressive behaviour presents itself. Second, an examination of the prevailing research methods used to study aggression is essential in order to facilitate a critical appraisal of the current body of knowledge. Amongst psychologists, it is trivial to state that research findings are dependent to a large extent on the specific measures by which they are obtained. However, in public debate about aggression, conclusions about causes and consequences of aggression are typically traded without much concern for their methodological foundations. A case in point is the controversy about detrimental effects of media violence, in which each side refers to select research results to corroborate their views without reflecting that differences in conclusion often result from differences in methodology. Therefore, it seems appropriate that a review of the scholarly literature on aggression should start by examining the advantages and limitations of the main methodological strategies used in this research.

Defining aggression

As an academic discipline, social psychology is concerned with the many facets of people's social lives, their thoughts, feelings, and behaviours towards other people, and the impact of those others on the way they themselves feel, think, and act. Describing and explaining these social processes is by no means the prerogative of the scientist but an integral part of everybody's psychological functioning. Therefore, it is not surprising that both social psychology and everyday discourse often use the same terms to describe social phenomena. This is certainly true for the term *aggression*, which is as firmly established in ordinary language as it is in the technical vocabulary of social psychologists. Unfortunately, using the same term does not necessarily imply agreement on the exact meaning that it is meant to denote. For example, when prompted for their understanding of aggression, lay persons often talk about "good" or "healthy" aggression in contrast to "bad" aggression, a distinction that most social psychologists would reject. Instead, there is a consensus in the academic field to define aggression as a negative or antisocial behaviour that has little to do with psychological health and well-being.

Beyond this basic consensus, there is, however, a need to define more precisely the criteria that have to be met by a specific behaviour to be categorised as "aggressive". A classic definition was proposed by Buss (1961, p. 1), who characterised aggression as "a response that delivers noxious stimuli to another organism." However, it has been pointed out that this purely behaviourist definition is too broad in some ways. It includes many forms of behaviour that should not be categorised as aggression, while being too narrow in other respects, for example excluding all non-behavioural processes, such as thoughts and feelings. Additional aspects were subsequently included to arrive at a more balanced definition (see also Tedeschi & Felson, 1994, Chapter 6, for a comprehensive discussion): For a person's behaviour to qualify as aggression, the behaviour must be carried out with the *intention* to inflict negative consequences on the target, which, in turn, presupposes the *expectancy* that the action will produce a particular outcome. This specification excludes behaviours that result in unintended harm or injury, e.g., by accident or through negligence or incompetence. At the same time, it includes behaviours aimed at harming another person which, for whatever reason, do not lead to the intended consequences: a gunshot that misses its target represents an aggressive act even though no hair may have been harmed on the target's head. Focusing on the person's intention to harm also allows for non-action, such as failure to help a person in need, to be classified as aggressive. A further specification refers to the willingness on behalf of the target person *to avoid* the harmful treatment. This is to exclude the case of self-directed aggression in

TABLE 1.1

Aspects of a typology of aggressive behaviour

Response modality	Verbal vs. physical
Response quality	Action vs. failure to act
Immediacy	Direct vs. indirect
Visibility	Overt vs. covert
Instigation	Unprovoked vs. retaliative
Goal direction	Hostile vs. instrumental
Type of damage	Physical vs. psychological
Duration of consequences	Transient vs. long-term
Social units involved	Individuals vs. groups

which the roles of aggressor and target coincide, such as suicide or injury inflicted in the context of sadomasochistic sexual practices.

A concise definition that takes these considerations into account is offered by Baron and Richardson (1994, p. 7). They suggest to use the term aggression to describe *"any form of behavior directed toward the goal of harming or injuring another living being who is motivated to avoid such treatment."* This definition has also been adopted for the present volume. It represents a kind of minimal consensus in social psychological aggression research and leaves room for a variety of additional dimensions, summarised in Table 1.1, for characterising different forms of aggression.

Although most of the distinctions in Table 1.1 are self-explanatory, the differentiation between hostile and instrumental aggression requires some further comment. This distinction refers to the psychological *function* of the aggressive behaviour for the actor. The primary motive for the aggressive behaviour may be either the desire to harm another person as an expression of negative feelings, as in hostile aggression, or the aim to reach an intended goal by means of the aggressive act, as in instrumental aggression. The two types of motivation for aggressive behaviour may frequently coexist. Nevertheless, we shall see in discussing theories of aggressive behaviour that it makes sense to tease them apart because different psychological processes may be involved.

An additional feature to be considered in defining aggression refers to the normative appraisal of the behaviour in question. There has been some controversy as to whether or not the aspect of *norm violation* should be included among the defining features of aggression. Disciplinary measures taken by teachers or acts of physical self-defence are examples of behaviours that satisfy the criteria of intention, expectancy, and target's desire to avoid them and should, accordingly, be classified as aggressive. Yet they are covered by social norms that turn them into accepted forms of social behaviour. Therefore, it has been argued, behaviour should only be considered aggressive if it involves the violation of a social norm. However, as Berkowitz (1993) has pointed out, defining aggression in terms of norm-violating or socially disapproved behaviour ignores the problem that the normative evaluation of a behaviour frequently differs depending on the perspectives of the parties involved. For example, some people regard corporal punishment as an acceptable and effective child-rearing practice, while others consider it to be an unacceptable form of aggression.

A related point can be made with regard to the distinction between *legitimate* and *illegitimate* aggression. Capital punishment, for example, satisfies all the elements in Baron and Richardson's definition: Actions are carried out with the intention and expectancy to inflict harm on the convicted person, who is motivated to avoid such treatment. However, these actions are legitimised in the laws of many countries. Therefore, is it appropriate to regard them as aggression—provided the legal procedures are properly conducted? Although many people will reject this idea, others may have a different view. In the absence of explicit legal regulations, the question of legitimacy becomes even more difficult. Are violent acts committed by separatist movements or marginalised minorities legitimate or illegitimate forms of aggression? It is obvious that the answer to this question will be affected to a large extent by the position a person takes in the underlying controversy. Therefore, while issues of norm violation and legitimacy are highly relevant, for example when it comes to analysing dynamics of intergroup encounters or justifications for aggressive behaviours, they are difficult to accommodate as critical features in a basic definition of aggression.

Before turning from the definition to the measurement of aggressive behaviour, we should briefly look at the meanings of two related terms: coercion and violence. *Coercion* is defined by Tedeschi and Felson (1994, p. 168) as "an action taken with the intention of imposing harm on another person or forcing compliance." Coercive action can take the form of threats, punishments, or bodily force. According to Tedeschi and Felson, there are several advantages in replacing aggression by the concept of coercion: (a) coercion includes the use of contingent threats to gain another person's compliance, which cannot easily be reconciled with the minimal definition of aggression; (b) coercive actions are interpreted as a form of social influence, which highlights the social nature of this type of behaviour and brings it conceptually closer to processes of communication and interaction not previously examined in the context of aggression; (c) coercion is recommended as less value laden than aggression because it avoids the issue of legitimacy. According to Tedeschi and Felson, "the interactions and motives of parents who use coercive actions to control or change the behavior of their children are not fundamentally different from the actions of a robber who seeks compliance and booty from a victim" (Tedeschi & Felson, 1994, p. 176). We will return to their social interactionist theory of coercion later in the next chapter.

In contrast to coercion, which is broader than aggression, the term *violence* denotes a subtype of aggression referring to extreme forms of physical aggression. Violence is defined as "the infliction of intense force upon persons or property for the purposes of destruction, punishment, or control" (Geen, 1995, p. 669). Archer and Browne (1989, p. 11) suggest to define as violence "physically damaging assaults which are not socially legitimised in any way." These definitions cover instances of personal violence, committed by an individual actor or group of identifiable individuals. A functional typology of violence is presented by Mattaini, Twyman, Chin, and Lee (1996), who identify six potential functions of violent behaviour: (1) change of, or escape from, aversive situations; (2) positive reinforcement, i.e., attainment of a particular goal; (3) release of negative affective arousal; (4) resolution of conflict; (5) gaining of respect; and (6) attack on a culturally defined "enemy", i.e., a member of a devalued outgroup.

A special form of violence has been called *structural violence* and denotes societal conditions that entail harmful consequences for certain social groups. Structural violence is seen as a latent feature of social systems that leads to social inequality and injustice, e.g., through institutionalising a power hierarchy between men and women that leaves women largely unprotected against male sexual coercion (see also Lubek, 1995). In the present volume, the focus will be on personal violence, but issues of structural violence will also be touched upon in several places in the course of the analysis.

The measurement of aggression

Since aggression has been defined as a form of social *behaviour*, measurement strategies are required that provide information at the

TABLE 1.2

Summary of methods for studying aggression

Observation	Naturalistic observation
	Field experiments
	Laboratory experiments
	• Teacher–learner paradigm
	• Essay evaluation paradigm
	• Competitive reaction time paradigm
	• Bobo doll paradigm
	• Verbal aggression
Asking	Behavioural self-reports
	Peer/other nominations
	Archival records
	Personality scales
	Projective techniques

behavioural level. The range of methodological options for obtaining such information is constrained by the inherently harmful nature of aggressive behaviour: researchers are under the obligation to ensure at any stage of their investigations that no damage is caused to their participants or another party. Records of aggressive behaviour can be obtained through two general approaches: *observation* and *asking* (Baron & Richardson, 1994). The variety of specific approaches available under these two headings are summarised in Table 1.2.

Observation

Observational measures facilitate the recording of aggressive behaviour as it occurs in a natural context, such as among children in a school playground, or in a contrived laboratory setting, e.g., in response to a staged provocation by an experimental confederate. Observing aggression in natural contexts has the advantage that behavioural information can be collected in an unobtrusive way without people realising that their behaviour is being recorded. With a social behaviour like aggression known to be socially undesirable, this is a particular asset because it avoids the problem of measurement *reactivity*, i.e., respondents' adjustment of their behaviour to the social norms perceived to be attached to that behaviour.

Natural observation. One aim of observation in natural contexts is to obtain a picture of the various forms of aggression in a particular setting and the frequency with which they are performed. This approach is commonly referred to as *naturalistic observation*. For example, Humpert and Dann (1988) recorded aggression-related interactions during school lessons with a specifically developed coding system comprising 10 categories of aggressive behaviour (e.g., damaging classmates' belongings, snatching things from others, threatening and blackmailing fellow pupils). In this type of research, the natural flow of behaviour is first recorded, then broken down into more fine-grained units of analysis, and finally assigned to the predefined categories. Questions of when and where to sample behaviour and how to define the basic units of analysis are central to this methodological approach (e.g., Wehby & Symons, 1996). Moreover, it is important to check how reliably the units can be assigned to the different categories by examining the correspondence achieved by two independent coders.

Field experiments. Another line of research using observation in natural contexts is directed at exploiting inconspicuous everyday situations to examine the link between certain antecedent conditions and subsequent aggressive responses. These studies incorporate the variation of an independent variable (e.g., strength of a frustration) and its effect on a dependent variable (e.g., intensity of the aggressive response) and thus meet the criteria of *field experiments*. Using a common traffic situation, for example, drivers' aggressive reactions, defined in terms of latency and duration of horn honking, was studied in response to a frustration in the form of a confederate who failed to move his car when the traffic lights turned green (Baron, 1976). Similarly, people waiting in a queue were frustrated by a queue-jumping confederate, and their aggressive responses were studied as a function of how close they had been to the head of the queue (Harris, 1974).

Despite their advantages in terms of allowing the analysis of naturally occurring behaviour uncontaminated by social desirability concerns, many additional variables may operate in field situations that are not under the experimenter's control. Suppose, for example, you were to use the queue-jumping approach to study the aggressive responses of people waiting for a bus. You would have a problem if in some of your trials the bus that people were waiting for was 15 minutes late at the time of the experimental intervention, creating an additional and powerful source of frustration.

Laboratory experiments. This lack of control over extraneous variables as well as over the assignment of respondents to experimental treatments is the prime reason why the vast majority of observational studies on aggressive behaviour have been conducted as *laboratory experiments*. Here, situations are created by the investigator to meet three essential criteria: that (a) respondents are exposed to an experimental manipulation aimed at influencing their aggressive response tendencies; (b) they can be randomly assigned to one of the experimental conditions; and (c) any distorting influences can be controlled. A critical decision involves the choice of behavioural indicators of aggression, which have to be valid measures of the underlying construct and, at the same time, must not involve damage to the target person. Five types of experimental procedures have been particularly prominent in aggression research:

(1) The *teacher–learner* paradigm. This paradigm uses the set-up of an alleged learning experiment in which one person adopts the role of a teacher and presents a word association task to another person, who is in the role of the learner. Errors made by the learner are punished by the teacher by administering adverse stimuli to the learner. In fact, the assignment to the two roles is rigged so that the naive respondent always ends up as the teacher, whose choice of punishment intensity is the critical index of his or her aggressive behaviour. In the most common version of this paradigm, punishments are delivered in the form of electric shocks whose strength is determined by the teacher. This procedure, probably better known from Milgram's (1974) famous study of obedience than from the context of aggression research, was pioneered by Buss (1961). He developed an "aggression machine", which enabled respondents to choose the *intensity* and the *duration* of electric shocks that they thought would be delivered to the learner (no shocks were actually delivered, but respondents received mild shocks in a trial run to convince them that the device was genuine). The teacher–learner paradigm thus provides an experimental framework in which a variety of variables may be studied in their effects on aggression (see Baron & Richardson, 1994). Differences in aggressive responding may be examined, for example, as a function of respondents' group membership (male versus female; prisoners versus students) or situational manipulations (different degrees of frustration or physiological arousal). Some studies have used a slightly modified procedure in which electric shocks are replaced by other adverse stimuli, such as loud noise or uncomfortable heat.

(2) The *essay evaluation* paradigm. This paradigm is used primarily to investigate aggressive behaviour in response to prior

frustration or provocation and was first introduced by Berkowitz (1962). Subjects are told that they are to provide a written solution to a problem-solving task, which will then be evaluated by a fellow subject who is, in fact, a confederate of the experimenter. They are also informed that the evaluation will be expressed in terms of the number of electric shocks delivered by the evaluator, with one shock indicating the best and ten shocks indicating the worst possible evaluation. Irrespective of the quality of their solution, subjects then receive either one or seven shocks, depending on whether they are in the provocation or control condition, respectively. In the second and main phase of the experiment, roles are reversed and the subject gets a chance to evaluate the solution provided by the other person. The number of shocks administered by the subjects is the dependent variable and indicates the strength of their aggressive response. Typically, more shocks are administered to a target person who is seen responsible for a negative evaluation of the actor in the first round of the experiment. Beyond addressing the role of provocation, this experimental design allows researchers to examine additional variables moderating the provocation–aggression link. A case in point is Berkowitz and LePage's (1967) well-known study on the so-called weapons effect, which will be examined in more detail in Chapter 2. They showed that provocation leads to stronger aggression in the presence of an aggression-related cue (such as a weapon) than in the presence of a neutral object (such as a badminton racket).

(3) The *competitive reaction time* paradigm. Like the first two approaches, this paradigm, developed by Taylor (1967), also uses electric shocks as indicators of aggression. Subjects are told that they compete with a partner (again typically an experimental confederate) on a reaction time task. The slower partner on each trial receives an electric shock whose intensity is set by the faster competitor. Since success and failure of the naive subjects are in fact predetermined by the experimenter, each genuine participant receives as well as delivers a set number of shocks in the course of the task. In order to make sure that the shocks received by the subjects are aversive but not painful, each participant's threshold of unpleasantness is established in a pilot phase. As the naive subjects are always allowed to win the first trial, their decision about the first shock level reflects their unprovoked aggressive responses. After they received the first shock from their opponent, subsequent choices reflect the strength of retaliative aggression. This approach also facilitates the examination of a variety of variables affecting

aggressive responses, such as the way in which subjects adjust their shock levels to the decisions made by their opponents or the impact of an audience on the choice of shock intensities.

(4) The *Bobo doll* paradigm. In the paradigms discussed so far, subjects are limited in the expression of their aggressive tendencies to a single behaviour, e.g., the administration of electric shocks. In contrast, the Bobo doll approach first used by Bandura, Ross, and Ross (1963) is designed to give children an opportunity to show a range of aggressive behaviours towards a large, inflatable clown figure called Bobo. In a typical experiment, readiness to act aggressively is first induced in the children. This is achieved most commonly by exposing them to a model who acts aggressively towards the Bobo doll. Subsequently, the children's behaviour towards Bobo is observed and assessed in terms of the frequency of aggressive acts. Differences in aggressive responses can thus be studied as a function of a variety of variables, such as characteristics of the model or the observed consequences of the model's behaviour in terms of vicarious reinforcement or punishment.

(5) *Verbal aggression*. Apart from physical responses, verbal measures have been used frequently as indicators of aggression (see Baron & Richardson, 1994). Typically, subjects are first exposed to a manipulation designed to instigate aggressive responses. Then, their verbal reactions are recorded, either as free responses, which are later analysed in terms of their aggressive contents, or as standardised evaluations of the person who provoked the aggressive reaction. For these evaluations to qualify as aggressive responses, subjects must be led to believe that their negative evaluation will entail harmful consequences for the other person, such as curtailing his or her chances of winning a job appointment or a promotion.

Finally, a new method has recently been introduced to the experimental study of aggression by McGregor et al. (1998) and Lieberman, Solomon, Greenberg, and McGregor (1999). In their studies, subjects' aggressive tendencies were measured in terms of the amount of hot sauce administered to another person assumed to dislike spicy food. The hot sauce measure yields an easily quantifiable index of aggressive behaviour. Moreover, it is ethically feasible because it does not lead to any harmful effects other than temporary discomfort.

Although the experimental procedures discussed in this section account for a large majority of the available evidence, their prominence has been by no means uncontroversial. The main challenge refers to their validity, i.e., the extent to which (a) they represent the underlying theoretical construct of aggression (construct validity), and (b) they can explain aggressive behaviour occurring outside the laboratory in the "real world" (external validity). In terms of construct validity, each of the four approaches using electric shocks is potentially susceptible to alternative interpretations of what is taken to be aggressive behaviour: in the teacher–learner paradigm, high levels of shock may be chosen because subjects want to help the learner to accomplish his learning task more effectively. In the essay evaluation task, high shock intensities may similarly reflect compliance with the cover story: to provide critical feedback on a person's problem solving success. In the competitive reaction time task, subjects' responses may be motivated by competitiveness rather than aggression, and finally, behaviour against the Bobo doll is directed against an inanimate object and thus is not covered by the standard definition of aggression. As far as external validity is concerned, critics point out that the artificial and impoverished nature of many laboratory settings is a far cry from those contexts in which aggression manifests itself as a social problem in the outside world. Thus, it has been questioned that evidence gained from laboratory studies can contribute to a better understanding of aggression as it occurs in natural contexts.

Without having space to review the controversy in detail (see Anderson & Bushman, 1997; Berkowitz, 1993; Lubek, 1995, for comprehensive treatments), two main lines of argument have been advanced in defence of laboratory experiments for the study of aggression:

(1) Experimental procedures for measuring aggression can be said to have high construct validity, i.e., to tap the same underlying construct, to the extent that subjects' responses to those procedures are (a) correlated across different indicators of aggression, such as duration, intensity, and number of shocks versus written expressions of aggression, and (b) affected by the same set of antecedent conditions. For example, if person A delivers more intensive electric shocks than person B, then A should also score higher than B in terms of shock duration or in written expressions of aggression. In terms of the second requirement, if the induction of negative affect is found to be an antecedent condition of shock intensities, then different strategies for inducing negative affect, such as angering or frustrating subjects, should have parallel effects on subsequent aggressive responses. Moreover, they should have similar effects on physical as well as verbal measures of aggression.

Integrating results from over 100 published studies, Carlson, Marcus-Newhall, and Miller (1989) supported these aspects of construct validity and concluded "that critics have gone too far in rejecting outright the thesis that specific aggression measures typically index a common behavioral disposition" (p. 386).

(2) The second criticism refers to a lack of external validity, i.e., the failure to generalise to aggression in the real world. This criticism was tackled by Anderson and Bushman (1997; Bushman & Anderson, 1998). They conducted a meta-analysis including 53 studies of laboratory and real-world aggression to explore the correspondence between the two sources of data across a range of independent variables. (Meta-analysis is a statistical procedure in which the results from a number of individual studies are converted to a common metric and then integrated into a quantitative index of effect size, indicating how large the difference between two variables, such as location of a study in the lab versus the real world, is across the entire range of studies; Glass, McGaw, & Smith, 1981).

More specifically, Anderson and Bushman looked for converging evidence concerning the role of individual difference variables (sex, trait aggressiveness, and Type A personality) and situational variables (provocation, alcohol, media violence, anonymity, and temperature) as determinants of aggressive behaviour. With the exception of temperature, where the laboratory evidence was inconsistent both in itself and with field research, they found substantial convergence across the two data sources. In both laboratory and field research, aggression was found to increase as a function of provocation, alcohol consumption, anonymity, and exposure to violent media contents. Aggression was also found to be higher in both settings for men (physical aggression only) and for individuals with high trait aggressiveness and Type A behaviour patterns. It is worth noting, however, that the magnitude of the effects varied across the two approaches. For example, the effect of violent media contents was found to be higher in laboratory experiments than in field studies, while the link between trait aggressiveness and behavioural aggression was stronger in field studies than in the laboratory. As Bushman and Anderson (1998) point out, these differences are conceptually plausible. They argue that the stronger effect size for the impact of trait aggressiveness on aggressive behaviour found in field studies was to be expected because laboratory studies mostly involve relatively homogeneous samples of college students, whereas variability in trait aggressiveness is greater among the largely unselected samples recruited in many field studies. In contrast, the effect of media violence on aggressive behaviour was expected to be stronger in the laboratory because the time interval between exposure to media violence and measurement of subsequent aggression is typically shorter in laboratory experiments and extraneous influences that might undermine the impact of the media presentation can be controlled more effectively in the lab.

In conclusion, Anderson and Bushman's (1997) analysis shows that the unquestionable advantage of laboratory experiments, i.e., their ability to test causal hypotheses in a custom-tailored context, is not necessarily undermined by a lack of external validity (see Berkowitz, 1993, for a similar conclusion). Therefore, laboratory studies are of prime importance in illuminating conceptual links between eliciting variables, aggressive behaviour, and consequences. They are seriously limited, on the other hand, when it comes to studying severe manifestations of aggressive behaviour that would be unethical to instigate deliberately. Therefore, there is clearly a place for both experimental and field approaches in the study of aggression.

Asking

Obtaining behavioural records through direct observation is not always feasible. As noted above, the dangerous and potentially damaging nature of aggressive acts prevents researchers from creating conditions under which such behaviours might be observed. Moreover, many aggressive acts occur without prior warning and/or only come to light after they have been performed. This is typically the case for acts of violence, such as physical assault, rape, or homicide. In these cases, researchers have to rely on methods that *ask* for reports of aggressive behaviours rather than gaining first-hand evidence of their occurrence. In other contexts, research questions may be focused not on behaviours, but on internal variables, such as aggressive thoughts and fantasies, which cannot be observed either. An overview of different strategies for asking about the commitment of aggressive acts is presented in the lower half of Table 1.2. Since these strategies are not specific to the aggression domain but represent methods of data collection employed in many areas of psychological research, they will be familiar to most readers. Therefore, a brief description of each strategy, including illustrative examples from aggression research, should be sufficient in the present context.

Behavioural self-reports. In this approach, subjects are asked to provide verbal accounts of their own aggressive behaviour, either in the context of large-scale surveys or as part of hypothesis-testing research. Depending on the aim of the inquiry, they can be asked to report general patterns of aggressive behaviour or specific acts in a particular domain. A general measure of aggressive behaviour is provided, for example, by the physical and verbal aggression scales of Buss and Perry's (1992) "Aggression Questionnaire", which is a revised version of the earlier and widely used Buss–Durkee (1957) Hostility Inventory (see also Archer, Kilpatrick, & Bramwell, 1995; Blickle, Habasch & Senft, 1998). On the physical aggression scale, respondents are required to indicate, for example, to what extent a statement like "Once in a while I can't control the urge to strike another person" is characteristic of them. An example from the verbal aggression scale is "I can't help getting into arguments when people disagree with me." Recording behavioural self-reports of aggression is not limited to the perpetrator perspective. It is also a viable strategy for collecting evidence on victimisation by aggressive others. For example, Mynard and Joseph (2000) developed a multidimensional scale tapping different forms of children's victimisation by aggressive peers.

An example of a domain-specific self-report measure is provided by the "Sexual Experiences Survey" (Koss & Oros, 1982), which elicits self-reports of sexually aggressive acts (see also Chapter 8). For example, male respondents are asked to answer "yes" or "no" to the following question: "Have you ever had sexual intercourse with a woman when she didn't want to because you used some degree of physical force (twisting her arm, holding her down, etc.)?"

Self-reports of aggressive behaviour can be combined with other-reports (i.e., reports of another person's behaviour) to examine the interdependency of aggressive actions and to assess the correspondence between self- and other-reports. This type of approach is prominently represented by the "Conflict Tactics Scales" developed by Straus (1979) to measure domestic violence. In their recently revised version, the Conflict Tactics Scales 2 (CTS2), respondents are asked to indicate which of a list of behaviours representing psychological aggression, physical assault, sexual coercion, and negotiation they inflicted on their partner in the past year (Straus, Hamby, Boney-McCoy, & Sugarman, 1996). In addition, they are asked to indicate, for the same range of behaviours, whether their partner showed the respective behaviour towards them. A corresponding scale addressing aggression in parent–child interactions has recently been provided by Straus et al. (1998).

Given that aggression is a negatively valued behaviour and respondents are typically aware of this, an obvious drawback of self-reports is their susceptibility to response biases in the direction of social desirability. This drawback is most serious when the aim of the research is to establish the frequency of particular aggressive acts, such as the number of rapes committed each year, and can only be compensated by referring to other data sources. Unfortunately, as the case of sexual violence illustrates, alternative sources, such as crime statistics, are often affected by other, equally serious reporting biases, which make it extremely difficult to obtain valid estimates of the scale of certain forms of aggression.

Peer/other nominations. The problem of social desirability is somewhat less pertinent when informed others are asked to contribute behavioural information about a target person. Teachers, parents, and peers, who have first-hand knowledge of a target person's aggressive behaviour, are asked to provide behavioural records, which can then be examined for their convergence with each other and with the person's self-reports. Peer ratings have been used successfully in personality measurement to provide independent ratings of personality traits to complement self-ratings (see Krahé, 1992, for a summary). In aggression research, this approach has been used by Eron, Huesmann and their colleagues in a longitudinal study linking peer nominations of aggression to preference for violent media programmes (e.g., Eron, Huesmann, Lefkowitz, & Walder, 1972). For each child, they obtained peer ratings of aggressiveness, mothers' reports of most frequently watched TV programmes, and self-reports of programme preference. In addition, violence ratings for each TV programme were determined independently. From this database, Eron et al. were able to show for their sample of 8-year-old boys that peer-nominated aggression was linked to the level of violence inherent in their favourite and most frequently watched TV programme (Huesmann & Miller, 1994). It is clear, though, that the use of ratings by informed others is a time-consuming and expensive strategy. Moreover, it has to be made sure that nominations from different raters show sufficient convergence to provide a reliable approximation to the target person's behaviour.

Archival records. Rather than asking individuals about their own or others' behaviours, researchers can derive information about aggressive behaviour from archival data originally collected for other purposes. Crime statistics and temperature records are particularly relevant in the context of aggression research. A series of studies by Anderson and his colleagues have utilised these two data sources to explore the relationship between temperature and violent behaviour (Anderson, 1989; Anderson & Anderson, 1996; Anderson, Bushman, & Groom, 1997). They found, for example, that the incidence rates of serious and deadly assault were higher in years with a higher average temperature, whereas robbery figures remained unaffected by temperature (Anderson, Bushman, & Groom, 1997, Study 1; see Chapter 4 for a more detailed discussion of this research). In the domain of sexual violence, archival data has been used in the United States to demonstrate a link, within different states, between the circulation rate of pornographic magazines and the incidence of rapes documented in annual crime statistics (e.g., Jaffee & Straus, 1987; Scott & Schwalm, 1988). These studies, however, nicely illustrate the problem of inferring causal pathways from associations between frequency data of this kind: It may not be unreasonable to suspect that both the popularity of pornographic magazines and the incidence of rape are expressions of a third variable, such as the prevalence of a macho gender stereotype among the male population, which was not captured by the design of the study.

Personality scales and projective techniques. Beyond asking for reports of aggression at the behavioural level, researchers have frequently been interested in studying the cognitive and affective concomitants of aggressive behaviour and in identifying stable individual differences in the disposition for aggressive action. To meet these objectives, two approaches have been used. The first consists in the development of standardised personality scales in which respondents are asked to describe their current internal states or their more enduring dispositions. Buss and Perry's (1992) "Aggression Questionnaire" contains two such scales, measuring dispositional anger (e.g., "I sometimes feel like a powder keg ready to explode") and hostility ("I am sometimes eaten up with jealousy"). The distinction between current states and stable traits is reflected in the State–Trait Anger Scale by Spielberger, Jacobs, Russell, and Crane (1983). It yields two scores for each respondent, representing the intensity of currently experienced anger (state measure) and the frequency with which that state is experienced in general (trait measure). The validity of these personality scales has been established by showing their convergence with other measures of aggression (see Bond et al., 1997).

The second approach for exploring the intrapersonal under-pinnings of aggressive behaviour involves the use of projective techniques. Subjects are provided with ambiguous stimulus material, such as the well-known ink-blots of the Rorschach test, and asked to provide their thoughts on the material. These are then scored for aggressive contents by trained raters. In the case of the Rosenzweig Picture Frustration Test (Rosenzweig, 1981), developed specifically for the measurement of aggression, respondents are presented with cartoons depicting situations involving some form of frustration. The person who caused the frustration, e.g., by calling a wrong number in the middle of the night, makes a comment that is designed to attenuate, or add to, the initial frustration. The subject, adopting the perspective of the frustrated recipient of the call, has to suggest a verbal response. Responses are coded for direction and type of aggression. Apart from the time-consuming task of coding free-response statements into a manageable set of categories, the reliability of such codings, i.e., their consistency across independent raters and across repeated codings by the same rater, has been difficult to achieve. Moreover, responses to the Picture Frustration Test have been found to be affected by social desirability concerns. Taken together, these problems explain why the use of projective techniques is no longer widespread in the social psychological analysis of aggression.

This chapter was designed to create a basis for the understanding and critical appraisal of empirical research to be discussed in the course of this volume. Moreover, a typology was outlined that high-lights central dimensions for classifying aggressive acts and provides a framework for the systematic description of different forms of aggressive behaviour. The body of research strategies reviewed in this chapter clearly shows that a variety of methods is available for the social psychological analysis of aggression. Which method will be chosen is determined by the specific questions researchers want to address and by the ethical constraints imposed on them by the inherently negative quality of aggressive behaviour.

Summary

- A definition of aggression was presented that focuses on the three aspects of *harmful consequences, intent and expectancy to harm* and *desire* by the target person to avoid the harmful stimuli.

- To measure aggression, a range of strategies for observing behaviour in natural contexts as well as under controlled laboratory conditions have been developed and used in a large body of research.
- Evidence was presented showing that findings from studies conducted in the real world correspond in many areas to relationships obtained in contrived laboratory settings.
- Among strategies asking for information about aggressive behaviour, self-reports, peer nominations, and the study of archival records have a firm place in social psychological aggression research. Standardised personality scales and projective techniques are designed to study the stability of individual differences in aggressive tendencies.

Suggested reading

Anderson, C.A., & Bushman, B.J. (1997). External validity of "trivial" experiments: The case of laboratory aggression. *Review of General Psychology, 1,* 19–41.

Bond, A.J., Lader, M.H., & Da Silveira, J.C. (1997). *Aggression: Individual differences, alcohol, and benzodiazepines* (Ch. 3). Hove, UK: Psychology Press.

Tedeschi, J.T., & Felson, R.B. (1994). *Violence, aggression, and coercive actions* (Ch. 6). Washington, DC: American Psychological Association.

Theories of aggressive behaviour 2

Given the harmful nature of aggressive behaviour and its pervasiveness in human societies, it is not surprising that the search for explanations of *why* people engage in such behaviour has always been a top priority in aggression research. Rather than coming up with one all-inclusive theoretical model, this search has produced a variety of theoretical approaches, each focusing on different mechanisms involved in the manifestation of aggressive behaviour. It is neither possible nor necessary to present these approaches in full detail (see Berkowitz, 1993; Tedeschi & Felson, 1994; Geen, 1998a, for detailed presentations, as well as any textbook of social psychology for brief summaries). However, it does seem important at this point to discuss their main ideas with two primary aims in mind: (a) to document the range of available explanations of aggressive behaviour that account for a substantial proportion of aggression research and without which any introduction to the field would be incomplete; and (b) to establish a common stock of theoretical constructs that are drawn upon by researchers trying to explain vastly different forms of aggressive behaviour.

As a starting point, Table 2.1 presents a list of the major theoretical perspectives in aggression research, denoting the way they conceptualise aggression and the emphasis they place on the stability versus variability of aggressive behaviour.

While the first three approaches are based on biological concepts and principles, the remaining explanations are located in a psychological frame of reference. Rather than seeing them as competing or even mutually exclusive, in most cases they are best regarded as complementary, stressing different aspects involved in aggression as a complex form of social behaviour. The next sections will introduce each of the approaches in turn, paying special attention to the answers they entail to two closely related questions: (1) Is aggression an innate quality of human nature? and (2) Is there a chance for aggressive behaviour to be pre-empted or controlled?

TABLE 2.1

Theoretical explanations of aggression

Theoretical perspective	Aggression conceptualised as . . .	Focus on stability (s) vs. variability (v)
Biological explanations		
Ethology	. . . internal energy	s
Sociobiology	. . . product of evolution	s
Behaviour genetics	. . . hereditary disposition	s
Psychological explanations		
Freudian psychoanalysis	. . . destructive instinct	s
Frustration–aggression hypothesis	. . . goal-directed drive	v
Cognitive neoassociationism	. . . response to negative affect	v
Excitation transfer model	. . . reinforced through neutral arousal	v
Social-cognitive approach	. . . function of information processing	v
Learning theory	. . . learned through reinforcement and imitation	v
Social interactionist model	. . . result of a decision-making process	v

Biological explanations

In this section, we will look at three models that refer to biological principles in explaining aggression: the ethological approach, the sociobiological approach, and the behaviour genetic approach. A fourth line of inquiry that is concerned with the influences of hormones on aggressive behaviour is particularly relevant to the issue of gender differences in aggression and will be discussed in that context (see Chapter 3). Biological approaches to aggression share the basic assumption that the roots of aggressive behaviour lie in the biological nature of humans rather than their psychological functioning.

The ethological view: Aggression as an internal energy

Among the biological approaches to aggression, an important contribution came from the field of ethology, which is concerned with the comparative study of animal and human behaviour. As one of the field's pioneers, Lorenz (1974) offered a model of aggression that dealt specifically with the issue of how aggressive energy is developed and set free in both animals and humans. His core assumption is that the organism continuously builds up aggressive energy. Whether or not this energy will lead to the manifestation of aggressive behaviour depends on two factors: (a) the amount of aggressive energy accumulated inside the organism at any one time; and (b) the strength of external stimuli (e.g., the sight or smell of a predator) capable of triggering an aggressive response. These two factors are inversely related: The lower the energy level, the stronger the stimulus required to elicit an aggressive response, and vice versa. If the energy level becomes too high without being released by an external stimulus, it will overflow, leading to spontaneous aggression. Lorenz likens this process to the operation of a steam boiler in which pressure is continually rising until it is either released in a controlled fashion or escapes in a spontaneous explosion.

In transferring this model from animal to human aggression, several additional assumptions have to be made. Most notably, it has to be explained why the inhibition against killing members of their own species, widely observed among animals, obviously fails to generalise to humans. Here, Lorenz (1974) argues that strong inhibitions against intraspecies killing were superfluous in the early history of mankind when fists and teeth were the only, relatively innocuous, weapons with which to attack one another. With the development of ever more sophisticated and lethal weapons, the fact that there is no innate inhibition to counterbalance the potential for destroying one's own species has given rise to basically uncontrolled levels of aggression and violence.

According to Lorenz's theorising, aggression must be regarded as a pervasive and inevitable feature of human nature. However, he sees the possibility of releasing aggressive energy in a controlled and socially acceptable way, e.g., through sports competitions. In this way, levels of aggressive energy can be kept below the critical threshold above which violent outbursts and other highly destructive forms of aggression would become likely.

Psychologists have challenged Lorenz's application of his findings from animal studies to human aggression on conceptual as well as empirical grounds (Mummendey, 1996). One criticism refers to the lack of an operational definition of aggressive energy: It is impossible to measure the amount of aggressive energy present in the individual at a given time. Another criticism is directed at the assumption that once the internal reservoir of aggressive energy has been used up in an aggressive act, it is impossible to trigger another aggressive response until a sufficient energy level is re-established. There is ample evidence that humans can perform several aggressive behaviours in quick succession and that one aggressive act frequently serves to precipitate rather than suppress further aggressive acts.

The sociobiological view: Aggression as a product of evolution

As a subdiscipline of evolutionary biology, sociobiology is concerned with applying the logic of evolutionary theory to the explanation of social behaviour. Sociobiology also offers an explanation of aggression that refers to both human and animal behaviour, focusing on the long-term development of aggression in the process of evolution. Rooted in Darwin's (1859) theory of "the origin of species", evolutionist thinking is based on the idea that in order for a characteristic or behaviour to survive within a species it has to be *adaptive*. Behaviours are adaptive to the extent that they enhance the chances of survival of the species as a whole and of individual members within the species.

Concise presentations of the evolutionist position have been provided by Daly and Wilson (1994) and Buss and Shakelford (1997; see also Archer, 1995). In this approach, aggressive behaviour directed at fighting off attackers as well as rivals in mate selection is seen as adaptive in the sense of enhancing the reproductive success of the aggressor. By virtue of their ability to control access to female mating partners, the more aggressive members of a species are likely to be more successful in passing their genes onto the next generation, thus favouring the natural selection of aggressive behaviour. Their genetic make-up will slowly spread at the expense of less aggressive and less reproductively successful members. According to the sociobiological view, aggressive behaviour is not only caused by "proximate" factors, such as short-term processes within the organism or social conditions, but also driven by "ultimate" causes shaping the development of both human and animal behaviour in the process of evolution.

In current aggression research, the most visible and comprehensive impact of the sociobiological approach has been in explaining the occurrence of sexual aggression (Malamuth & Heilmann, 1998). Sexual aggression is conceptualised as an optional, if high-risk mating strategy for those men who have limited opportunities for reproduction in consensual sexual relationships (Thornhill & Thornhill, 1991). This view implies that the potential for rape is part of the evolutionary inheritance of all males. It also implies that reproduction is the main functional basis for rape, not necessarily in the rapist's conscious awareness, but in terms of the evolutionary significance of his behaviour. To substantiate their arguments, proponents of a sociobiological explanation of rape refer to two main sources of data: (a) animal studies interpreted as showing evidence of forcible mating behaviours in different species (e.g., Ellis, 1989); (b) crime statistics that show that the vast majority of rape victims are young women at the height of their reproductive capacity and that men of low socio-economic status account for a disproportionate percentage of convicted rapists. Both data sources have been fundamentally challenged by critics of the sociobiological approach (e.g., Harding, 1985), and the controversy is far from being settled. We will return to the arguments in this debate in more detail in Chapter 8.

In general, sociobiologists look at aggression as a form of behaviour that has evolved in animals as well as humans because of its potential to enhance an individual's reproductive success, thereby facilitating the selective transmission of his or her genes to future generations. To what extent this evolutionary process is shaped by cultural influences, giving rise to cross-cultural variability in aggression, is an issue still unresolved between biologists and social psychologists.

Behaviour genetics: Is aggression hereditary?

As noted above, the sociobiological argument holds that aggression has evolved because it is instrumental in enhancing the reproductive success of an individual. Central to this line of reasoning is the proposition that the propensity for aggressive behaviour is part of an individual's genetic make-up. This proposition has been addressed in the field of behaviour genetics, which is directed at exploring the role of genetic similarity in explaining personal characteristics and behaviour. Specifically, behaviour geneticists have sought to demonstrate that genetically related individuals are indeed more similar in terms of their aggressive tendencies than individuals who are not genetically related. Because most children are brought up by their biological parents, to whom they are genetically related, the effects of "nature" and "nurture" normally coincide in individual development. Therefore, special research strategies are needed to tease apart the influences of family environment and heritability.

One such strategy involves the study of adopted children whose aggressive tendencies can be assessed relative to both their adoptive and their biological parents. The similarity between the children and their adoptive parents can then be regarded as reflecting the impact of the family environment uncontaminated by genetic factors, whereas the similarity with the biological parents indicates the impact of genetic factors uncontaminated by environmental influences. A second strategy involves the comparison of identical and fraternal twins in terms of the similarity of their aggressive tendencies. Identical twins share 100% of their genetic make-up, while fraternal twins only have a 50% genetic similarity. Therefore, evidence that identical twins are more similar than fraternal twins in their aggressive behaviour would support the idea that aggression is to some extent genetically transmitted.

Evidence from both twin and adoption studies was reviewed by Miles and Carey (1997). They conducted a meta-analysis of 22 studies in which ratings of aggressive or antisocial behaviour had been obtained either from the respondents themselves or—in the case of young children—from their parents. Two further studies were included that had observed actual aggressive behaviour. The authors conclude from their findings that shared genetic make-up accounts to a significant extent for similarities in self-ratings as well as parent ratings of aggressiveness, explaining up to 50% of the variance. Taking into account the different age groups included in the meta-analysis, they suggest furthermore that the relative importance of genetic and environmental influences in shaping aggression may change in the course of development: Shared genes were found to be more powerful than shared environmental influences in explaining similarities in aggression in adulthood, while the reverse pattern was found for children and adolescents. However, an important qualification of these conclusions comes from the two studies that used behavioural observation as measures of aggression. In these studies, the impact of shared environment was substantially greater than that of genetic similarity.

DiLalla and Gottesman (1991) make a similar point with respect to the heritability of antisocial behaviour, where genetic similarity was found to be more influential on questionnaire measures than on behavioural indicators, such as criminal convictions. At the same time, they conclude from their review of adoption studies that genetic factors do play a role in criminality in conjunction with environmental factors: Individuals whose biological as well as adoptive parents were criminal had the highest likelihood of becoming criminal themselves, followed by individuals whose biological parents, but not adoptive parents, had criminal records. The risk of the latter group of becoming criminal was found by several studies to be substantially higher than that of the group whose adoptive parents were criminal but whose biological parents were not, suggesting that genes are relatively more influential than shared environment.

On balance, the available evidence suggests that genetic make-up must be considered as a potentially important source of individual variation in aggression. A precise assessment of the magnitude of its impact relative to environmental influences is difficult, hampered by various methodological problems noted throughout the literature (see Tedeschi & Felson, 1994, Chapter 1). For example, studies analysing genetic versus environmental influences on criminality often fail to distinguish between violent and non-violent crimes. This distinction is crucial if the aim is to determine the heritability of aggressive behaviour in particular rather than of antisocial or deviant behaviour in general. Furthermore, studies combining both self-report and observation are needed to resolve the issue of why the two measurement strategies produce diverging evidence on the strength of genetic influences.

With regard to the question of whether or not aggression is an inevitable part of human nature and individual character, research showing the impact of genetic factors has sometimes been construed as suggesting a deterministic, and thus pessimistic, view: If an individual carries the aggressive genes, then he or she will grow up to be aggressive and violent. Such a view, however, is rejected by behaviour geneticists. They stress that an individual's genetic make-up ("genotype") may dispose him or her towards becoming an aggressive person ("phenotype"), but that environmental factors play a crucial role in determining whether that disposition will be reinforced or counteracted.

Psychological explanations

The theoretical approaches considered so far all refer to biological processes in explaining aggression. We will now turn to contributions concentrating on psychological mechanisms involved in aggressive behaviour. It is worth noting, though, that the earliest line of theoretical development in this tradition, Freud's psychoanalytic account of aggression, also started off from a biological construct by conceptualising aggressive behaviour as the expression of a genetically rooted *instinct*.

Freudian psychoanalysis: Aggression as a destructive instinct

In his dual instinct theory, Freud (1920) proposed that individual behaviour is driven by two basic forces that are part and parcel of human nature: the life instinct (eros) and the death instinct (thanatos).

Whereas *eros* drives the person towards pleasure seeking and wish fulfilment, *thanatos* is directed at self-destruction. Due to their antagonistic nature, the two instincts are a source of sustained intrapsychic conflict, which can be resolved only by diverting the destructive force away from the person onto others. Thus, acting aggressively towards another person is seen as a mechanism for releasing destructive energy in a way that protects the intrapsychic stability of the actor. In his notion of *catharsis*, Freud acknowledged the possibility of releasing destructive energy through non-aggressive expressive behaviour (e.g., jokes), but with only temporary effects. According to this view, aggression is an inevitable feature of human behaviour beyond the control of the individual, and it is interesting to note that Freud revised his earlier model, centring on *eros* only, by adding a destructive force after witnessing the violence of World War I. Empirical evidence in support of Freud's theorising is scarce, resting largely on case studies without stringent operationalisations of the major theoretical constructs. Nonetheless, his ideas have played a significant role in promoting the understanding of aggression in so far as they inspired the influential frustration–aggression hypothesis, which will be considered next.

The frustration–aggression hypothesis: Aggression as a goal-directed drive

The reception of instinct-related explanations of aggression has been a critical one for several reasons, not least because of a shortage of empirical evidence to support them (see Baron & Richardson, 1994). However, the idea that there is a force within the organism that, in conjunction with external events, leads to aggressive behaviour has been retained by an influential line of research postulating an aggressive *drive* as motivating aggressive behaviour. Unlike an instinct, a drive is not an ever present, continuously increasing source of energy but is activated only if the organism finds itself deprived of means to satisfy a vital need. A drive then serves as an energising force directed at terminating the state of deprivation.

In the original *frustration–aggression hypothesis* (Dollard et al., 1939), aggression is explained as the result of a drive to end a state of frustration, whereby frustration is defined as external interference with the goal-directed behaviour of the person. Thus, the experience of frustration activates the desire to act aggressively against the source of the frustration, which in turn precipitates the performance of aggressive behaviour.

It is clear, though, that not every frustration leads to an aggressive response. Alternatively, frustrated individuals may withdraw from the situation or become depressed. Moreover, not every aggressive act is the result of a preceding frustration. Acts of instrumental aggression carried out to achieve a particular goal, such as robbing a bank to resolve a desperate financial situation, do not necessarily entail a previous frustration. Therefore, the earlier proposition of a deterministic relationship between frustration and aggression was soon changed into a probabilistic version by Miller (1941), one of the authors of the original theory. He stated that "frustration produces instigations to a number of different types of response, one of which is an instigation of some form of aggression" (p. 338). In this revised view, aggression is not the only, but a possible response to frustration. To the extent that the aggressive act reduces the strength of the underlying drive, it becomes self-reinforcing: The likelihood increases that an aggressive response will be shown following subsequent frustrations.

Whether or not frustration will result in an aggressive response depends on the influence of moderating variables. Fear of punishment for overt aggression or unavailability of the frustrator are moderators that inhibit aggression. These moderators may also explain why aggression is frequently "displaced" away from the frustrator onto a more easily accessible or less intimidating target. In a recent meta-analysis, Marcus-Newhall, Pedersen, Carlson, and Miller (2000) found consistent evidence for the displacement of aggression from the source of the frustration onto a less powerful or more accessible target across a total of 49 studies.

In contrast to factors which lead to the suppression or displacement of aggressive responses to frustration, the presence of aggression-related cues is a promoting factor. In a much-cited study, Berkowitz and LePage (1967) demonstrated the significance of aggression-related cues as moderators of the frustration–aggression relationship. Subjects who had previously been frustrated administered more electric shocks (as a measure of aggression) in the presence of a firearm, i.e., an aggressive cue, than in the presence of a badminton racket, i.e., a neutral object. The availability of aggressive cues had no effect on the aggressive behaviour of subjects who had not been previously frustrated. Although subsequent studies not always replicated the effect—some failing to find a weapons effect and others finding an effect in the non-frustrated subjects as well—overall support for the role of aggression-related cues in facilitating aggressive behaviour is impressive. From their meta-analysis of 57 studies, Carlson, Marcus-Newhall, and Miller (1990, p. 632) conclude that "aggression-related cues present in experimental settings act to increase aggressive responding." Thus, starting off as a drive model, the frustration–aggression hypothesis has developed into a more complex approach, stressing the cognitive appraisal of situational cues as a crucial mediator between a frustrating event and an aggressive response. This development was carried further by Berkowitz (1989) in his cognitive neoassociation model summarised in the next section.

Cognitive neoassociationism: The role of negative affect

In trying to explain why frustration leads to aggression in some circumstances but not in others, Berkowitz (1989) proposed that negative affect in the form of anger is an important mediator between frustration and aggression. Frustrations lead to aggression only to the extent that they arouse negative affective states. For example, frustrations perceived as deliberate or illegitimate usually give rise to more anger than frustrations perceived as accidental or legitimate, and they lead to stronger aggressive responses. Frustrations arising out of competitive interactions are also particularly prone to trigger aggressive responses via the elicitation of negative emotional arousal. Viewed in this way, frustrations can be seen as just one of different aversive events that elicit negative affect. Other types of aversive stimulation, such as fear, physical pain, or psychological discomfort, through their capacity to elicit negative affect, are also recognised as powerful instigators of aggression (see Berkowitz, 1997, 1998a).

In his cognitive neoassociationist model, Berkowitz (1989, 1993) presents an elaborate account of the pathway from encountering an aversive event to experiencing anger (Figure 2.1). When individuals encounter an aversive event, they initially experience an undifferentiated negative affective state. This reaction evokes two impulsive reactions: fight and flight. Fight is associated with aggression-related thoughts, memories, and behavioural responses; flight is associated with escape-related responses. These responses serve to channel the initially undifferentiated negative affect into the more specific emotional states of (rudimentary) anger or (rudimentary) fear. To accentuate these rudimentary feelings into more elaborate emotional states, further cognitive processing takes place that comprises an evaluation of the initial stimulus situation, potential outcomes, memories of similar experiences, and the social norms associated with the

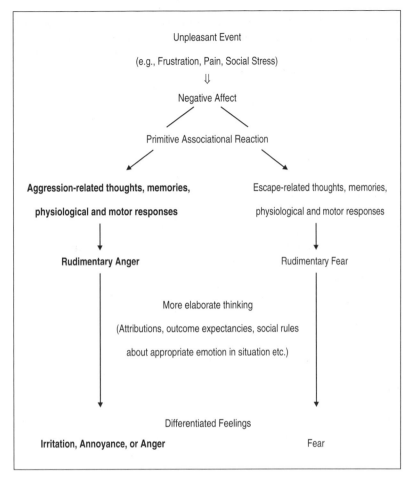

Unpleasant Event

(e.g., Frustration, Pain, Social Stress)

⇓

Negative Affect

Primitive Associational Reaction

Aggression-related thoughts, memories,

physiological and motor responses

Escape-related thoughts, memories,

physiological and motor responses

Rudimentary Anger

Rudimentary Fear

More elaborate thinking

(Attributions, outcome expectancies, social rules

about appropriate emotion in situation etc.)

Differentiated Feelings

Irritation, Annoyance, or Anger

Fear

FIG. 2.1. Berkowitz's "cognitive neoassociation model" of aggression (adapted from Berkowitz, 1993, p. 57, reproduced with permission of The McGraw-Hill Companies).

expression of different emotions. The final emotional state is "a collection of particular feelings, expressive motor-reactions, thoughts and memories that are associated with each other" (Berkowitz, 1993, p. 59). Because all the components of the emotional experience are associated with each other, activating one component is assumed to trigger other components relative to the strength of their association. For example, activating memories of past aversive events can give rise to aggressive thoughts and feelings that increase the likelihood of aggressive behaviour in a new situation or towards a target who is completely unrelated to the initial aversive event.

From the above discussion of Berkowitz's model it is clear that aggression is but one possible response to aversive stimulation. This implies that aggression is not an inevitable, but a potential feature of human behaviour, which can be promoted or suppressed by the emotional experience elicited by the aversive event.

Excitation transfer theory: Anger and the attribution of arousal

Whether or not an individual will react with an aggressive response to an aversive stimulation depends to a high degree on how the stimulation is interpreted by the recipient. As we saw above, frustrations are especially likely to elicit anger if they are interpreted as deliberate and unjustified interferences with the actor's goal-directed activities (see also Geen, 1990, on the role of attributional mediators of aggression). In his excitation transfer model, which builds on Schachter's (1964) two-factor theory of emotion, Zillmann (1979) proposes that the intensity of an anger experience is a function of two components: the strength of the physiological arousal generated by an aversive event and the way in which the arousal is explained and labelled. For example, every motorist knows the sudden increase in physiological arousal after a narrow escape from a dangerous traffic situation, such as stopping one's car inches away from a pedestrian who stepped out on the road from behind parked cars. Whether or not this arousal will be interpreted as anger depends to a significant extent on the appraisal of the situation. If the pedestrian is an adult, then the driver's arousal is likely to be experienced as anger over the other person's carelessness. If that person is a young child, then feelings of relief are likely to prevail over feelings of anger. Thus, the attribution of physiological arousal elicited by an aversive event is crucial in determining the link between the aversive event and a potential aggressive response.

Moreover, Zillmann postulates that if emotional arousal is unspecific and its origins not readily apparent to the individual, he or she tries to make sense of the arousal by drawing on informational cues present in the current situation. He argues that physiological arousal from a neutral or irrelevant source may be transferred to the arousal elicited by an aversive stimulation through a process of mis-attribution. Arousal generated by a source unrelated to the aversive stimulation may be falsely attributed to the aversive event and thus serve to intensify the anger elicited by that event. However, it is important that awareness of the original source of the arousal has faded, so that the individual still feels the arousal but is no longer conscious of its origin. In support of his model, Zillmann (1979) showed that individuals who carried residual arousal from a physical activity into an unrelated social situation in which they were exposed to a provocation were more likely to respond aggressively to the provocation than non-aroused individuals. The affectively neutral arousal serves to intensify the negative arousal caused by the provocation in that it is interpreted in the light of the salient situational cue, i.e., the provocation. As Zillmann (1994) notes, if the residual arousal does not stem from a neutral source, but from preceding anger, its anger-enhancing effect in the new situation is likely to be even stronger, leading to an escalation of angry aggression.

The excitation transfer model deals in particular with the combination of physiological arousal and cognitive appraisal involved in the emotional experience of anger. By influencing attributions of physiological arousal, aggressive response tendencies can either be strengthened, as explained above, or weakened. If people are led to believe that their arousal was caused by a pill rather than the provocation they experienced from another person, they see themselves as less angry and react less aggressively than those who are not offered a neutral explanation for their arousal (Younger & Doob, 1978). Therefore, this approach also supports the view of aggression as a potential, but by no means inevitable, manifestation of human behaviour.

The social cognitive approach: Aggressive scripts and social information processing

The importance of cognitive processes in the formation of an aggressive response has been stressed throughout the preceding sections. The way in which people think about an aversive event and about the emotional reaction they experience as a consequence is critical in determining the manifestation and strength of an aggressive response. The social cognitive approach further extends this perspective by studying individual differences in aggression as a function of differences in social information processing. In particular, two issues have been explored by this research: (a) the development of cognitive schemata that guide the performance of aggressive behaviour; and (b) characteristic ways of processing social information that distinguish between aggressive and non-aggressive individuals.

Cognitive schemata referring to situations and events are called "scripts". Scripts consist of knowledge structures that describe "appropriate sequences of events in a particular context" (Schank & Abelson, 1977, p. 41). These knowledge structures are acquired through experience with the respective situations, either first-hand or vicarious, such as via the media. In his social cognitive approach, Huesmann (1988, 1998) proposes that social behaviour in general, and aggressive behaviour in particular, is controlled by behavioural repertoires acquired in the process of early socialisation. From these behavioural experiences, scripts develop as abstract cognitive representations containing the characteristic features of the critical situation, expectations about the behaviour of the participants involved, as well as about the consequences of different behavioural options.

For example, if children have repeatedly responded (or seen others responding) to conflict situations by showing aggressive behaviour that settled the conflict to their advantage, they are likely to develop a generalised cognitive representation in which conflict and aggression are closely linked. In future conflict situations, this representation is likely to be activated, leading to further aggressive responses. Inherent in aggressive scripts are normative beliefs that guide the individual's decision about whether or not a specific response is appropriate under the given circumstances. Thus, children may develop the normative belief that you can hit back if attacked by a peer in a fight, but not if hit by an adult as a disciplinary measure. In a recent study, Huesmann and Guerra (1997) found a significant correlation between the endorsement of normative beliefs approving of aggressive behaviour and actual aggressive behaviour. Failure to learn the normative restrictions imposed on the manifestation of overt aggression will lead to the repeated performance of inappropriate aggression, which may form the basis for long-term adjustment problems (Eron, 1987).

Whether or not an aggressive script is activated and guides the person towards responding in an aggressive fashion depends to a significant extent on the cognitive processing of the initial social information that precedes the behavioural performance. Following the perception of another person's behaviour, the individual looks for an interpretation of that behaviour. Several studies show that individuals with a history of aggressive behaviour selectively prefer interpretations that attribute the other's behaviour to hostile intentions, especially when the actor's behaviour is ambiguous (Geen, 1998a). This "hostile attribution bias" may then activate an aggressive script and enhance the probability that an aggressive reaction will be selected from the individual's response repertoire.

In addition to the hostile attribution bias, other cognitive limitations have been shown to be characteristic of highly aggressive individuals, such as difficulties in remembering the details of conflict scenarios as well as generating non-confrontational and compromise-oriented solutions to those conflicts (see Lochman & Dodge, 1994).

Even though these socio-cognitive limitations may, in principle, be targeted by specific interventions, Eron (1994) notes that such interventions have largely been unsuccessful. In his view, the main reason why maladaptive forms of information processing are so resistant to change lies in the fact that aggressive scripts are learned very early on and applied successfully in the course of development: "The payoff is very good so that despite occasional or even frequent punishment it is difficult to unlearn and thus the behavior persists under the regulation of well-established cognitions" (Eron, 1994, p. 8).

Learning to be aggressive: The role of reinforcement and imitation

The specific mechanisms leading to the acquisition of aggressive scripts and behaviours have been studied with reference to two general principles of learning: instrumental conditioning and modelling. Unlike the view that aggression is an innate feature of human character, learning theorists have stressed that aggressive behaviour is produced to a large extent by "nurture", i.e., acquired through learning processes like most other forms of social behaviour (e.g., Bandura, 1983). Both instrumental conditioning, i.e., learning through reinforcement and punishment, and modelling, i.e., learning through the observation of models, have been shown as powerful mechanisms for the acquisition and performance of aggressive behaviour. To the extent that individuals are rewarded for aggressive behaviour, the likelihood is increased that the same or a similar behaviour will be shown again in the future. For example, if a child realises that he or she can win the upper hand in a dispute with a peer by pushing him to the ground, the successful outcome of the behaviour will lead the child to respond aggressively if a similar situation comes up again.

Another way in which aggressive behaviour can be learned is by observing others behaving in an aggressive fashion. In the classic study by Bandura et al. (1963), children were shown films of two adult models behaving either in an aggressive or a non-aggressive way towards a large inflatable doll. When the children were subsequently given the opportunity to play with the same doll, those who had watched the aggressive model showed more aggressive behaviour towards the doll than those who had watched the non-aggressive model. These findings suggest that observing an influential model (such as a person of high status or competence, a well-liked model, or a popular TV character) may lead to the *acquisition* of the observed behaviour even if the model has not been reinforced for his or her behaviour. In predicting whether or not the learned behaviour will actually be *performed*, the perceived consequences of the model's as well as the observer's behaviour do play an important role. The more positive the consequences of the aggressive behaviour for the model, the greater the likelihood that it will be imitated by the observer. The model's behaviour as well as its consequences serve as external stimuli that elicit aggressive response tendencies in the observer. The observers' normative standards as to the adequacy of the observed behaviour and their self-efficacy beliefs (i.e., the conviction that they are capable of performing the behaviour with the intended effects) serve as internal mechanisms regulating aggressive behaviour.

The social learning perspective has been a major theoretical approach for conceptualising the effects of media violence on aggressive behaviour, which can be regarded as a paradigmatic case of observational learning and vicarious reinforcement and will be considered in more detail in Chapter 5.

The social interactionist model: Aggression as coercive social influence

The last, and most recent, theoretical contribution to be reviewed in this chapter was proposed by Tedeschi and Felson (1994) to extend the analysis of aggressive behaviour into a broader "social inter-actionist theory of coercive actions." They prefer the concept of coercive action over the traditional notion of aggression, (a) because they see it as less value laden, avoiding the qualification of harm-doing as legitimate or illegitimate, and (b) because it includes threats and punishments as well as bodily force as important strategies of inflicting harm or gaining compliance from an unwilling target.

Most of the approaches reviewed in the previous sections focused on hostile or impulsive aggression. In contrast, the social interactionist model is concerned with the instrumental function of coercive actions. It postulates that coercive strategies are used by the actor to inflict harm on the target or to make the target comply with the actor's demands in the service of three major goals: to control the behaviour of others, to restore justice, and to assert and protect positive identities (Tedeschi & Felson, 1994, p. 348). Coercive actions are conceptualised as outcomes of a decision-making process in which the actor first decides to use coercive influence strategies rather than non-coercive ones and then chooses a particular form of coercion from the range of available options. For example, a person whose goal it is to make a wealthy relative change his will in his or her favour has to decide first

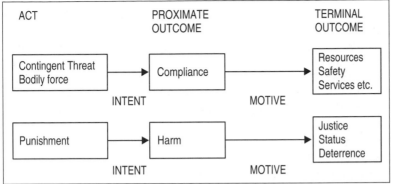

ACT	PROXIMATE OUTCOME		TERMINAL OUTCOME
Contingent Threat Bodily force	→ Compliance	→	Resources Safety Services etc.
INTENT		MOTIVE	
Punishment	→ Harm	→	Justice Status Deterrence
INTENT		MOTIVE	

FIG. 2.2. The motivational foundations of coercive actions (reprinted with permission from Tedeschi & Felson, 1994, p. 164; copyright © 1994 by the American Psychological Association).

whether to use non-coercive social influence, such as ingratiation and gentle persuasion, or coercive strategies, such as threats or physical harm. If a decision is made in favour of coercive influence, then the next step is to decide what particular form of coercion will be most successful in reaching the intended goal.

Three forms of coercive actions are at the core of the theory: (a) *threat*, i.e., the communication of an intention to harm the target person, with special emphasis on contingent threat that makes the infliction of harm contingent upon the target's refusal to comply with the aggressor's demands; (b) *punishment*, i.e., an act performed with the intention to inflict harm on the target person; and (c) *bodily force*, i.e., the use of physical contact to compel or constrain the behaviour of another person. The choice of a coercive strategy is determined by the intention to achieve a particular immediate or "proximate" outcome, which in turn is motivated by the aim to reach a valued terminal goal. These motivational underpinnings of coercive actions are illustrated in Figure 2.2.

A person's decision to use threats or bodily force is seen as prompted by the intent to obtain compliance from the target person with his or her demands. However, compliance is not a goal in itself but is motivated by the desire to reach a terminal outcome, such as getting the target to part with resources or provide services to the aggressor. In contrast, punishment is carried out as a coercive action with the intent to harm the target person with the ultimate goal of restoring justice, defending one's superior status, or deterring the person from carrying out particular unwanted actions.

To explain the nature of the decision-making process that leads to the performance of coercive actions, Tedeschi and Felson draw on several lines of theorising, some of which have been discussed earlier in this chapter. Weighing the costs and benefits attached to each option plays an important role in the decision-making process. The subjective value of the intended goal, the probability that it will be reached successfully by the particular action considered, and the magnitude and probability of potential negative effects are considered by the actor. Past learning experiences in similar situations hold vital cues in assessing the probability of different outcomes as well as their costs and benefits. Moreover, the actor's attitudes and values determine whether a particular behaviour, such as corporal punishment of children, is seen as an acceptable coercive strategy. Referring to sociocognitive processes, the ease with which scripts for different types of coercive versus non-coercive courses of action are cognitively accessible to the actor is seen as another critical factor. For example, if an individual habitually uses coercive strategies, coercive scripts will be activated more readily in a new situation because they have been rehearsed more frequently in the past.

The important contribution of the social interactionist approach is to place aggression in the context of other forms of social behaviour designed to exert influence over others. It stresses that aggression, as a particular form of coercive action, is but one potential influence strategy and that the individual decides in a rational choice process whether or not to use that strategy in a given situation. Therefore, rather than being driven to aggressive behaviour by innate instincts or intense negative affect, the individual is seen here as having control over his or her aggressive response repertoire and being able to choose non-aggressive alternatives.

Altogether, the approaches reviewed in this chapter reflect the diversity of theoretical accounts of how and why aggressive behaviour occurs. In particular, the psychological approaches have highlighted the interplay of affective states, cognitive processes, and behavioural decisions on the implementation of aggressive responses. The "General Affective Aggression Model (GAAM)" developed by Anderson and his co-workers is a recent addition to the range of theoretical conceptualisations of the antecedents of aggression and offers an integrative framework for many aspects from previous theories (Lindsay & Anderson, 2000). The GAAM is presented in Figure 2.3.

Anderson and his co-workers (e.g., Anderson, Anderson, & Deuser, 1996; Anderson, Benjamin, & Bartholow, 1998) have presented a range of studies exploring elements of the model, in particular the role of trait hostility and trait aggressiveness on aggressive behaviour (see Chapter 3) and the impact of situational factors, such as temperature and aggressive primes (see Chapter 4).

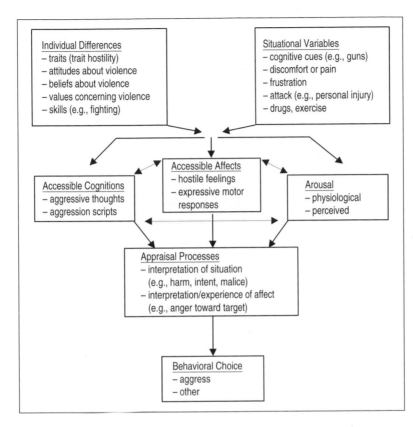

FIG. 2.3. The General Affective Aggression Model (from Lindsay & Anderson, 2000, *Personality and Social Psychology Bulletin*, *26*, 533–547, copyright © 2000 by Sage Publications; reprinted by permission of Sage Publications, Inc.).

In comparing the different conceptualisations of aggression, one important point of comparison refers to their implications concerning the controllability and reduction of aggressive behaviour. The early instinct- and drive-related approaches entail a basically pessimistic view, but the lack of empirical support for their central constructs has led them to be largely disregarded in modern aggression research. As Berkowitz (1993, p. 387) points out, "people have a *capacity* for aggression and violence, but not a biological urge to attack and destroy others that is continually building up inside them." This view is supported by theories stressing the mediating role of cognitions and learning as well as decision-making processes. They entail the possibility of strengthening the inhibitory forces against the perform-ance of overt aggression and acknowledge the individual's freedom to decide against the performance of aggressive behaviour in favour of alternative courses of action.

Summary

- Theoretical approaches aimed at explaining aggressive behaviour include both biological and psychological lines of thinking and research.
- The biological models refer to evolutionary and genetic principles to explain aggression. The sociobiological approach postulates that aggression has developed as an adaptive form of social behaviour in the process of evolution. The ethological perspective explains the manifestation of overt aggression as a function of an internal aggressive energy that is released by aggression-related external cues. Evidence from the field of behaviour genetics suggests that the disposition to act aggressively is at least partly determined by genetic influences.
- Early psychological models also assumed aggression to be an innate response tendency. Freud's view of aggression as an instinct to serve the fulfilment of the pleasure principle inspired the frustration–aggression hypothesis, which saw aggression as driven by a desire to overcome frustration. Subsequent psychological approaches widened the frustration–aggression link into a more general model of negative affect and highlighted the role of cognitive factors, learning experiences, and decision-making processes in predicting aggressive responses.
- The psychological explanations of aggression share the assumption that aggressive behaviour is not inevitable, but that the likelihood of its occurrence depends on the operation of a variety of promoting and inhibiting factors located both within the person and the environment.

Suggested reading

Berkowitz, L. (1998a). Affective aggression: The role of stress, pain, and negative affect. In R.G. Geen & E. Donnerstein (Eds.), *Human aggression: Theories, research and implications for social policy* (pp. 49–72). San Diego, CA: Academic Press.

Geen, R. (1998a). Aggression and antisocial behavior. In D.T. Gilbert, S.T. Fiske, & G. Lindzey (Eds.), *The handbook of social psychology* (4th ed., Vol. II, pp. 317–356). Boston, MA: McGraw-Hill.

Tedeschi, J.T., & Felson, R.B. (1994). *Violence, aggression, and coercive actions*. Washington, DC: American Psychological Association.

Individual differences in aggression 3

The theories reviewed in the previous chapter have offered a range of explanations of how aggressive tendencies are acquired and expressed. In this chapter, we will explore empirical evidence addressing the origins of individual differences in aggressive behaviour. In the first section, we will examine developmental approaches looking at the emergence of aggressive behaviour in a child's repertoire of social behaviour. In particular, characteristic pathways of aggression from childhood to adolescence will be described along with factors that discriminate between those different pathways. The second section will review evidence on the relationship between stable personality traits and individual differences in aggression in adulthood. Finally, the third section will look at differences in aggressive behaviour as a function of a particular individual characteristic, i.e., gender. Here, we will ask whether there are differences in aggressive behaviour between men and women and, if so, how they are best explained. Only research focusing primarily on individual differences in aggression will be included in this chapter. Studies that consider individual difference variables alongside or secondary to other issues will be reviewed in their respective contexts (see, for example, the discussion of gender differences in response to media violence in Chapter 5).

The development of aggressive behaviour

As Loeber and Hay (1997) have pointed out, aggression is to a certain extent age-normative among children and adolescents. This means that behaviours carried out with the intention to harm another person are shown at least occasionally by many, if not most members of these age groups. However, there is a proportion of children and adolescents who deviate from this normal course of development by showing high and persistent levels of aggressive behaviour, which can no longer be seen as age-normative. It is the behaviour of these individuals that the developmental analysis of aggression is particularly interested to understand.

In trying to explain why children develop non-normatively strong aggressive tendencies and how these tendencies extend into subsequent periods of development, the following questions are of key importance (Loeber & Hay, 1997):

(1) When does aggressive behaviour first appear and what forms does it take in childhood, adolescence, and early adulthood?
(2) How stable are early manifestations of aggressive behaviour as children get older?
(3) Does the development of aggressive behaviour follow a pattern of escalation whereby milder forms of aggression are followed by more severe aggressive behaviours?
(4) What are the emotional and cognitive antecedents of aggressive behaviour?
(5) What is the role of the social environment (parents, peers, and neighbourhoods) in the formation and persistence of aggressive behaviour patterns?

We will summarise the evidence regarding each of these questions, guided by two recent state-of-the-art reviews by Coie and Dodge (1998) and Loeber and Hay (1997).

Manifestations of aggressive behaviour from childhood to young adulthood

The first precursor of aggressive behaviour is the recognition of anger in adults' facial expression, which infants are capable of from as early as 3 months. This is followed by the expression of anger by the child in response to frustration, which starts in the second half of the first year. Behavioural patterns of aggression in conflicts with peers and adults emerge during the second and third years of life in the form of temper tantrums and the use of physical force (e.g., hitting, pushing, kicking). In the early school years, gender differences in aggression become apparent, with boys generally showing higher levels of physical aggression than girls. Girls, however, do show both verbal aggression (swearing, name calling) and relational aggression (peer exclusion, gossiping) to a substantial degree (Crick & Grotpeter, 1995; Rys & Bear, 1997). Even though aggressive behaviour tends to decrease from early to middle childhood as a function of increasing

THE INDEPENDENT

Tuesday 25 January 2000 *

NEWS 3

Johnny and Luther are 12-year-old twins. Yesterday their army took 700 hostages

FIG. 3.1. An example of the early manifestation of severe aggression (reprinted with permission from The Independent Syndication).

self-regulatory and social skills, this does not seem to apply to sibling aggression, which both genders report to be common.

Loeber and Hay (1997) note that aggressive behaviour changes its level and pattern in adolescence and young adulthood. Aggressive behaviour tends to become more harmful, not least due to the high prevalence of firearms and other weapons among adolescent males (Verlinden, Hersen, & Thomas, 2000). An extreme example of juvenile aggression is presented in Figure 3.1. The headline refers to the actions of two 12-year-old commanders of a rebel army in Sri Lanka who took an entire hospital population hostage, killing several of their captives.

In the Carolina Longitudinal Study conducted by Cairns and Cairns (1994), more than half of the boys under the age of 16 said they owned a firearm and 81% reported that firearms were present in their household. These are alarming figures, not only from a European perspective where gun control legislation is much stricter than in the United States. Loeber and Hay also point out that the dramatic increase in juvenile homicide in the United States over the past decade can be attributed to a large extent to the widespread availability of firearms, which were involved in more than half of all juvenile killings.

An important change in the pattern of aggressive behaviour from childhood to adolescence is that aggression and violence tend to become more socially organised. Juvenile gangs assemble adolescents who are socially rejected by their less aggressive peers. They are attractive to highly aggressive individuals and account for a high proportion of juvenile aggression, including in-fighting between rival gangs. While gang violence is still largely seen as a male phenomenon, reports of girl gangs capable of serious aggression are becoming increasingly frequent (see also Chapter 6 for a discussion of group violence). However, there does seem to be a gender difference in that girls' aggressive behaviours are replaced by non-aggressive strategies of conflict resolution to a greater extent, while boys' tendencies to use aggression to resolve social conflicts more frequently persist into adolescence and early adulthood.

Stability of aggressive behaviour from childhood into adolescence and young adulthood

An important question concerning the implications of non-normatively high aggressive tendencies in childhood is whether or not they remain consistently high in subsequent periods of development. Longitudinal studies have produced evidence that aggressive behaviour is, indeed, relatively stable over time (see Laub & Lauritsen, 1995, for a review). Based on data from 16 studies exploring the stability of male aggressiveness, Olweus (1979) estimated stability coefficients of $r = .76$ over a one-year period, $r = .69$ over a period of 5 years, and $r = .60$ over an interval of 10 years (see also Zumkley, 1994). These figures suggest that aggression is almost as stable as intelligence, even over extended periods of time. One implication of this conclusion is that aggression at a young age is not a problem that children are likely to grow out of as they get older, unless they are targeted by specific intervention programmes. Loeber and Hay note that stability is likely to be highest for those individuals who represent the extremes of the aggression continuum, i.e., are the least or the most aggressive at Time 1.

However, the fact that high stability coefficients were found for aggressive behaviour from childhood into adolescence and early adulthood should not lead investigators to overlook the variability in aggressive behaviour between individuals. Even when stability coefficients are high at a group level, some individuals may change their patterns of aggressive behaviour over time. For example, a person who was non-aggressive at Time 1 may show an increase in aggression at Time 2, i.e., a late onset of aggression. Alternatively, a person who was aggressive at Time 1 may no longer be aggressive at Time 2, showing desistance from aggressive behaviour. There is evidence to support both forms of change. For example, Kingston and Prior (1995) measured aggression in a group of Australian children on three occasions between the ages of 2–3 and 7–8. They found that 55% of the boys and 41% of the girls who were aggressive at the age of 2 were still aggressive at age 8, i.e., showed stability. In contrast, 31% of the aggressive boys at age 2 and 24% of the aggressive girls were no longer aggressive at age 8, i.e., had desisted from aggression. In addition, they found that about a quarter of the aggressive children at age 8 first appeared as aggressive at age 5. Each of the latter two groups displayed instability in their aggressive behaviour over time, albeit in different directions.

Escalation of aggressive behaviours

Overall, there is evidence of a continuous decline in aggression as a function of age (see Loeber & Stouthamer-Loeber, 1998), so desistance may reflect the age-normative pattern of development with regard to aggressive behaviour. However, it is equally clear that a substantial proportion of aggressive children carry on being aggressive. Given that aggression manifests itself in different forms, varying in the extent of violence involved, it is important to examine whether or not the level of aggression remains stable for these individuals or whether their aggressive behaviour tends to escalate from less serious to more serious forms of aggression in the course of development. *Long-term escalation* refers to the gradual increase in the severity of aggressive actions from childhood to adolescence, while *short-term escalation* denotes a rapid increase in violence among individuals who only start becoming aggressive at a later stage. At a group level, evidence of a long-term escalation effect comes from studies exploring the cumulative onset curves for different forms of aggression varying in severity. An example of this approach is provided in Figure 3.2, presenting Loeber and Hay's analysis of the age at which minor aggression, physical fighting, and severe violence become apparent in boys' behaviour.

Figure 3.2 reveals that minor forms of aggression (annoying others, bullying) showed the earliest onset, followed by physical fighting. Despite its later onset, physical fighting shows a steeper increase than minor aggression, and by the age of 15 the two curves have reached similar prevalence levels. The latest and slowest-rising onset was observed for violence (strong-arming, assault, and forced sex). As would be expected, its prevalence at age 16, though impressive at almost 20%, was substantially lower than prevalence rates for the two less serious forms of aggression.

At an intra-individual level, there is conclusive evidence that a high proportion of violent individuals previously showed mild and/or moderate forms of aggression. Moffitt et al. (1996) showed that 73% of the boys who had a conviction for violent offences at age 18 also had a history of persistent antisocial behaviour from childhood onwards. However, it is equally true that individuals may become violent without having a history of previous aggression. In the Moffitt et al. study, 23% of violent offenders had not displayed antisocial

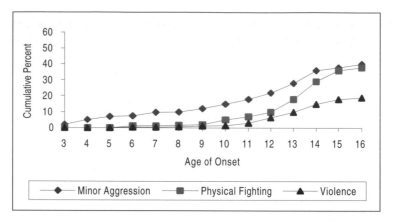

FIG. 3.2. Cumulative onset of minor aggression, physical fighting, and violence in boys (adapted from Loeber and Hay, 1997, p. 379; with permission, from the *Annual Review of Psychology*, Volume 48 © 1997 by Annual Reviews www.AnnualReviews. org).

conduct problems prior to adolescence. Why some individuals start becoming highly aggressive in adolescence without showing a gradual escalation of aggressive behaviour patterns from childhood is not entirely clear. Some authors suggest that late-onset violent individuals are often over-controlled, trying to suppress their aggressive tendencies and only showing aggression if aggressive stimulation (frustration, anger arousal) is sufficiently strong to overcome those inhibitions. Another possibility is that the social organisation of violence in adolescence in the form of youth gangs may attract individuals who are vulnerable because of other, non-aggression-related problems, such as low self-esteem or social isolation.

Emotional and cognitive antecedents of aggressive behaviour

A further central issue in understanding individual differences in aggressive behaviour in childhood and adolescence refers to the role of personal characteristics, most notably emotional control and cognitive functioning. Children who show deficits in affective regulation and impulse control are more likely to develop and sustain aggressive behaviour patterns. These children are often perceived as having a difficult temperament and they find it hard to constrain their aggressive impulses in an age-appropriate way (Kingston & Prior, 1995). Differences in temperament emerge at an early age and affect the way in which children are treated by their social environment.

At the level of general cognitive functioning, the possible impact of low intelligence and attention deficit disorders has been addressed by a limited number of studies. Available evidence suggests that both variables may be linked to aggression, but the exact nature of the link and interactions with other variables still need to be clarified. Among more specific cognitive precursors to aggression, aggression-related attitudes were found to play an important role. For example, Erdley and Asher (1998) found that children who saw aggression as a legitimate form of social behaviour showed higher levels of actual aggressive behaviour (as evidenced in peer ratings and in the children's own responses to ambiguous provocation described in hypothetical scenarios). The difference in aggressive behaviour as a function of legitimacy beliefs was found for both boys and girls, but levels of aggression were generally lower for girls than for boys.

Beliefs about the legitimacy of aggression can be seen as part of an individual's aggressive script, developed on the basis of direct and vicarious learning experiences (see Chapter 2 for a discussion of the script approach and Chapter 5 for a discussion of media presentations of legitimate aggression). Another feature of the scripts of children who show high levels of aggression may be the perception of hostile intent in others. These children interpret their peers' behaviour in the light of a pre-existing knowledge structure suggesting hostile intent, and they are more likely to act aggressively in response to that perception. Every time hostility is perceived and aggressive behaviour shown as a reaction, the link between the perception of hostile intent and aggression is reinforced, a cycle which may account for the long-term stability of aggressive behaviour. This line of reasoning was corroborated in a longitudinal study by Burks et al. (1999). They obtained mother and teacher ratings of aggressive behaviour in kindergarten and Grade 8. In Grade 8, they also assessed children's attributions of hostile intent in response to hypothetical conflict scenarios and their hostile knowledge structures (i.e., the salience of hostility-related thoughts). In support of their hypotheses, Burks et al. found that children who had hostile knowledge structures were more likely to attribute hostility in a specific social encounter and were also rated as more aggressive by their mother and teacher. In addition, they found that the link between early aggression and aggressive behaviour in Grade 8 was mediated by hostile knowledge structures. Thus, individual differences in aggression may be the result of schematic, i.e., habitual ways of information processing that suggest aggression as an adequate response to social stimuli.

Social influences on the development of aggression

A variety of adverse social conditions have been examined as potentially responsible for individual differences in aggression. Harsh

parental discipline was found to be linked to higher levels in children's subsequent aggressiveness, not least because physical punishment comes across to the child as an acceptable form of conflict
resolution. In the same way, children exposed to abuse and neglect
were shown to display higher levels of aggression (see Coie & Dodge,
1998; Englander, 1997; and Chapter 7). Furthermore, the role of
learning by observation is underscored by findings that witnessing
violence, both immediately in the family and indirectly in media
portrayals, enhances the likelihood of aggressive behaviour (Widom,
1989, and Chapter 5).

Peer relationships constitute another powerful source of social
influence relevant to aggression. Aggressive children are rejected by
their peers from as early as the age of 6, and rejection is associated
with subsequent increases in aggression. The more a child's behaviour is dominated by aggression, i.e., the less he or she displays non-
aggressive forms of behaviour, the more unanimous the rejection
and the more extreme the resulting social isolation. To the extent
that aggressive children are socially isolated by their non-aggressive
peers, they are likely to associate with other aggressive peers,
entering social systems, such as violent gangs, which further
promote aggressive behaviour. Thus, they get trapped in a situation
where social acceptance depends on the commitment of further acts
of aggression. Nonetheless, for some aggressive individuals,
association with aggressive peers and the reinforcement of aggressive response will be limited to adolescence and not necessarily
extend into adulthood. Loeber and Hay (1997) note that violence
rates peak in adolescence or early adulthood and then decrease with
age. Nonetheless, adults differ as much as children and adolescents
in their aggressive response tendencies. The next section will therefore examine the relationship between personality and aggression in
adulthood.

Personality and aggression in adulthood

Social psychological aggression research has traditionally devoted
more attention to the variability of aggressive behaviour as a function
of situational influences (see Chapter 4) than to the consistency with
which people behave aggressively across time and situations and the
extent to which they differ from others in their aggressive tendencies.
Therefore, the body of evidence concerning the role of personality in

aggression is limited compared to the host of research addressing the impact of situational factors on aggression (see Chapters 4 and 5). Nonetheless, several personality constructs have been suggested to explain individual differences in aggression, and measures to assess these constructs have been developed (Baron & Richardson, 1994, Chap. 6; Berkowitz, 1998b; Geen, 1998b; see also Berkowitz, 1993, for the relationship between psychopathy and aggression). In this section, we will take a brief look at the following constructs: irritability, emotional susceptibility, dissipation–rumination, hostile attribution bias, and the self.

Irritability refers to the habitual "tendency to react impulsively, controversially, or rudely at the slightest provocation or disagreement" (Caprara, Perugini, & Barbaranelli, 1994, p. 125). Habitually irritable people, as identified by the Caprara Irritability Scale (Caprara et al., 1985) consisting of items like "I think I am rather touchy", were found to show increased levels of aggression compared to non-irritable individuals. The difference was particularly pronounced if the respondents had previously been frustrated. Similarly, irritability augmented the differences in aggressive behaviour observed in response to the exposure of aggressive cues (see Caprara et al., 1994, for a summary).

Emotional susceptibility is defined as an individual's tendency "to experience feelings of discomfort, helplessness, inadequacy, and vulnerability" (Caprara et al., 1994, p. 125). Like irritability, it is presumed to indicate a generally higher readiness (or lower response threshold) for aggressive behaviour. Findings reported by Caprara and his colleagues largely parallel the effects found for irritability. Emotionally susceptible subjects showed more aggressive behaviour, particularly following prior frustration. They also showed a larger increase in aggression following physical exercise, lending support to Zillmann's "excitation transfer model" (see Chapter 2). The two constructs of irritability and emotional susceptibility thus seem to be associated with individual differences in affective or hostile aggression.

Dissipation versus rumination represent the poles of a continuum describing the extent to which people are preoccupied with aggressive cognitions following an aggression-eliciting stimulus. High dissipators/low ruminators quickly get over a provocative or hostile encounter without investing much time and effort in thinking about the experience. Ruminators, on the other hand, remain cognitively pre-occupied with the hostile experience and are more likely to plan and elaborate retaliative responses. In order for ruminative versus dissipative tendencies to show an effect, sufficient time must be allowed between the hostile or provoking stimulus event and the aggressive response. The more time elapses, dissipators should become less likely to show an aggressive response, while ruminators should become more likely. Because they are related to differences in the level of cognitive activity, Caprara et al. (1994) argued that differences in rumination–dissipation should be particularly likely to show up in response to stimuli that trigger cognitive rather than affective reactions. In an experiment that used threat to self-esteem (as a cognition-eliciting stimulus) rather than frustration (as an affect-eliciting stimulus), ruminators were found to show more aggression than dissipators. However, a close look at the operationalisation of frustration (failure in a learning task) versus threat to self-esteem (negative or positive evaluation by a confederate) suggests that the distinction may not yet have been clearly drawn (see also Collins & Bell, 1997). Nevertheless, it may be concluded that individual tendencies to respond to aggression-eliciting stimuli with dissipation or rumination are associated with differences in aggressive responding (see Caprara, Barbaranelli, & Zimbardo, 1996, for an integration of these aggressive response dispositions into the famous "Big Five" factor model of personality).

Hostile attributional style is another individual difference variable related to aggressive behaviour. It refers to a person's habitual tendency to interpret ambiguous stimuli in terms of hostility and aggression. Earlier in this chapter, we looked at a study by Burks et al. (1999), which showed that hostile knowledge structures lead children to interpret social stimuli in a more negative way and make them more likely to respond in an aggressive fashion. Dill, Anderson, Anderson, and Deuser (1997) complement this evidence by two studies that demonstrate the effect of a hostile attributional style on aggression in adults.

It is important to note that attributional style not only affects the way in which individuals interpret actions directed at them personally but also shapes their social perceptions in general. As Dill et al. (1997, p. 275) graphically describe it, these people "tend to view the world through blood-red tinted glasses." Attributional style is a cognitive disposition and does not depend on the experience of affective arousal, i.e., anger, as a result of being personally affected by others' apparently hostile actions. However, this cognitive disposition may go hand in hand with affect-based dispositions towards aggression. Dill et al. (1997) showed that irritability and trait aggressiveness predicted the extent to which subjects attributed aggressive thoughts to the actor in a scenario describing an ambiguous social interaction. In a second study, they showed that differences in the attribution of aggressive feelings and behaviours were not only apparent when the stimulus material was ambiguous with respect to aggressive meaning but also occurred for unambiguously aggressive interactions.

Whereas the hostile attribution bias enhances aggressive behaviour, *perspective taking* is a cognitive variable associated with the inhibition of aggressive responses. Perspective taking refers to a person's ability to orient him/herself non-egocentrically to the perspective of another person (Richardson, Green, & Lago, 1998). The role of perspective taking in inhibiting aggressive behaviour has been established by a variety of studies (Miller & Eisenberg, 1988). For example, Richardson et al. (1994) showed that individuals high on dispositional perspective taking were less likely to report aggressive behaviour and also less likely to respond in an aggressive way to a provocation. In a more recent study, Richardson et al. (1998) found that individuals high on dispositional perspective taking were more likely to choose a non-aggressive response to a verbal attack (as opposed to an aggressive response) than low perspective takers. This was only true, however, if the attacker's verbal insults increased in aggressiveness from the beginning to the end of the interaction. When it decreased from high to low levels of verbal insults, no effect of perspective taking emerged. The need to understand an aggressive opponent's behaviour is probably greater if the opponent's aggression becomes more extreme in the course of the interaction than when initially aggressive opponents become less aggressive over time. Therefore, high perspective takers may have chosen non-aggressive, i.e., de-escalating responses to a greater extent when the opponent showed increasing levels of aggression.

The findings on both perspective taking and hostile attribution bias show that individual differences in the cognitive processing of social information are relevant to the understanding of individual differences in aggressive behaviour.

Self-esteem has long been considered an important factor explaining individual differences in aggression. Traditionally, it has been assumed that low self-esteem would precipitate aggressive behaviour, that negative feelings about the self would make an individual more likely to hit out against others. Several studies have claimed support for this conception. More recently, however, Baumeister and Boden (1998) have questioned the empirical foundations of that view and proposed a different perspective on the link between self-esteem and aggression. They argued that individuals with high self-esteem are more prone to aggressive behaviour, particularly in response to stimuli (negative feedback, provocation) perceived as a threat to their high self-esteem. Their view is that "aggression follows from an explosive combination of favorable self-appraisals and external threat" (Baumeister & Boden, 1998, p. 115). The authors review evidence from a wide range of areas, including laboratory aggression, domestic violence, murder and assault, and even violence exerted by political groups (see also Baumeister, Smart, & Boden, 1996). In all of these areas, there is evidence to suggest that individuals who commit aggressive acts are more likely to have a positive rather than a negative self-image. However, Baumeister and Boden point out that it is important to consider the basis of high self-esteem to arrive at more accurate predictions of its impact on aggression. High self-esteem that is inflated (i.e., considerably higher than reflected in others' appraisals) and unstable (i.e., fluctuates over time) is particularly likely to lead to aggression when threatened by external appraisal. In line with Berkowitz's cognitive neoassociation model of aggression (see Chapter 2), Baumeister and Boden (1998) stipulate that threat to self-esteem precipitates aggression by eliciting negative affect, i.e., anger. To the extent that negative appraisal is perceived as unjustified, it evokes anger, which, in turn, enhances the probability of an aggressive response.

Another aspect of the self relevant to the understanding of individual differences in aggression is *self-control*. This construct refers to internal restraints that should prevent the release of aggressive response tendencies. Several authors have suggested that some people's chronic deficits in self-control are responsible for their criminal behaviour. The fact that many criminals commit a variety of different offences, together with the observation that criminal behaviour is often paired with lack of self-control in other activities (heavy smoking, excessive alcohol consumption), supports the idea of a general self-control problem underlying aggressive behaviour (see Baumeister & Boden, 1998).

The evidence reviewed in this section points to a number of personal characteristics associated with relatively stable individual differences in aggression. This line of research is important in explaining why individuals behave differently even when exposed to the same situational conditions. In the following section we will summarise key findings from an extensive literature that has been devoted to a particular individual characteristic and its impact on aggressive behaviour.

Gender differences in aggressive behaviour

The assumption that men are generally more aggressive than women is well established in everyday observation, crime records, as well as lay conceptions about gender. Men consistently outnumber women by a wide margin as perpetrators of criminal offences. The German Official Crime Statistics for 1999 reveal that women accounted for only 10.9% of all criminal suspects (Bundesministerium des Inneren [Interior Ministry], 2000). Similar figures can be found in the Anglo-American literature (e.g., Archer & Lloyd, in press; Kruttschnitt, 1995). For example, Chesney-Lind (1997, p. 15) quoted figures from the US Federal Bureau of Investigation for 1994, which show that men outnumbered women by 4.4 to 1 in arrests for aggravated assault and by 2.8 to 1 in arrests for other assaults. Reviewing arrest rates for juvenile violence, Scott (1999) found young males to be more than six times more likely than females to be arrested for criminal violence. Findings based on self-reports support these conclusions. The widespread prevalence of physical aggression in male social behaviour is illustrated, for example, by Archer, Holloway, and McLoughlin (1995). They found that 61% of a sample of male students had been involved in a fight during the 3 years prior to the study. A substantial number of respondents reported that either they (11%) or their opponent (18%) had drawn blood. In 15% of all fights, the police had been involved, and in 8% arrests had been made. Unfortunately, no comparable data on women's involvement in fights were reported. Men are also far more likely to own a gun than are women. Earlier, we quoted the longitudinal study by Cairns and Cairns (1994), which found that 51% of boys under the age of 16 reported owning a gun. The parallel figure for girls was just 5%.

Developmental research reveals that gender differences in aggressive behaviour emerge early in life, from about the third year onwards (Coie & Dodge, 1998; Maccoby, 1998). Loeber and Stouthamer-Loeber (1998) summarised the evidence on gender differences in aggressive behaviour in different developmental periods, as shown in Table 3.1.

Table 3.1 reveals that gender differences in aggression are apparent from pre-school age onwards, the direction of these differences being towards higher levels of aggression in boys. Moreover, Loeber and Stouthamer-Loeber report that the developmental course of aggressive behaviour seems to differ for boys and girls: A greater proportion of girls start becoming aggressive in adolescence without a prior history of aggression, and girls' involvement in serious

TABLE 3.1

Evidence for gender differences in aggression in childhood and adolescence

Developmental period	Manifestation	Gender differences
Infancy	Frustration and rage	No
Toddlerhood	Instrumental aggression	Few
Pre-school	Personal aggression	Yes
	Physical fighting	
Elementary school	Indirect aggression	Yes
Middle and high school	Group and gang fighting	Yes
	Aggravated assault	
	Sexual violence	
	Homicide	

Reprinted with permission from Loeber and Stouthamer-Loeber (1998, p. 253); copyright © 1998 by the American Psychological Association.

violence peaks earlier than that of boys. Paralleling gender differences in aggressive *behaviour*, boys and girls were found to differ in their approval of aggression as a means of conflict resolution (Huesmann & Guerra, 1997).

Evidence for higher aggression in adult males

Concerning overall differences between men and women in aggressive behaviour, the available evidence from both individual studies and meta-analytical reviews is remarkably clear: Men show higher levels of aggression across the board, but the difference is not dramatic (e.g., Eagly & Steffen, 1986; Hyde, 1984). Findings from cross-cultural studies also support this conclusion (e.g., Archer & McDaniel, 1995).

However, a closer inspection of the evidence suggests several important qualifications. Most importantly, gender differences in aggression vary as a function of the type of aggressive behaviour studied. Gender differences are typically larger on measures of physical as compared to verbal aggression, and on measures of direct as compared to indirect aggression. Moreover, the way in which aggression is measured (through peer nominations, observations, or experimental behaviour) affects the magnitude of gender differences. A contentious issue has been whether or not gender differences in aggression have become smaller over time. Several reviewers found that earlier studies tended to show larger differences than more recent publications (e.g., Hyde, 1984), and some have taken this finding to suggest that socialisation is more important in eliciting gender differences than biological processes. However, Knight, Fabes, and Higgins (1996) demonstrated that earlier and later studies not only differ with regard to their publication date, but also in terms of their use of different methodologies. Different methodologies, in turn, were found to be systematically related to different magnitudes of gender differences. When these methodological differences were taken into account in Knight et al.'s re-examination of studies included in Hyde's (1984) meta-analysis, the "year of publication effect" disappeared.

Even though there is consistent evidence that men are more aggressive than women, this is not to say that female aggression is non-existent (Keeney & Heide, 1994; White & Kowalski, 1994). Björkqvist and Niemelä (1992) provide a comprehensive coverage of the different aspects of female aggression, including both biological and cross-cultural analyses. This evidence suggests that girls may be more likely to engage in more indirect forms of aggression, such as relational aggression (e.g., excluding others and spreading gossip). Among adults, women still scored higher than men on a measure of relational aggression in a study by Björkqvist, Österman, and Lagerspetz (1994). While indirect aggression was found in this study to be common in men as well, it was more likely to take the form of rational-appearing aggression. This category includes aggressive acts for which a rational basis might be construed (e.g., unfairly criticising someone, limiting another person's chances to express him/herself).

Explaining gender differences in aggression

Unlike the evidence on the existence of sex differences in aggression, which is fairly clear-cut in suggesting higher levels of aggression in males, the task of explaining why these differences occur is far from being resolved. Three main lines of explanation have been suggested to account for the observed gender differences in aggression: the hormonal explanation, the sociobiological model, and social role model.

(1) The *hormonal* explanation attributes increased aggressive tendencies to the male sex hormone testosterone. According to this view, sex differences in aggression are due at least in part to higher levels of testosterone in males. Studies involving subhuman species provide some support for the role of testosterone in aggression shown by male animals (Archer, 1988). To demonstrate the link between testosterone and aggression in humans, men who differ in

terms of aggressive behaviour have been compared with regard to their levels of testosterone. Overall, these cross-sectional studies have failed to substantiate the proposed importance of testosterone in male aggression (see reviews by Archer, 1991; Archer, Birring, & Wu, 1998; Benton, 1992). In addition, the claim that testosterone plays a crucial role in aggression would require evidence that intra-individual variations in testosterone levels are accompanied by corresponding fluctuations in aggression. In particular, the dramatic increases in testosterone in puberty should lead to parallel increases in aggressive behaviour. In a longitudinal study that followed boys from the beginning to the end of puberty, Halpern, Udry, Campbell, and Suchindran (1993) failed to find a covariation of testosterone and aggression.

(2) The *evolutionary* or sociobiological account stresses the adaptive value of male aggression in securing access to attractive (i.e., highly reproductive) females (e.g., Thornhill & Thornhill, 1991; Wilson & Daly, 1985; see also Chapter 2). The finding that it is primarily *young* men who are responsible for higher rates of male aggression, as reflected in crime statistics as well as controlled studies, is quoted in support of this reasoning. According to the evolutionary perspective, men's display of aggression is designed to demonstrate their status and power and thereby to enhance their success in the reproductive competition with other men. Therefore, situations involving a threat to a man's status should be particularly likely to elicit aggression as a means of restoring power and status. Similarly, men whose status is continuously low or under threat should be more violent than high-status men. Support for this proposition is offered by Archer, Holloway, and McLoughlin (1995) who found that compared to students (a relatively high status group), unemployed men were significantly more likely to have been involved in a fight following public humiliation or a dispute over money or property.

(3) The *social role* model posits that aggressive behaviour is acquired as part of the masculine gender role in the process of socialisation. This model argues that stronger male tendencies towards aggression and stronger female inhibitions against aggression are largely the result of gender role socialisation (Eagly, 1987). Findings that show that women more frequently report feelings of guilt and anxiety as accompanying responses of aggressive behaviour support this line of reasoning. In addition, women have been found to be as aggressive as men when role constraints prohibiting aggression are removed. For example, Bettencourt and

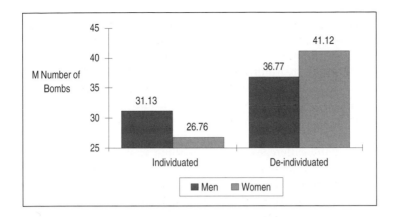

FIG. 3.3. Gender differences in aggression as a function of individuation vs. de-individuation (adapted from Lightdale and Prentice, 1994, *Personality and Social Psychology Bulletin, 20,* 34–44, copyright © 1997 by Sage Publications; reprinted by permission of Sage Publications, Inc.).

Kernahan (1997) found that men were more aggressive than women in the presence of aggression-related cues when no prior provocation had taken place. However, when they had previously been provoked, women were no less aggressive than men. This conclusion is in line with the meta-analytic findings reported by Bettencourt and Miller (1996). Similarly, Lightdale and Prentice (1994) found gender differences to disappear when subjects were de-individuated, i.e., tested under anonymity. Their respondents had to play a video game in which they could attack their opponents by dropping bombs. Figure 3.3 displays the findings for men and women under de-individuated versus individuated conditions.

While men's aggressive behaviour was significantly higher than women's under individuated conditions (i.e., when they were personally identified by large name badges), both sexes were equally aggressive under de-individuated conditions. (The difference in means between men and women in this condition was not significant.) It may be argued that aggression in response to provocation or under anonymity is less at odds with female role prescriptions and that the disappearance of gender differences in these circumstances attests to the sensitivity of those differences to the influence of social norms.

The impact of masculine sex role socialisation on men's aggressive behaviour has been examined in the context of the so-called "macho personality pattern" (Mosher & Sirkin, 1984). This construct seeks to explain individual differences between men in terms of their aggressive behaviour. The macho personality pattern consists of three related components: (a) calloused sexual attitudes towards women; (b) the perception of violence as manly; and (c) the view of danger as exciting. Since aggression is deeply ingrained in the male gender stereotype, macho men are expected to show aggressive behaviour to a greater extent than men not endorsing this hypermasculine style. In support of this reasoning, endorsement of the macho personality pattern was found by Mosher and Sirkin (1984) to correlate positively with aggression, impulsivity exhibition, and play, and negatively with understanding, harm avoidance, and cognitive structure.

The extent to which evolutionary and social role explanations offer fundamentally different and incompatible views has been the object of some debate, not only with regard to aggression, but more generally with regard to gender differences in social behaviour. Eagly and Wood (1999) have offered a comparative appraisal of the two approaches. They point out that both approaches are similar in that they explain gender differences as a function of different challenges to men and women to adapt to environmental demands. However, the evolutionary approach sees the roots of this adaptive process in the early history of the human species, focusing on differences in reproductive strategies between men and women. This view leaves little room for variations in aggression across cultures and historical periods and, indeed, views evidence of cross-cultural similarity in aggression as supportive of its claims. In contrast, the social role approach explains gender differences in social behaviour as the result of the individual's adaptation to particular social structural conditions and role requirements, varying over time and across societies. The two approaches, while differing in fundamental ways in the significance attached to biological versus social origins of sex differences, become compatible if they are placed along a continuum from distal to proximal influences. The evolutionary account is concerned with so-called distal factors explaining the long-term emergence of gender differences in the human species, whereas the socialisation approach emphasises the proximal influences impinging on individuals in the course of their development. Both approaches enhance the understanding of gender differences in aggressive behaviour, which represent one of the most consistent bodies of evidence in the social psychology of aggression.

Summary

- Aggressive behaviour is shown from early childhood, with boys generally displaying higher levels of aggression than girls from pre-school age onwards. In adolescence, aggression starts declining, giving way to non-aggressive strategies of conflict resolution. If aggressive behaviour persists, however, it becomes more harmful in its consequences and is more often socially organised in the form of gangs and group violence.

- Individual differences in aggression remain largely stable from childhood to early adulthood. Nonetheless, a substantial minority of aggressive children stop being aggressive as they grow older, while others show a late onset of aggression in adolescence without a previous history of aggressive behaviour. Acceptance of aggression as legitimate and the habitual perception of hostile intent in others were found to be important cognitive antecedents of aggression in childhood and adolescence. Exposure to violence in the family, including harsh parental punishments, and peer rejection are environmental factors linked to individual differences in aggression.

- Adults display individual differences in aggression in much the same way as children and adolescents. Individual differences in irritability, emotional susceptibility, and dissipation versus rumination following an aggression-eliciting stimulus have been linked to differences in aggression. Moreover, hostile attributional bias, i.e., the tendency to interpret others' behaviour as hostile, was found to predict adults' aggressive behaviour. Finally, a new perspective on the role of self-esteem claims that it is not low but unrealistically high self-esteem that makes individuals vulnerable to aggression. Individuals holding inflated and/or unstable views of themselves are more easily threatened in their self-esteem and are more likely to show aggression to restore positive self-appraisal.

- Research on gender differences in aggression has found with high consistency that men are more physically aggressive than women, even though the difference is only moderate in size. Men still exceed women on measures of verbal aggression, but the difference is smaller than for physical aggression. However, recent research on aggressive women suggests that women may choose indirect, relational forms of aggression to a greater extent than men. While little support was found for the role of the male sex hormone testosterone in explaining higher levels of male aggression, the debate on how to explain gender differences in aggression has centred on the evolutionary versus the social role approach. The evolutionary approach attributes gender differences in aggression to differential reproductive strategies in men and women, whereas the social role approach emphasises the significance of gender-specific roles and norms to which men and women have to adapt in their social behaviour.

Suggested reading

Archer, J., & Lloyd, B.B. (in press). *Sex and gender* (3rd ed., Chap. 6). New York: Cambridge University Press.

Baumeister, R.F., & Boden, J.M. (1998). Aggression and the self: High self-esteem, low self-control, and ego-threat. In R.G. Geen & E. Donnerstein (Eds.), *Human aggression: Theories, research and implications for social policy* (pp. 111–137). San Diego, CA: Academic Press.

Coie, J.D., & Dodge, K.A. (1998). Aggression and antisocial behavior. In W. Damon & N. Eisenberg (Eds.), *Handbook of child psychology* (5th ed., pp. 779–862). New York: Wiley.

Loeber, R., & Hay, D. (1997). Key issues in the development of aggression from childhood to early adulthood. *Annual Review of Psychology, 48,* 371–410.

Situational influences on aggression 4

In the previous chapter, we looked at the development of aggressive behaviour and at individual characteristics that account for relatively stable differences in people's aggressive response tendencies over time. The present chapter will focus on situational influences on aggressive behaviour. We will examine research about those aspects of a situation that trigger or exacerbate aggressive actions. First, we will explore the significance of aggression-related cues, i.e., stimuli present in a given situation that direct the individual's attention towards aggression as a potential response. In the second section, we will look at the role of alcohol in connection with aggressive behaviour. The third section will examine current evidence on the impact of temperature on aggression, and the chapter will conclude with a brief review of crowding, noise, and air pollution as further environmental stressors relevant to aggressive behaviour. A complementary perspective on the link between situational characteristics and aggression is to ask what features of a situation are likely to reduce or inhibit aggression. This question is closely linked to the issue of aggression prevention and control and will be discussed in that context in Chapter 9.

Aggressive cues

As part of the frustration–aggression hypothesis (see Chapter 2), it has been claimed that aggression is a likely, but not inevitable consequence of frustration. The task arising from this proposition is to identify those circumstances under which the experience of frustration—or more generally, negative arousal—is likely to lead to aggressive behaviour. To predict when exactly frustration will give rise to aggression, Berkowitz and LePage (1967) conducted an experiment that highlighted the importance of *aggressive cues in the environment* in triggering aggressive responses. They showed that subjects who had previously been frustrated and were thus in a state of negative arousal were more likely to act aggressively towards the frustrator in the presence of a weapon than in the presence of a neutral object (a badminton racket). Many subsequent studies have supported the conclusion that when faced with a range of response options, frustrated individuals are influenced in their behaviour by aggression-related cues that make aggression salient as a behavioural option. Despite a number of disconfirming studies, Carlson et al. (1990) concluded from their extensive meta-analysis that there was overall support for the so-called "weapons effect". Moreover, other aggression-related cues, such as names associated with unpleasant experiences of violent incidents, were also found to act as mediators between frustration and aggression. In addition, Carlson et al. (1990) identified an effect, albeit weaker, of aggressive cues on subjects in a neutral mood state. This finding suggests that negative arousal is not a necessary condition for situational cues to affect aggressive behaviour. It seems that aggressive cues within a situation activate ("prime") cognitive schemata related to aggression and thus increase the salience of aggressive response options, even in the absence of negative affective arousal. However, a meta-analysis by Bettencourt and Kernahan (1997) shows that gender plays an important role in the extent to which aggressive cues elicit aggressive behaviour in unprovoked subjects. They found that in the absence of prior provocation, men's responsiveness to violent cues was substantially higher than women's. If provoked, however, exposure to violent cues led to equal levels of aggression in both men and women.

Using a standard reaction time paradigm, Anderson et al. (1998) showed that exposure to weapons does, indeed, enhance the accessibility of aggression-related cognitions, even in subjects who were not previously angered or frustrated. They presented their subjects with series of word pairs, with the first word of each pair acting as a prime. Primes were either aggression related (weapon words) or neutral (animal words). Following the silent reading of the prime word, subjects were instructed to read the second word of the pair out loud as fast as they could. Reaction times for reading the second word were used as the dependent variable. The second word was either aggression-related or neutral. As aggressive primes were assumed to activate aggressive thoughts, it was predicted that weapon primes would lead to shorter reaction times in reading aggressive words as compared to neutral words and as compared to animal primes. The findings from the study are presented in Figure 4.1.

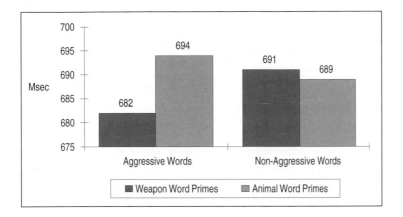

FIG. 4.1. Effects of aggressive versus non-aggressive primes on reaction times for aggressive and neutral words (based on Anderson, Benjamin, & Bartholow, 1998, Study 1).

As Figure 4.1 shows, subjects were significantly faster in reading out aggressive words when they had been primed by a weapon word than when the prime had been an animal word. Moreover, reaction times within the aggressive prime group were shorter for the aggressive than for the non-aggressive words. A second study conducted by Anderson et al. (1998) using visual stimuli as primes (pictures of weapons versus pictures of plants) confirmed this result.

The literature on the weapons effect suggests that the very fact that a weapon is visually present within the situation increases the likelihood of aggressive responses. Further research has demonstrated that the effect is not limited to weapons, but extends to other aggression-related stimuli as well. People associated with aggressive events, e.g., because they happened to be present in a particular situation or featured in a particular aggressive film, can acquire aggressive cue value and increase the salience of aggressive thoughts through their mere presence (Baron & Richardson, 1994; Carlson et al., 1990). The literature on aggressive cues has important practical implications concerning the availability and accessibility of weapons and other aggression-related objects in a wide variety of social contexts, both in real life and in the media.

Alcohol

While alcohol is not an external situational influence in the same way as aggressive cues, it still induces a situation-specific, transient state that may explain why individuals show aggression in a particular situation and not in others. It is part of everyday psychological wisdom that people tend to become more aggressive under the influence of alcohol. In the present section, we will examine the empirical basis for this proposition. In addition, we will review evidence that seeks to identify the mechanisms involved in the alcohol–aggression link and to clarify the pathways through which alcohol affects aggressive tendencies.

There is evidence from a variety of domains to document the co-occurrence of alcohol and aggression. Alcohol was shown to play an important role in the perpetration of violent crime, including homicide (Murdoch, Pihl, & Ross, 1990; Parker & Auerhahn, 1999). A large number of studies have identified alcohol as a risk factor for domestic violence, including the physical and sexual abuse of children, sexual aggression, and wife battering (e.g., Wiehe, 1998). Furthermore, alcohol has been pinpointed as a central factor in many forms of group violence, such as sports violence, rioting, and vandalism (e.g., G.W. Russell, 1993). From the evidence available to date, it seems safe to conclude that "more than a very little alcohol leads to increased aggressive behavior" (Baron & Richardson, 1994, p. 278).

However, the finding that alcohol is often involved in the performance of aggressive behaviour does not necessarily suggest that alcohol is *causally* and/or *directly* responsible for an individual's aggressive actions. It may be the case that both the tendency to get intoxicated and the performance of aggressive behaviour are caused by a third variable, such as lack of impulse control, or that alcohol affects the likelihood of aggressive behaviour in an indirect way, e.g., by lowering a person's frustration level. In addition, it is possible that the aggression-promoting effects of alcohol consumption only occur in the presence of particular features of the situation, such as provocation or prior frustration. To make things even more complicated, there are at least two ways in which alcohol can affect aggressive behaviour. The first is through its pharmacological effects, which influence the physiological functioning of the body. The second is through its psychological effects, creating expectancies that the consumption of alcohol will lead to certain changes in feeling, thinking, and behaviour. Alcohol-related expectancies can affect aggressive responding by providing actors with an excuse for behaving in an aggressive fashion.

To obtain a clearer picture of the nature of the alcohol–aggression link (causal versus correlational, direct versus indirect), and of the role of pharmacological versus psychological effects, experimental designs have been developed that allow researchers to test causal hypotheses about the effect of alcohol on aggression and to separate the different mechanisms involved. Bushman and Cooper (1990) have

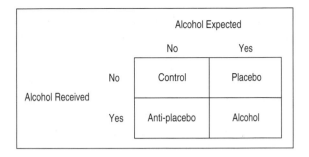

FIG. 4.2. The balanced placebo design for studying the alcohol-aggression link (based on Bushman & Cooper, 1990).

described the prototypical methods used in experimental research on the alcohol–aggression relationship:

- *The placebo design*: Studies using this design inform their subjects that they will receive an alcoholic drink. Only one group (alcohol group) then receives alcohol, while the other receives a non-alcoholic drink (placebo group).
- *The placebo plus control design*: In addition to the alcohol and placebo groups, these studies include a control group, which expects *and* receives a non-alcoholic drink.
- *The balanced placebo design*: In this design, a further group is included, which is led to expect a non-alcoholic drink, but is, in fact, given an alcoholic drink (anti-placebo group).

The balanced placebo design, which represents the most comprehensive experimental approach to studying the effects of alcohol on aggression, is depicted in Figure 4.2.

By comparing the placebo group with the control group, the significance of alcohol-related expectancies can be assessed: Neither group has received alcohol, so there can be no pharmacological effects, but subjects in the placebo group *believe* they have consumed alcohol. Thus, if the placebo group shows more aggression than the control group, this can be attributed conclusively to the impact of cognitive variables, i.e., expectancies. In contrast, comparing the anti-placebo and the control groups isolates the pharmacological effects of alcohol. Neither group thinks they have received alcohol, cutting out alcohol-related expectancies, but the anti-placebo group does, in fact, receive an alcoholic drink. If the anti-placebo group shows more aggression than the control group, the difference can be explained as a result of the physiological changes brought about by the alcohol.

Bushman and Cooper (1990) conducted a meta-analysis that included 30 studies addressing the impact of alcohol on aggression.

They found the largest effect size, i.e., the extent to which aggression differed across the studies as a function of alcohol consumption, between the alcohol group and the placebo group. This finding suggests that the pharmacological changes caused by alcohol consumption lead to an increase in aggressive responses, because alcohol-related expectancies are held constant across the two groups. At the same time, no significant difference was found between the placebo and the control groups. Neither group had received alcohol, but subjects in the placebo group were led to believe they had. Thus, it seems that alcohol-related expectancies, in the absence of actual alcohol intake, have little impact on aggressive tendencies. However, the meta-analysis failed to obtain a significant difference between the anti-placebo and control groups: Subjects in both groups believed they had not received alcohol, but the anti-placebo group had in fact been given an alcoholic drink. If the effects of alcohol were purely pharmacological, more aggression should have been shown by the subjects in the anti-placebo group, who were unaware of their intoxication.

A second significant, but much smaller effect size was found by Bushman and Cooper (1990) for the comparison of the alcohol versus control group: Consuming alcohol (and knowing about it) was associated with stronger tendencies to act aggressively than consuming a non-alcoholic drink (and knowing about it). In this comparison, the pharmacological and expectancy effects of alcohol cannot be separated, because the alcohol group both expects and receives alcohol, whereas the control group both expects and receives a non-alcoholic drink. However, this comparison may still be the most relevant one in terms of real-life significance: As Bushman and Cooper (1990) point out, the pharmacological and psychological effects of alcohol consumption typically co-occur outside the laboratory: People usually know whether or not they have consumed alcohol, enabling them to form expectancies on how they are likely to be affected by its pharmacological effects.

Leonard and Roberts (1998) addressed the issue of pharmacological versus expectancy effects of alcohol in a naturalistic laboratory experiment involving married couples with or without a history of husband physical aggression towards the wife. Using the placebo plus control group design, husbands in one group received an alcoholic drink and were correctly informed about it (alcohol group), husbands in a second group were led to believe they would receive an alcoholic drink but, in fact, received a non-alcoholic drink (placebo group), and husbands in a third group expected and received a non-alcoholic drink (control group). Then, all couples engaged in a discussion of the most controversial issue in their relationship, which had previously been identified for each couple. Observations of the couples' discussion behaviour yielded three scores for each partner: (a) a negativity score, composed of negative reactions towards the partner; (b) a problem-solving score, comprising attempted solutions to the conflict; and (c) a positivity score, including behaviours such as smiles and laughter. In the present context, the negativity scores are of greatest interest. To establish baseline levels of negativity unaffected by alcohol, couples discussed the second most controversial issue in their relationship prior to the introduction of the alcohol manipulation. Figure 4.3 shows how negativity scores for husbands and wives were affected by the alcohol manipulation.

For husbands in the alcohol group, a significant increase in negativity towards the partner was observed after the administration of alcohol. In contrast, the placebo group did not increase their negativity scores from baseline level. Similarly, no differences were observed in the control group between baseline and drinks administration, as expected.

It is interesting to note that wives in the alcohol condition, who had been exposed to an intoxicated husband but not received any drinks themselves, showed parallel changes in negativity scores to their intoxicated partners. This finding is interpreted by Leonard and Roberts (1998) as an indication of the negative reciprocity in dyadic conflict. In contrast, wives in the placebo condition who merely believed that the husband had received alcohol were not affected in their negativity scores. As expected, under the control condition no changes were observed in wives' negativity scores. Finally, it should be noted that both couples with and without a history of previous aggression were affected by the alcohol manipulation in the same way, disconfirming the authors' initial hypothesis that alcohol should have a greater effect on couples with an already heightened potential for aggression. With regard to the question of how alcohol operates to elicit aggression, this experiment also suggests that the pharmacological effects of alcohol are primarily responsible for alcohol-dependent changes in aggressive behaviour.

With regard to the effect of alcohol dose, the evidence is not completely clear. Bushman and Cooper (1990) found no effect of alcohol dose across four studies. However, in their meta-analysis of a larger sample of 49 studies, Ito, Miller, and Pollock (1996) did find that the differences in aggression between sober and intoxicated individuals increased as a function of alcohol dose.

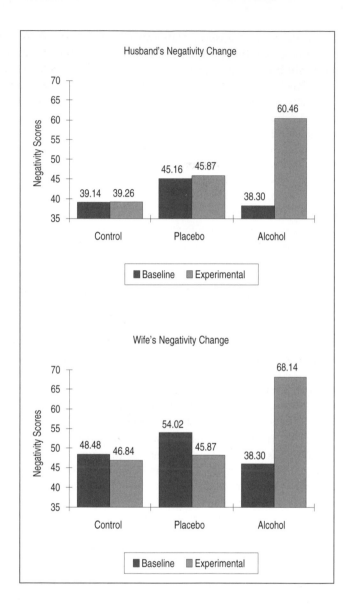

FIG. 4.3. Increase in negativity scores in married couples as a function of husband's intoxication (adapted with permission from Leonard & Roberts, 1998; copyright © 1998 by the American Psychological Association).

One methodological issue in the experimental literature on the alcohol–aggression link refers to the fact that the most clear-cut effects of alcohol in increasing aggression were found in studies that did not provide subjects with a non-aggressive response alternative. In these studies, respondents could only be relatively less aggressive, i.e., by administering fewer or shorter electric shocks, but they could not avoid giving an aggressive response altogether (see Bushman & Cooper, 1990, Table 2). In their meta-analysis, Ito et al. (1996) found that the effect of alcohol on aggression was indeed stronger in studies that did not include a non-aggressive response alternative. However, intoxicated persons were still more aggressive than sober persons in studies that did provide subjects with a choice to respond in a non-aggressive fashion.

Few studies are available that examine the effects of drugs other than alcohol on aggressive behaviour (Bushman, 1993). The limited evidence suggests that for drugs that depress the central nervous system in a similar way to alcohol, comparable effects on aggressive behaviour can be expected (Taylor & Chermack, 1993; Yudofsky, Silver, & Hales, 1993).

Moderators of the alcohol–aggression link

Despite the strong support for the alcohol–aggression link, it is clear that not all intoxicated individuals become aggressive. Therefore, it is important to identify variables that act as "moderators" of the effect of alcohol on aggression, i.e., facilitate predictions as to when intoxicated individuals are likely to act more aggressively than sober individuals, and when they are not. Four situational moderators have received particular attention in the literature: (a) provocation, (b) frustration, (c) self-focused attention, and (d) the presence of aggressive versus non-aggressive situational cues.

Concerning the effect of *provocation*, Gustafson (1994) reviewed evidence on the role of alcohol in eliciting unprovoked aggression. He concluded that intoxicated and sober subjects generally showed little difference in aggressive behaviour in the absence of provocation. If confronted with a mild provocation, however, intoxicated subjects increased the frequency and intensity of their aggressive responses, whereas sober subjects remained largely unaffected. Similarly, Bushman (1997) reported results from a meta-analysis showing that provocations have a greater effect on intoxicated subjects than on sober persons. However, this evidence was challenged on both empirical and conceptual grounds by Ito et al. (1996). In terms of empirical evidence, Ito et al.'s meta-analysis established an effect of provocation in the opposite direction from that found by Gustafson: While intoxicated subjects were generally more aggressive than sober subjects, the differences were *more* pronounced under low as compared to high provocation. Ito et al. also provide a conceptual explanation why alcohol should affect aggressive behaviour to a greater extent in the absence of provocation. They argue that sober persons should be aware of the normative constraints prohibiting unprovoked aggression, whereas intoxicated persons should be more oblivious of such constraints. In contrast, showing aggression in response to prior provocation is more socially accepted and does not require observation of social norms to the same extent. Therefore, the difference between sober and intoxicated individuals should be less pronounced under provocation.

A similar pattern was predicted by Ito et al. (1996) for the effects of *frustration* on the aggressive tendencies of sober and intoxicated individuals. Unlike provocation, which is caused by the actions of another person, frustration can arise from any obstacle blocking the individual's attainment of a particular goal. Ito et al. expected small differences between sober and intoxicated subjects following frustration (when both sober and intoxicated subjects were thought to perceive aggression as a justified response), but larger differences in the absence of frustration when intoxicated subjects were thought to be less aware than sober participants of the inappropriateness of aggressive responses. However, the findings from their meta-analysis point in the opposite direction: Intoxicated subjects were even more aggressive than sober subjects following high as compared to low levels of frustration. While Ito et al. (1996) provide several methodological explanations for the divergent findings concerning provocation and frustration, they also suggest an interesting conceptual distinction: Provocation may be more likely to give rise to anger arousal leading to affective aggression, while frustration may be more likely to elicit instrumental aggression, i.e., aggression directed at removing the perceived obstacle to successful goal attainment. This difference in the motives for aggression triggered by provocation versus frustration may form the basis for explaining the differential effects of the two moderators on the alcohol–aggression link, but further research is needed to follow this lead.

Self-focused attention, the third moderator variable considered by Ito et al. (1996), is generally thought to be impaired under the influence of alcohol (e.g., Hull, Levenson, Young, & Sher, 1983). When intoxicated, individuals are thought to be less able to concentrate on the self and monitor their behaviour than when sober. However, inducing self-focus in intoxicated subjects who are aware of their alcohol consumption (i.e., in the alcohol condition of the balanced placebo design) might lead these subjects to try extra hard to compensate for alcohol-related cognitive impairment. Therefore, differences between sober and intoxicated subjects in terms of aggressive behaviour should be less pronounced under high as compared to low self-awareness. This prediction was confirmed in Ito et al.'s (1996) meta-analysis when all 49 studies were considered simultaneously. However, when the amount of alcohol administered was used to classify studies into high versus low dosage groups, an interesting pattern emerged: Under low doses of alcohol, differences in aggression between sober and intoxicated subjects *decreased* as self-awareness *increased*. In contrast, when high doses of alcohol were administered, the intoxicated subjects become more aggressive relative to sober subjects as a function of increasing self-awareness. This finding suggests that efforts to counteract the deleterious effects of alcohol through increased self-attention are successful only at low levels of intoxication.

The presence of *aggressive versus non-aggressive cues* has been examined as a further moderator of the effects of alcohol on aggression. We saw earlier in this chapter that aggression-related cues may serve to highlight aggression as a behavioural option, but does this effect apply in the same way to sober and intoxicated persons? Research examining the impact of threats present in a situation, such as an opponent's indication that he or she will set high shock levels, shows that threat increases aggression in both sober and intoxicated individuals, but that it leads to a much higher increase in aggressive responses in intoxicated as compared to sober subjects (e.g., Taylor, Gammon, & Capasso, 1976). Other evidence suggests that intoxicated persons only respond to explicit, salient external cues (Leonard, 1989). If these cues highlight aggression, such as aggressive behaviour from a fellow participant, then an aggressive response is likely to be shown. If, however, salient cues are non-aggressive, such as social pressure to set low levels of shock, then behaviour becomes less aggressive. Because sober persons can attend to a greater variety of situational stimuli as well as personal norms, their behaviour is less affected by the salience of cues.

Finally, one potential moderator that was found by a majority of studies *not* to predict differences in aggression as a function of alcohol consumption was gender. Reviews converge on the conclusion that the aggression-enhancing effect of alcohol is similar for men and women (Bushman & Cooper, 1990; Gustafson, 1994). However, findings by Giancola and Zeichner (1995) suggest that men and women may express their aggressive tendencies differently under the influence of alcohol: In their study, men showed increased levels of shock intensity *and* shock duration as a function of alcohol consumption, whereas women only chose longer shock durations when intoxicated.

Explanations of the alcohol–aggression link

Several theoretical assumptions have been proposed to explain *how* the tendency to show aggressive behaviour is affected by alcohol consumption. Three main approaches will be briefly described here (see Chermack & Giancola, 1997; Ito et al., 1996; and Seto & Barbaree, 1997, for summaries of other approaches).

The first approach focuses on the *pharmacological* effects of alcohol. It comprises several hypotheses addressing different consequences of alcohol consumption. The "disinhibition hypothesis" claims that alcohol directly affects the centre of the brain that controls aggressive behaviour. This view holds that aggressive impulses are set free by alcohol because it demobilises the individual's ability to suppress and avoid aggressive tendencies. However, the finding that subjects who received alcohol but were unaware of it (the anti-placebo condition of the balanced placebo design) were not found to be more aggressive than subjects who neither expected nor received alcohol (the control condition) speaks against the assumption of such a direct link between alcohol and aggression. The "arousal hypothesis" suggests that the stimulant effects of alcohol are responsible for its aggression-enhancing effect. However, evidence concerning alcohol-induced arousal and aggression is limited, and results on other stimulant drugs are described by Chermac and Giancola (1997) as inconsistent.

The second approach is concerned with the psychological mechanisms triggered by alcohol-related expectancies. The *expectancy hypothesis* proposes that the effects of alcohol on aggression are due at least in part to people's knowledge that they have consumed alcohol. This knowledge is associated with alcohol-related expectancies, which include cultural norms excusing or condoning aggressive behaviour under the influence of alcohol ("blaming the bottle"). As we saw above, the failure to find significant differences as a function of alcohol-related expectancies (comparing the placebo and control groups) indicates that these psychological variables are not centrally important in the alcohol–aggression link. However, critics have pointed out that there is a lack of convincing manipulation checks for the elicitation of alcohol-related expectancies. It seems questionable that subjects can easily be fooled about their alcohol intake, both in the placebo and the anti-placebo groups, especially since substantial doses of alcohol are required to produce clear pharmacological effects (Bushman & Cooper, 1990).

Finally, the third approach attributes the aggression-enhancing affect of alcohol to the disruption of cognitive information processing. The *attentional hypothesis* suggests that alcohol has an indirect effect on aggression by reducing the attentional capacity of the individual, hampering a comprehensive appraisal of situational cues. As a result, only the most salient cues present in a situation will be attended to, and if these cues suggest aggressive rather than non-aggressive responses, aggressive behaviour is likely to be shown. This view receives support from evidence, reviewed earlier in this chapter, concerning the impact of aggression-related cues. Moreover, Laplace, Chermack, and Taylor (1994) proposed that attentional impairment should be more pronounced in people not used to drinking alcohol, who should therefore be more aggressive following a high dose of alcohol intake than moderate or heavy drinkers. The findings from their study support this proposition.

Altogether, several conclusions can be derived from the current literature on alcohol-related aggression:

(1) There is ample evidence to show that, when intoxicated, individuals show more aggressive behaviour than when sober. This evidence comes from controlled laboratory studies, including research using a balanced placebo design, as well as from studies in a variety of real-life contexts, using both self-reports and observational methods.

(2) It seems clear that the pharmacological effects of alcohol are largely responsible for its aggression-enhancing effect. However, due to methodological limitations, such as frequent failure to check the effectiveness of placebo and anti-placebo manipulations, the role of alcohol-related expectancies, deriving from the knowledge of having consumed alcohol, has not yet been fully explored.

(3) Alcohol does not directly lead to aggressive behaviour, but affects aggression in an indirect way. Cognitive interpretations are seen as the most promising explanations of the effects of alcohol on aggression. They emphasise that alcohol impairs a person's information-processing capacities, including attention to the normative constraints that would suppress aggressive responses in a sober state.

(4) Finally, the link between alcohol and aggression is affected by variations in the situation. Provocation, frustration, and self-focused attention have been examined as relevant variables accounting for differences in the effect of alcohol on aggressive responses.

Temperature

Ambient temperature is a further situational determinant of aggression widely explored in the literature. Most of this research refers to the so-called "heat hypothesis", which states that "uncomfortably high temperatures increase aggressive motives and aggressive behavior" (Anderson, Bushman, & Groom, 1997, p. 1213). Since the late nineteenth century, scientists have observed that aggression levels vary as a function of temperature, being higher under hot than under comfortable temperatures. More recent research has adopted fine-grained empirical methods to explore the relationship between temperature and aggression. Anderson and Anderson (1998), who provide an up-to-date and comprehensive account of research on the heat hypothesis, describe three main methodological approaches towards studying the temperature–aggression link.

The first approach is concerned with identifying *geographic region effects*, i.e., with showing that aggression is more prevalent in hotter as compared to cooler geographical regions.

The second approach is designed to identify *time period effects*, i.e., examines variations in the level of aggression as a function of temperature changes over time (seasons, months, times of day).

Finally, there are studies which look for *concomitant heat effects*, i.e., measure temperature and aggressive behaviour at the same time and observe the effects of variations in temperature on the likelihood of aggressive behaviour. While geographic region and time effect studies mostly rely on archival evidence, e.g., relating official crime report figures to meteorological records, concomitant heat effects are commonly studied under laboratory conditions where the effect of temperature variation can be observed largely uncontaminated by other factors. Evidence from each of the three approaches has been reviewed by Anderson (1989) and, more recently, by Anderson and Anderson (1998). The reviews also highlight the methodological problems inherent in each approach. Before we present a summary of the main findings, it is important to clarify what exactly has been examined as aggressive behaviour in these studies. In keeping with the proposition that uncomfortably high temperature creates negative affect, affective (or hostile) aggression is most pertinent to the heat hypothesis. Aggressive acts with a strong affective component of anger and hostility, such as homicide, assault, rioting, and rape, are therefore expected to be more strongly affected by temperature than acts of instrumental aggression, such as robbery, theft, or, possibly, international warfare.

Evidence for the heat hypothesis

Studies based on the *geographic region approach* have shown with high consistency that violent crime is, indeed, more widespread in hotter than in cooler regions. It is important to stress that geographic region studies typically compare temperature-related differences in aggression within the same country to avoid the influence of different political, economic, and social conditions. Nevertheless, even within a country, variations in geographical location are often associated with other social structural variables that may be responsible, solely or in part, for observed differences in aggression. Therefore, researchers soon realised the necessity to control for the potential influence of demographic and socio-economic factors, such as population size, ethnic composition, unemployment rate, educational background, and age composition. However, the link between temperature and violent crime remained across a range of studies even after these factors were taken into account. One alternative explanation to the heat effect in comparing Northern versus Southern regions in the United States was proposed by Nisbett (1993). He argued that higher rates of violent crime in the South result from a particular "Southern culture of violence" or "Southern culture of honour", traced back to the historical roots of settlement and survival in the South. The Southern culture of violence is characterised by a greater acceptance of the use of violence, both for self-protection and in response to an insult or provocation as a way of restoring one's honour. At the behavioural level, Nisbett (1993) reported that Southerners showed greater anger in response to a provocation and were more likely to produce aggressive solutions to an interpersonal conflict following a provocation. Similarly, Cohen, Nisbett, Bowdle, and Schwarz (1996) showed that following an insult Southerners were more upset and more likely to engage in aggressive behaviour than Northerners (see, however, Anderson & Anderson, 1996, for a challenge of the Southern culture of violence as an alternative framework to the heat hypothesis).

A potential drawback of the geographic region approach lies in the fact that it can only provide correlational data about the co-occurrence of high temperature and violent crime. Moreover, it supports the temperature–aggression link at a highly aggregated level, i.e., at the level of entire regions and large populations. Therefore, it does not allow immediate inferences about the link between exposure to high temperature and aggression within the individual person, as it is stated in the heat hypothesis. On the other hand, geographic region studies have the advantage of providing large and reliable data sets about the criterion variable, i.e., violent crime. Murder and assault rates, for example, are reported and recorded continuously over time. Therefore, geographic region studies are able to complement evidence from other sources in evaluating the heat hypothesis (see also Anderson, Bushman, & Groom, 1997, for a more detailed critique of the geographic region approach).

Time period studies avoid some of the methodological problems of the geographic region approach. They examine variations in aggression over the year within a given population and are therefore unaffected by the confounding effects of socio-structural variables. However, they carry their own problems, in that seasonal variations are associated with variations in activity patterns relevant to violent crime rates. For example, drink-driving offences typically go up before Christmas, not as a function of temperature, but as a function of the social institution of Christmas parties. In the summer, people spend more time outside their homes and may therefore be more likely to be involved in aggressive incidents. One way round this problem is to compare hotter and cooler years, based on average annual temperatures, or hotter versus cooler days within a season, in their effects on violent crime. Each of these variants of the time period approach, i.e., comparisons of hotter versus cooler years, seasons, and days, has yielded consistent support for the heat hypothesis, as summarised by Anderson and Anderson (1998). For example, rates for murder, assault, and rape were found to be highest in the summer months across several studies. The daily rates of emergency calls to police stations were found to increase as temperatures went up. Comparing years with different average temperatures and with hotter versus cooler summers, Anderson, Bushman, and Groom (1997) found further support for the heat hypothesis and its focus on affective aggression: Both homicide and serious assault were more prevalent in hotter years and hotter summers, but property-related crime was unaffected by variations in temperature.

The third approach addressing the heat hypothesis is the *concomitant heat paradigm*. It comprises studies that examine temperature and aggression simultaneously and look for variations in aggression as a function of variations in temperature. Here, intra-individual regularities are observed between exposure to heat and aggressive behaviour, using very different behavioural criteria of aggression (mostly electric shocks) from the other two paradigms. A methodological limitation of this approach is that subjects know that their behaviour is observed by the experimenter, and that they may often see through the link between artificially created high temperatures

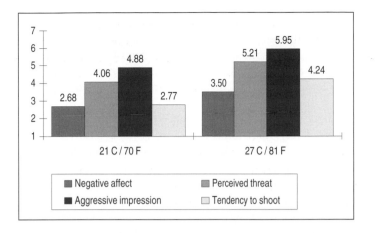

FIG. 4.4. Effect of room temperature on police officers' responses to a burglary scenario (based on Vrij, van der Steen, & Koppelaar, 1994).

and the tasks they are expected to perform. Given that it seems part of intuitive psychological wisdom that aggression increases with temperature (see Anderson & Anderson, 1998, Study 1), it cannot be ruled out that subjects' intuitive theories about the heat–aggression relationship affect their behaviour in the experiment.

The concomitant heat approach is nicely illustrated in a study by Vrij, van der Steen, and Koppelaar (1994), who exposed a sample of police officers to a virtual reality display of a burglary that involved a face-to-face confrontation with the suspected burglar. Subjects were asked to respond to the incident as they would do in reality, using laser beams as weapons. Room temperature while subjects were responding to the scenario was varied, with one group being exposed to a comfortable temperature of 21°C (70°F), and the other being tested in an uncomfortably hot room at 27°C (81°F). The main dependent measures were (a) ratings of the negative affect elicited by the confrontation with the burglar; (b) perceptions of the burglar as aggressive; (c) perceived threat from the burglar; and (d) self-rated tendency to shoot. The findings on how these judgements were affected by temperature are displayed in Figure 4.4.

All four dependent variables showed a significant effect of room temperature: Subjects tested under high room temperatures perceived the suspected burglar as more aggressive, reported more negative affect, and perceived greater threat. In support of the heat hypothesis, they also indicated higher intentions to use their firearms against the suspect than subjects tested under comfortable room temperatures.

This finding of a positive relationship between temperature and aggression has also been corroborated by other experimental studies.

However, it has not been supported with the same consistency that we have seen for the geographic region and time period studies. Quite a few laboratory experiments found an inverted U-shaped curve of the temperature–aggression link, with aggressive responses first increasing with temperature and then dropping again when temperatures reached a high level. This research, summarised by Baron and Richardson (1994), found that subjects who were previously provoked were more likely than unprovoked subjects to show a decline in aggressive behaviour under aversively high temperatures. One possible explanation of this finding is that the higher the negative effect (through the combined effect of provocation and heat), the stronger the motive to escape from the situation may become, overriding aggressive impulses. In summary, it must be concluded that evidence from the concomitant heat paradigm is inconclusive as to the exact nature of the impact of heat on aggression.

Before we move on to explanations of the mechanisms underlying the temperature–aggression link, it should be noted that evidence addressing this link has—with very few exceptions—been limited to the aggression-enhancing effects of uncomfortably *high* temperatures. A pragmatic reason for this limitation is offered by Anderson and Anderson (1998), who point out that is has always been easier for people to protect themselves against the cold than to escape from the heat. Therefore, discomfort resulting from low temperatures is not experienced to the same extent as discomfort from high temperatures.

Explanations of the heat–aggression link

Given the consistent support for the heat hypothesis from studies using the geographic region and the time period approaches and at least some support from experimental studies, the question remains why high temperatures lead to increased aggression. Several answers have been proposed to this question (see Anderson & Anderson, 1998), none of which can claim, however, to account for evidence from all three research paradigms. One model, *routine activity theory* (Cohen & Felson, 1979), posits that changes in aggression in relation to temperature occur because the routine activities of people change as a function of temperature. For example, seasonal variations in everyday behaviour patterns, such as frequency of outdoor activities or alcohol consumption, may affect the chances of becoming involved in aggressive incidents and thereby act as mediators of the temperature–aggression link. While this theory can accommodate findings from the time period paradigm, it is unable to explain concomitant heat effects observed under laboratory conditions.

A second model, "negative affect escape theory" (Baron & Bell, 1976; Bell, 1992), proposes that high temperatures induce negative affect and that aggression is a response to this negative affective state. The model further assumes that if negative affect exceeds a certain level, for example if high temperatures co-occur with provocation or frustration as an additional source of negative affect, subjects' primary motive will be to escape from the situation rather than release aggressive tension. This model can explain the curvilinear relationship between temperature and aggression found in several laboratory studies for subjects who were exposed to both provocation and unpleasantly high temperature. It cannot, however, explain the linear increase in aggression as a function of heat found consistently in studies analysing regional and temporal variations of aggression as a function of different temperatures. Finally, Nisbett's (1993) "Southern culture of violence" model, described earlier, attributes temperature-related differences in aggression to the normative endorsement of aggression in Southern parts of the United States. This approach only pertains to regional variations in aggression and does not incorporate findings on temperature variations over time and evidence from the concomitant heat paradigm.

Thus, we are left to conclude that the empirical evidence for the heat effect is more convincing than the current range of theoretical explanations for its occurrence. One direction for promoting a theoretical understanding of the temperature–aggression link may be to move away from specific explanations directed at temperature effects towards a view of temperature as just one of several input variables that elicit negative affective arousal. This view, outlined by Anderson et al. (1996), integrates the heat hypothesis into Berkowitz's (1993) "cognitive neoassociation model" of affective aggression described in Chapter 2. Further conceptual and empirical work is required to see if this extended perspective will prove useful in understanding the significance of temperature for aggressive behaviour.

Other Environmental Stressors

In this concluding section, we will briefly examine the role of three further environmental stressors in instigating and promoting aggressive behaviour: crowding, noise, and air pollution.

Crowding refers to the perception of spatial density as unpleasant and aversive. Note that crowding is a subjective experience, while density is a physical concept definable in terms of the number of persons per space unit. This distinction is important because the same level of spatial density may give rise to feelings of crowding in some people but not in others. Similarly, the same level of spatial density may be perceived as pleasantly busy in some settings (e.g., in an open-air concert) and unpleasantly crowded in others (e.g., in a crammed train compartment). While density as such cannot be linked to aggression in a conclusive fashion, crowding has been found to increase the likelihood of aggression in a variety of settings, such as crowded living conditions of families, prison environments, and violations of personal space (Geen, 1990). Experimental evidence suggests that the aggression-enhancing effect of crowding is mediated by negative affective arousal elicited by the subjective perception of spatial constraint. Furthermore, it seems that men are more responsive to crowding than women in terms of aggressive behaviour (see Baron & Richardson, 1994). This finding is consistent with the negative affect explanation in that men have been found consistently to claim more personal space than women and are therefore more likely to be adversely affected by restrictions of their territorial claims (e.g., Leibman, 1970; Patterson, Mullens, & Romano, 1971).

Noise is another environmental stressor linked to aggressive behaviour. In its capacity as intensifier of ongoing behaviour, noise can reinforce aggressive behavioural tendencies already present in the actor. In a study by Geen and O'Neal (1969), subjects were shown either a violent or a non-violent film and subsequently instructed to deliver electric shocks to another person as a punishment for errors on a learning task. While they administered the shocks, half of the subjects were exposed to a loud noise. It was found that the noise manipulation only led to higher aggression in those subjects who had previously seen the violent film. Another consequence of noise is its impairing the person's tolerance for frustration, thereby increasing aggressive behavioural tendencies following a frustration (see Donnerstein & Wilson, 1976). Thus, noise operates as a reinforcer of aggressive response tendencies in persons who are already in a state of increased readiness for aggressive behaviour. However, it does not seem to be the noise per se that facilitates aggression but the fact that noise is often an uncontrollable aversive event. If the noise was perceived as controllable by the person, its impact on aggressive behaviour was substantially reduced (Geen & McCown, 1984).

Finally, *air pollution* has been found to be a reinforcer of aggressive response tendencies in much the same way as crowding and noise. Studies examining the effect of cigarette smoke on aggression found that subjects exposed to cigarette smoke showed more hostility towards others (not only towards the person producing the smoke) than a control group not exposed to smoky conditions (e.g., Zillmann, Baron & Tamborini, 1981). The role of unpleasant smells in promoting aggression has been examined in the context of the negative affect escape model (Baron & Bell, 1976), which was mentioned earlier in the context of the heat hypothesis. The model predicts that moderate levels of unpleasant smell lead to an increase in aggression, while aggression levels drop again as the unpleasant smell becomes more intense. Support for this prediction was found in a study by Rotten et al. (1979).

Summary

- Aggression-related cues, alcohol, and temperature have been identified as situational variables that exert a significant influence on the manifestation of aggressive behaviour. More limited evidence is available on the impact of other external stressors, such as crowding, noise, and air pollution, but the conclusions suggested by this evidence point in the same direction.
- The "weapons effect", first demonstrated by Berkowitz and LePage (1967), refers to situational cues, such as weapons or other violence-related primes, which enhance the cognitive availability of aggression as a response option. The weapons effect was found to be at its strongest with individuals who were previously angered or frustrated, and were therefore already in a state of heightened anger arousal. However, it has also been demonstrated to work for people who were in an affectively neutral state. So, the mere presence of an aggression-related cue seems to increase the probability of an aggressive response.
- The claim that people are more likely to act aggressively under the influence of alcohol has been supported with considerable consistency in the aggression literature. Alcohol affects aggressive behaviour primarily through its pharmacological effects, but psychological effects, i.e., alcohol-related expectancies, also

seem to play a role as cultural norms provide excuses and justifications for antisocial behaviour under the influence of alcohol. In understanding the pathway from alcohol consumption to aggressive behaviour, cognitive and attentional deficits are considered of primary importance. Under the influence of alcohol, the individual's span of attention is reduced, and only the most salient stimuli are attended to. In particular, attention to internal cues—such as the awareness of normative constraints suppressing aggressive behaviour—is reduced, impairing an important mechanism in the self-regulation of aggressive behaviour.

- The effect of temperature on aggression has also been demonstrated with consistency across different methodological paradigms. Comparing hot versus cold regions or hot versus cold time periods within a region, it was found that aggression, in particular violent crime, is generally more pronounced under conditions of high temperature, supporting the "heat hypothesis". Experimental studies exploring differences in aggression as a function of variations in temperature also provide some support for the heat hypothesis, but the evidence is less conclusive. Explanations of the effect of temperature suffer from the problem that most approaches can only account for findings from one methodological paradigm. So far, no comprehensive explanatory framework has been tested that would do justice to regional, temporal, and concomitant temperature effects.

- Finally, the general proposition that external stressors create negative affective arousal that gives rise to aggressive responses receives further support from studies looking at crowding, noise, and bad air quality in relation to aggression. While none of these stressors are considered to act as primary causes of aggressive behaviour, their role is seen as reinforcers of aggressive response tendencies.

Suggested reading

Anderson, C.A., & Anderson, K.B. (1998). Temperature and aggression: Paradox, controversy, and a (fairly) clear picture. In R.G. Geen & E. Donnerstein (Eds.), *Human aggression: Theories, research and implications for social policy* (pp. 247–298). San Diego, CA: Academic Press.

Bushman, B.J., & Cooper, H.M. (1990). Effects of alcohol on human aggression: An integrative research review. *Psychological Bulletin, 107,* 341–354.

Carlson, M., Marcus-Newhall, A., & Miller, N. (1990). Effects of situational aggression cues: A quantitative review. *Journal of Personality and Social Psychology, 58,* 622–633.

Chermack, S.T., & Giancola, P.R. (1997). The relation between alcohol and aggression: An integrated biopsychosocial conceptualization. *Clinical Psychology Review, 17,* 621–649.

Media violence and aggression 5

In the public debate on aggression and violence, media influences are commonly cited as one of the most powerful factors responsible for the apparently increasing levels of aggression, especially among children and adolescents. Indeed, a cursory and occasional "sampling" is sufficient to suggest to the everyday observer that television programmes are full of aggressive episodes, often of a highly violent nature, easily accessible even to young viewers. The same is true for home videos, cinema productions, comics, and, increasingly, computer games. In addition, surveys regularly present alarming figures of the average number of hours per week spent using such media by children from pre-school age onwards. These observations foster the conviction that the portrayal of violence in the media is responsible for a general increase in aggression in society. Some critics even claim that media consumption, irrespective of its aggressive contents, works as a contributory factor to aggression and antisocial behaviour.

In the present chapter, we will examine the basis for the claim that exposure to violent media contents enhances viewers' aggressive tendencies. Even though the discussion will be limited to aggression, it is important to acknowledge that eliciting aggressive behaviour is not the only detrimental effect ascribed to violent media depictions. Fear, for example, is another common and adverse result of exposure to media violence (Smith & Donnerstein, 1998). An extensive literature, both within psychology and in media science, is available to address the media–aggression link, focusing on television as the most widely used medium. The present chapter will look at three strands that have emerged from this literature:

(1) the study of immediate and *short-term effects* of violent media contents on aggressive behaviour;
(2) research on the *long-term consequences* of sustained and prolonged exposure to violent media contents; and

(3) the effects of a specific type of media content, i.e., *pornography*, on aggression in general and sexual aggression in particular.

It is important to note that the scientific debate about media-induced aggression is *not* based on the assumption of a simple mono-causal relationship between media violence and aggression. Such an assumption would hold that exposure to media violence causes aggression regardless of other influences. Instead, it is recognised in the debate that media violence is only one of many factors potentially leading to aggression. As will become clear in the course of our discussion, the detrimental effects of media violence may be exacerbated, e.g., when combined with exposure to real-life violence within the family, or attenuated, e.g., by highlighting the negative consequences of violence for actors and targets.

Short-term effects of media violence

The question addressed in this section is whether exposure to media aggression enhances viewers' aggressive response tendencies in the period following the presentation of the aggressive contents. The effects of media aggression on behaviour may manifest themselves in two ways: (a) in a specific way whereby the behaviour shown is a direct imitation of the behaviour presented; and (b) in a more generalised way whereby observation of a particular form of aggression leads to an increased likelihood of aggressive responses taking a different form from the behaviour presented.

Direct imitation, or copycat violence, features with some regularity in crime reports. Deliberate as well as accidental killings were shown to have resulted from children's re-enactments of scenes they had observed in the media. In adults, copycat imitations of specific fictional actions or widely publicised real events, such as hijackings, are also well documented in the literature, including the impact of spectacular self-killings on subsequent suicide rates (the "Werther effect"; see Jonas, 1992). Additional evidence by Miller, Heath, Molcan, and Dugoni (1991) identified a significant link between heavyweight boxing fights and increases in homicide rates.

Prevalence and consumption of media violence
A much larger database is available concerning the effects of media aggression on aggressive behaviour not identical to the observed acts.

In this work, researchers have looked for intra-individual links between exposure to media aggression and various forms of subsequent aggressive behaviour. Moreover, they have tried to answer the question of why certain individuals are more affected in their aggressive responses by exposure to media aggression than others.

There are two prerequisites to the claim that media violence leads to aggression in viewers. First, evidence is required that violence and aggression are widely present in media programmes. Secondly, it must be shown that exposure to such violent contents is substantial among both children and adults. The first issue is addressed by a wide range of studies providing content analyses of television programmes in a variety of countries. These studies, reviewed by Potter (1999), show that aggressive actions do, indeed, account for a substantial proportion of media contents. To name just two recent examples, the National Television Violence Study (1997) showed that 57% of the programmes sampled across 23 channels in the United States in 1994 and 1995 contained violent episodes. A comparable study conducted by Gunter and Harrison (1998) for eight UK channels (four terrestrial and four satellite) found a violence rate of 37%, which broke down into 28% for the four terrestrial channels and 52% for the four satellite channels. Similar prevalence rates of aggressive content were identified in German television programmes (Groebel & Gleich, 1993). Further evidence that aggression is widespread in the media comes from Comstock and Scharrer's (1999) review of violent contents in music television, home videos and pay-per-view channels.

With regard to the second question concerning exposure to violent media contents, regular surveys of television consumption reveal that both adults and children spend considerable amounts of time exposed to this medium. For example, Smith and Donnerstein (1998) quote survey data collected in 1996 showing that adults over the age of 18 spend about 32 hours per week watching television. Adolescents between 12 and 17 years watch television for about 20 hours a week, and children aged 2 to 11 have an average TV exposure of 22 hours per week. As research by Hamilton (1998) shows, children's television consumption is not restricted to programmes directed at young viewers—and the high amount of violence they contain (Potter, 1999)—but also extends to programmes directed at an adult audience. Table 5.1 illustrates how the audience of different types of aggressive media contents targeting adult viewers is distributed across age groups.

Table 5.1 reveals that even programmes directed at an adult audience attract a substantial proportion of their viewers from

TABLE 5.1

Age distribution (%) of viewers exposed to violent programmes targeted at adults

	Children 2–11	Teens 12–17	Women 18–49	Men 18–49	Women 50+	Men 50+
Violent series						
Acapulco H.E.A.T.	13	8	24	27	15	13
Cobra	11	6	25	26	17	14
Highlander	9	7	30	30	12	11
Kung Fu	11	7	25	28	16	12
Renegade	11	6	25	26	17	15
Violent reality						
Cops	11	8	27	27	15	13
Emergency Call	7	7	26	25	19	16
Real Stories of the Highway Patrol	7	7	28	29	14	16
Violent syndicated movies						
Nightmare on Elm Street 5	12	17	31	30	5	5
Amityville: The Evil Escapes	15	9	31	22	15	9
Crucifer of Blood	8	3	23	27	18	21

Note: For each programme, percentages across the different age groups add up to 100%. The figures, collected in November 1993, are based on national average audiences for each programme.

Adapted from Hamilton, James T., *Channeling Violence*; copyright © 1998 by Princeton University Press; reprinted by permission of Princeton University Press.

children and adolescents. Eleven per cent of viewers of programmes such as "Kung Fu" and "Renegade" were children up to the age of 11.

From the evidence reviewed in this section, it is clear that violence is both widely available and widely consumed in the media age. Given these facts, we can now turn to the central question of whether exposure to media violence leads to increased aggression in viewers.

Evidence for the media violence–aggression link

Studies examining the effect of media-presented aggression have provided overall support for the proposed aggression-enhancing effect of violent media contents. One source of evidence is provided by experimental studies on the media–aggression link that dominated the first phase of research into the effects of media violence until the early 1980s. Rather than recording respondents' natural viewing behaviour, these studies expose respondents to aggressive media contents in the experiment and then obtain behavioural observations of aggression. Aggressive responses shown by the experimental subjects are compared with those of a control group who did not receive aggressive contents (either saw a neutral film or no film at all) in order to examine the impact of media aggression on subsequent behaviour. Evidence from this methodology also suggests that exposure to aggressive media contents leads to a short-term increase in the observed level of aggressive behaviour (Geen & Thomas, 1986; Hearold, 1986). Reviewing evidence from a total of 23 experiments involving children and adolescents, Wood, Wong, and Chachere (1991) concluded "that media violence enhances children's and adolescents' aggression in interaction with strangers, classmates and friends" (p. 380).

Paik and Comstock (1994) conducted a comprehensive meta-analysis including 217 studies published between 1957 and 1990. They found a significant overall effect of exposure to media violence, indicating that across all 271 studies greater exposure to media violence was associated with higher levels of aggression. The obtained link was stronger for experimental studies (in which respondents' exposure to violent versus non-violent media contents was systematically varied) than in surveys (which related subjects' self-reported exposure to media violence to self-reported aggressive behaviour or intentions). Moreover, gender and age were found to be relevant moderator variables: The link between exposure to media violence and aggression was stronger for male than for female viewers and for children and adolescents as compared to adults. Furthermore, fictitious portrayals of violence in cartoon and/or fantasy programmes showed a stronger effect on aggression than more realistic presentations, such as action and crime programmes as well as news coverage of violent events.

Another meta-analysis by Hogben (1998), including evidence from a total of 30 different samples, largely supports these findings. His analysis also yielded a moderate, but consistent link between exposure to media aggression and aggressive behaviour. In addition it confirmed that the impact of aggressive media contents declines with viewers' age and is stronger for aggression presented in unrealistic/implausible manifestations or settings (see, however, Freedman, 1988, for a more critical appraisal of the evidence up to the mid-1980s).

In recent years, a new medium has transformed the media usage of children and adolescents: video games that are played on Game-boys, Playstations, and home computers. Evidence is gradually accumulating that video games containing violent themes trigger aggressive behaviour in much the same way as violence on television and in the cinema (Ballard & Lineberger, 1999; Dietz, 1998; Dill & Dill, 1998; Griffiths, 1997). Anderson and Dill (2000) found a correlation of $r =.46$ between long-term exposure to violent video games and aggressive delinquent behaviour in a sample of college students. Taking personality differences into account, they were able to show that people with high trait aggression were much more adversely affected by exposure to violent video games than those low on trait aggression. Comparing the effects of violent versus non-violent video games in a further experimental study, Anderson and Dill (2000) showed that subjects who had played a violent game and lost subsequently delivered longer blasts of aversive noise to an opponent in a reaction time task than those who had lost in a non-violent game. In discussing the implications of their findings, Anderson and Dill list three reasons why they consider the effects of violent video games to have an even greater potential for harm than violence in films or on television: (a) video games require the player to adopt the role of the aggressor and act from the aggressor's perspective throughout the game; (b) they involve active participation by the player rather than passive reception; and (c) are addictive in nature, providing a constantly available, reinforcement-providing medium.

Taken together, there is considerable consensus across a large literature that media aggression has a potentially detrimental effect by increasing the likelihood of viewers' subsequent aggressive behaviour. However, it is clear that this conclusion, derived from studies comparing groups of people exposed to violent media contents with those who did not see violence, does not mean that everyone exposed to violence will actually become more aggressive. Therefore, it is important to ask when, i.e., under what circumstances, media-presented aggression leads to more aggressive behaviour.

Several important conditions have been identified that facilitate the aggression-enhancing effect of media violence (see Berkowitz, 1993; Hogben, 1998; Potter, 1999):

(1) The *assignment of aggressive meaning* to an observed behaviour. For example, a rugby fan watching a rugby match on television is likely to see it as an exciting sports event, while another observer may see the same interactions as aggressive encounters between hostile opponents. The aggression-enhancing effect of the match is likely to be greater for the viewer who perceives the players' behaviour as aggressive rather than as part of a sportive exchange.

(2)   The *perceived positive consequences* of aggressive behaviour. Even if a particular behaviour is interpreted as aggressive, the effect on the viewer's own behaviour is likely to be affected by the perceived consequences of the witnessed aggression. If aggression is punished or fails to succeed, it is less likely to instigate aggressive responses in the viewer than if the actor gets away with it or is even rewarded by success. As an extensive study of 2500 hours of US television programmes showed, only 19% of aggressive actors were punished for their aggressive actions, a further 8% received both rewards and punishments in the course of events (National Television Violence Study, 1997). In a controversial computer game called "Carmageddon", the players' task is to knock down pedestrians with their cars. Bonus points can be earned for knocking down a blind victim and running him over a second time in reverse gear.

(3)   The *failure to present aggressive acts as "bad"*. Two issues are involved here. The first refers to the extent to which the negative consequences of aggressive acts are made salient in the presentation. Cartoon characters who jump up happily after having been flattened by a steam-roller or recover within seconds from being blown to pieces are cases in point. The idea that violent acts are irreversible and cause genuine pain and injury is obliterated—particularly, but by no means exclusively, for young viewers. The National Television Violence Study (1997) revealed that about half the aggressive episodes failed to show any suffering or physical injury of the target. If only children's programmes were considered, this figure even went up to 62%. Similarly a recent study analysing UK television violence found that almost 60% of all violence was not shown to produce any pain at all, and more than a third failed to lead to any discernible harm or injury (Gunter & Harrison, 1998). Hogben's (1998) meta-analysis established that the link between TV violence and aggression was stronger when no or inaccurate consequences of aggression were presented.

The second issue concerns the presentation of aggression as justified and therefore not reprehensible. Aggression is often employed in films and video games in the pursuit of an allegedly good cause, as in a deserved punishment for the "baddies" or as a retaliation for others' aggressive actions. In 44% of the aggressive episodes identified by the National Television Violence Study (1997), the aggressive acts were presented as justified. Such acts of justified aggression are more likely to elicit aggressive responses in the viewer (Hogben, 1998).

(4)   The *identification with the aggressor*. Aggression is often performed by characters who are particularly powerful and/or admirable and therefore serve as attractive role models. Obi-Wan Kenobi and Qui-Gon Jinn in the latest Star Wars craze illustrate this point. As social learning theory indicates, aggressive behaviour shown by an admired model is more likely to be imitated.

(5)   The viewer's *inability to distance him- or herself* from the media aggression. If viewers are able to distance themselves psychologically from the presented violence, the aggression-enhancing effect is suppressed. Distancing can be achieved by focusing on non-aggressive aspects of the media contents, such as a film's aesthetic qualities, or by trying to focus on the fact that the portrayed violence is fictional and not real. However, increasingly powerful forms of presenting media contents, such as 3-D movies, are designed to counteract such efforts by impinging with ever greater immediacy on the viewers' senses and undermining their awareness of external reality.

These five aspects delineate a set of conditions that make it particularly likely for media violence to increase aggressive response tendencies. The different aspects may add up and mutually reinforce each other, such that identification with aggressors may be stronger if their actions are presented as justified and successful, and distancing from the portrayed aggression may be more difficult if the viewer strongly identifies with the aggressor.

However, even when exposed to aggressive contents under the same conditions, not all individuals will react with an increase in aggressive tendencies in the same way. Therefore, another important issue is the identification of personal characteristics that make individuals particularly susceptible to the aggression-enhancing effects of media violence.

Individual differences in media-instigated aggression

Among the variables potentially moderating the effects of media violence on aggression, an individual's disposition to be aggressive, i.e., his or her relatively stable tendency towards aggressive behaviour, is of particular importance. Are people who are habitually more inclined to show aggression than others particularly affected by aggressive media contents?

Bushman (1995) explored this issue by exposing individuals with different levels of trait aggressiveness to violent media depictions and comparing their subsequent aggressive affect and aggressive behaviour. First, he demonstrated that high trait-aggressive respondents expressed greater desire to watch films containing violence and reported spending more time watching violent media programmes than respondents low on trait aggressiveness. Thus, high trait aggressiveness was linked to higher rates of habitual exposure to and stronger preference for violent media contents.

In the second study, Bushman (1995) examined the extent to which aggressive and non-aggressive individuals experienced aggressive affect, i.e., hostility, after watching a violent film. As predicted, aggressive individuals reported more hostility after watching a violent film than non-aggressive individuals. Following a non-violent control film, no differences in hostility emerged as a function of trait aggressiveness. Because differences in habitual exposure between aggressive and non-aggressive respondents were statistically controlled for and hostility ratings were also obtained prior to the film to establish a hostility baseline, the differences in aggressive affect following the violent film can be attributed conclusively to the impact of the film.

Finally, Bushman's third study explored the impact of media violence on aggressive behaviour shown by respondents high versus low in trait aggressiveness. The design of his study enabled him to measure unprovoked aggression (selecting aversive noise intensity for an ostensible opponent in a first move immediately following the film) as well as provoked aggression (selecting noise intensity after having received aversive noise ostensibly set by the opponent).

As far as unprovoked aggression was concerned, both aggressive and non-aggressive individuals were equally affected by the violent film in that they set higher noise levels than respondents exposed to a non-violent film. Following prior provocation, however, the aggression-enhancing effect of the violent film was significantly more pronounced for the aggressive than for the non-aggressive respondents. Figure 5.1 displays this interaction between trait aggressiveness and exposure to media violence on aggressive behaviour among the provoked respondents.

Taken together, Bushman's (1995) findings suggest the operation of a vicious cycle: Aggressive individuals have a preference for violent programmes, which in turn reinforce their aggressive disposition. Other studies corroborate the finding that dispositionally aggressive and emotionally disturbed individuals are more strongly affected in their aggressive response tendencies by violent media depictions (e.g., Comstock et al., 1978).

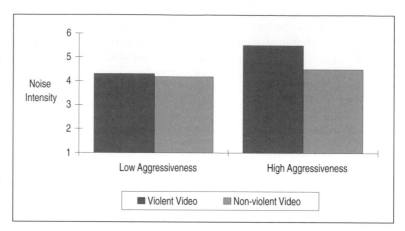

FIG. 5.1. Effects of media violence on aggression in low versus high trait-aggressive individuals following provocation (adapted with permission from Bushman, 1995, p. 958; copyright © 1995 by the American Psychological Association).

Further variables found to be related to individual differences in susceptibility to media violence, particularly among children, include gender, cognitive maturity, and family socialisation. Boys are more affected than girls, children with more advanced cognitive development are less susceptible, and children who have experienced and witnessed violence in their families are more susceptible to the aggression-enhancing effect of media violence (see Potter, 1999, Chap. 3). These factors need to be taken into account in assessing the detrimental effects of media violence on the individual viewer.

Long-term effects of media violence

A proper assessment of the effects of media violence needs to consider the long-term consequences of repeated exposure over and above the immediate effects demonstrated by the research reviewed in the previous section. It has already been pointed out that even very young children spend an average of around 3 hours per day watching television, and that the programmes they are exposed to, including those specifically directed at young audiences, contain a considerable amount of violence. Therefore, it is essential to examine the potential cumulative effects of exposure to media aggression. Longitudinal studies, following the same respondents over extended periods of time, are the method of choice to address this issue. In addition, longitudinal studies are better equipped than cross-sectional correlational analyses to address the issue of a *causal* link between media violence and aggression. After all, in contrast to the hypothesis that viewing violence leads to aggression, it could be argued that the link between media violence and aggression is due to aggressive individuals being more attracted to violent programmes.

Given the difficulties and costs involved in tracing large samples over long periods of time, it is not surprising that only a small number of longitudinal studies into the media–aggression link are available. These studies are, however, able to clarify some of the issues involved in the debate left unresolved by the cross-sectional evidence, most notably referring to the role of cumulative exposure over time.

A review of longitudinal studies into the effects of exposure to media violence is provided by Huesmann and Miller (1994). In a much-quoted study, Eron, Huesmann, and their colleagues conducted an extensive study, starting in 1960 with a sample comprising the entire population of third graders, then 8 years old, in Columbia County, New York. At the first data point, measures of aggressiveness (self-reports and peer ratings) and preference for violent TV programmes were obtained for each child. These measures were taken again 10 and 22 years later, complemented by additional indicators of aggression, such as delinquency and criminal convictions. Since gender turned out to be a relevant variable in the analyses, we will first look at the findings obtained for boys.

Boys' preference for violent programmes in third grade was significantly related to aggressiveness 10 years as well as 22 years on. No concurrent link was found at age 18 between preference for TV violence and level of aggression. The latter finding suggests that adolescents who were exposed to TV violence at age 8 were still more aggressive 10 years later even though their preference for TV violence was not apparent any more at age 18. The link between preference for TV violence at age 8 and aggression at age 18 was found to be even stronger than the concurrent link between TV violence and aggression at age 8 (see Huesmann & Miller, 1994, p. 169). Still more impressively, boys' preference for violent television programmes predicted the seriousness of criminal convictions at the age of 30 (Huesmann, 1986).

Figure 5.2 reveals that the criminal record of men who had expressed a strong preference for violent programmes at the age of 8 was more than twice as serious as that of men who were not attracted to violent programmes as 8-year-olds. Regarding the possibility that the causal direction goes from dispositional aggressiveness to preference for aggressive media contents, aggressiveness in Grade 3 was found to be unrelated to preference for TV violence a decade later. These findings suggest that television violence acts as a causal

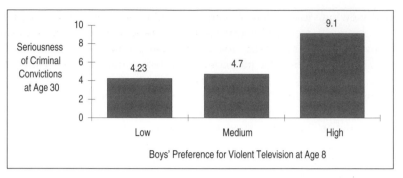

influence on aggressive behaviour rather than the other way round (Lefkowitz, Eron, Walder, & Huesmann, 1977). Concerning the issue of gender effects, the study found no links of exposure to media violence with aggression in girls, neither concurrently at age 8 nor at the later ages of 18 and 30. However, it should be noted that subsequent studies also showed an effect of exposure to television violence on the aggressive behaviour of girls.

In a cross-national study, Huesmann and Eron (1986) extended the longitudinal analysis of the media–aggression link to samples from five different countries (Australia, Finland, Israel, Poland, and the United States). In each country, children in Grades 1–3 were tested on three occasions separated by 1-year intervals. Aggression was measured by self-reports and peer nominations. Preference for TV violence was measured by asking children to select their favourite programmes from a list of programmes pre-rated for aggressive content. In four of the five countries (Australia being the exception), boys' preference for TV violence on the first two occasions was significantly linked to higher levels of aggressive behaviour at the third measurement point. In this study, girls were found to be equally affected by TV violence in three countries (Israel, Poland, and the United States). Again, the causal pathway from exposure to TV violence to subsequent aggression was stronger than the pathway from early aggression to subsequent preference for violent programmes. Two further studies, conducted in the United States (Milavsky, Kessler, Sipp, & Rubens, 1982) and in South Africa (Botha, 1990), also found parallel patterns of results for boys and girls.

In combination, longitudinal studies linking media violence and aggression, though not being numerous, corroborate the conclusions derived from cross-sectional analyses: Exposure to media violence is likely to increase aggressive tendencies, and the effects of early exposure are still noticeable more than 20 years later. What seems particularly important is that long-term exposure to TV violence does not appear to be necessary to uphold the detrimental effect of early preference for violent programmes. As noted above, higher levels of aggression among those boys who preferred TV violence at age 8 were still apparent 10 years later, even though their preference for TV violence showed no stability over the same period. Eron (1982) suggests that there is a sensitive period for exposure to TV violence, estimated between the ages of 8 and 12, after which violent media contents do not seem to have additional cumulative effects. It is argued that exposure to TV violence during this sensitive period affects the development of aggressive scripts in that children incorporate media depictions of aggression into the cognitive repertoires guiding their aggressive behaviour (see Chapter 2). Once the script is learned, it is consolidated through enactment and rehearsal and does not necessarily require further media input to be sustained. We will discuss the script framework as a comprehensive explanation of the effects of media violence in more detail later in this chapter. First, however, we should take a brief look at a type of media content which has generated particular controversy within the media violence debate.

The effects of pornography

Pornography may be broadly defined as "media material used or intended to increase sexual arousal" (Allen, D'Alessio, & Brezgel, 1995, p. 259). It includes presentations of nudity, consensual sexual interactions, and coercive or violent sexual interactions. A review of the different ideological positions concerning the effects of pornography and the appropriate societal responses to deal with them has been provided by Linz and Malamuth (1993). In the present section, we will focus on the empirical evidence generated by the debate about the harmfulness of pornography (see also D.H. Russell, 1993).

Two methodological strategies have dominated research on the link between pornography and aggression. The first is correlational and examines the link between consumption of pornography and aggression. Correlations are computed either at a societal level (by linking circulation rates of pornographic material to prevalence rates of violent crime and sexual offences; e.g., Gentry, 1991; Scott & Schwalm, 1988) or at an individual level (by relating self-reported consumption of pornographic material to some measure of aggressive behaviour; e.g., Boeringer, 1994; Demaré, Briere, & Lips, 1988). The second approach is experimental and involves systematic comparisons between individuals exposed to different media contents (pornographic versus neutral material; depictions of consensual versus coercive sexual interactions; sexually violent versus non-sexually violent material).

The issue whether or not pornography serves to promote aggressive behaviour needs to be broken down into several more specific questions:

(1) *Is there an effect of pornography on sexual aggression as well as on non-sexual violence?* As reviewers note, empirical evidence addressing this issue is far from conclusive (e.g., Bauserman, 1996; Donnerstein, 1984; Linz & Malamuth, 1993). Bauserman (1996) found no overall support for the proposition that sexual offenders have a history of higher exposure to pornographic material than comparison groups of non-offenders. Experimental evidence included in a meta-analysis by Allen, D'Alessio, and Brezgel (1995) did find an effect of exposure to pornography on subsequent (non-sexual) aggression in the laboratory, but the effects were heterogeneous (i.e., varied in strength) across the 30 studies included in the analysis.

(2) *Is there a difference between non-violent and violent pornography in affecting aggression?* Evidence on this issue is somewhat more conclusive: Pornographic material containing violence has been found to have a greater impact on subsequent aggression than non-violent sexual stimuli. The meta-analysis by Allen, D'Alessio, and Brezgel (1995) examined the pornography–aggression link separately for three types of stimuli: (a) presentations of nudity; (b) non-violent sexual behaviour; and (c) violent sexual behaviour. The findings from their analysis are presented in Figure 5.3.

Figure 5.3 shows that presentations of nudity actually decrease aggressive tendencies. Depictions of sexual behaviour are positively associated with aggression, but the link is stronger for violent than for non-violent interactions. However, the difference in effect size between non-violent and violent sexual interactions failed to reach significance, leading the authors to conclude that "violent content, though possibly magnifying the impact of pornography, is unnecessary to producing aggressive behavior" (Allen, D'Alessio, & Brezgel, 1995, p. 271; see also Paik & Comstock, 1994). Donnerstein (1984) suggests that non-violent pornography may only affect

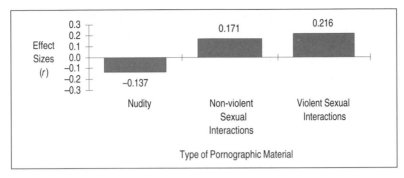

FIG. 5.3. Effects of different types of pornography on aggression in laboratory experiments (based on Allen, D'Alessio, & Brezgel, 1995, p. 271).

individuals whose threshold for aggressive behaviour is already low, e.g., due to previous frustration, alcohol, or arousal from a different source (see excitation transfer theory, Chapter 2). In interpreting findings from the experimental literature, it is important to bear in mind that these studies involve only brief exposure to violent pornography. The fact that measurable effects of such limited exposure were obtained suggests that even small effect sizes are not to be dismissed.

(3) *Is there a difference between violent pornography and portrayals of non-sexual violence in their effects on aggression?* This question is important because it pits the sexual against the violent aspects of pornography and addresses the role of sexual arousal in precipitating aggression. Donnerstein conducted a series of studies that compared subjects' aggressive responses following the presentation of a non-violent pornographic film, a violent pornographic film, and a non-sexual aggressive film (summarised in Donnerstein, 1984). In addition, some of the studies explored the effect of previous provocation—assumed to lower the threshold for aggressive behaviour—on responses to the different films. In one of the experiments, male subjects were either angered or not angered by a female confederate, then exposed to one of three films, and subsequently given the opportunity to aggress against the female confederate by electric shocks of varying intensity. The main results of this study are presented in Figure 5.4.

The findings in Figure 5.4, which are corroborated by similar studies, suggest that it is not so much the sexual but the aggressive contents of the materials that instigate aggression. The non-sexual violent film led to significantly more aggression than the non-violent sexual film. The highest levels of aggression were observed for the film that combined both sexual and violent contents. Prior

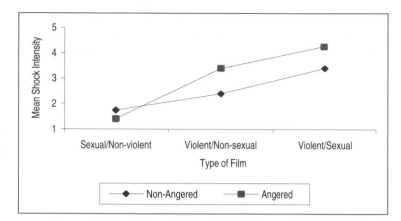

FIG. 5.4. Aggression against a female confederate as a function of anger and film type (adapted with permission from Donnerstein, 1984, p. 76).

provocation led to higher levels of aggression as a response to both types of aggressive films, but the pattern across the three films was not affected by provocation.

The primary dependent variable in this study was shock intensity, i.e., a non-sexual aggression measure. However, Donnerstein also measured sexually aggressive response tendencies following exposure to the films. Again, exposure to violence, even without sexual content, was associated with higher likelihood of aggression (willingness to use force and willingness to rape) than exposure to the non-violent sex film. However, it would be premature to conclude that non-violent pornography is innocuous with regard to aggression. Paik and Comstock's (1994) meta-analysis yielded a substantially higher effect size for violent and non-violent erotica, combined, than for non-sexual violence. This finding is in line with Zillmann's (1998) "sexual callousness model". Zillmann suggests that the degrading portrayal of women in pornography may promote sexual callousness towards women, which facilitates male aggression directed at female targets. His model points to the role of attitudinal variables as mediators between sexual/violent media contents and subsequent aggression, which is addressed in the next section.

(4) *Does pornography affect attitudes relevant to aggression, in particular rape-supportive attitudes?* This question reflects the possibility that pornographic media contents may have an indirect negative effect on aggression by promoting attitudes conducive to aggressive behaviour. For example, many pornographic films show violence against women that is seemingly enjoyed by the targets or portrays initially reluctant women changing their mind after

forceful attempts by the man to engage in sexual contact. Such presentations may foster the view that women enjoy aggressive sexual tactics and that they are usually willing to have sex even if they initially reject a man's advances. Reviews of the evidence from both correlational and experimental studies suggest that the distinction between non-violent and violent pornography is important again in this context.

Linz (1989) examined the experimental evidence on the effects of short-term (less than an hour) and long-term (above 1 hour) exposure to pornographic materials. Under short-term exposure, little evidence was found for an increase in rape-supportive attitudes and judgements following sexually explicit material compared to a control group exposed to a neutral film. Studies comparing short-term exposure to non-violent versus violent pornography yielded more consistent results: Violent pornography led to stronger rape-supportive and antisocial attitudes than non-violent sexual material. A parallel picture emerged with regard to the long-term effects: little evidence of non-violent pornography on rape-supportive beliefs and antisocial attitudes, more negative effects of violent as compared to non-violent pornography.

A subsequent review by Allen, Emmers, Gebhardt, and Giery (1995) included both experimental and correlational studies and used meta-analysis to provide quantitative assessments of the strength of pornography effects on rape-supportive attitudes. A total of 24 studies were entered in the analysis, 8 of which were correlational (i.e., self-reports of exposure to pornography were related to rape-supportive attitudes). The remaining 16 were experimental (i.e., exposure to pornography was manipulated and then related to measures of rape-supportive attitudes). As evidenced in an average effect size of $r = .018$, the correlational studies failed to support the claim that individuals with higher exposure to pornographic material hold more rape-supportive attitudes. In contrast, the experimental evidence did suggest a significant effect, albeit small (average effect size of $r = .146$). Again, violent pornography was more strongly related to rape-supportive attitudes than non-violent sexual depictions. However, even non-violent pornography was found in this review to have a small, but non-trivial effect on rape-related attitudes compared to control conditions.

While being a far cry from providing a conclusive answer to the question of how dangerous pornography really is in terms of aggression, the findings reviewed in this section allow some tentative conclusions: The first is that pornographic material that contains elements of violence is more likely to elicit aggressive behaviours and antisocial attitudes in viewers than non-violent pornography. The second is that the presentation of violence and of explicit sexual stimuli seem to have an additive effect: Non-sexual violence triggers more aggression than sexual stimuli without violence, but violent pornography, combining sexual and aggressive cues, produces a further increase. The third conclusion is that there seems to be an effect of violent pornography on rape-supportive attitudes that suggests the possibility of an indirect pathway from pornography to aggression. Given a substantial body of evidence showing that rape-supportive attitudes predict sexual aggression (e.g., White & Kowalski, 1998), the detrimental effect of pornography on those attitudes must be taken seriously.

Explaining the media violence–aggression link

So far, we have concentrated on evidence showing the existence of a link between media violence and aggression. In this section, we will try and answer the question of *how* the observation of violent inter-actions works to increase aggressive tendencies in the observer. Several interlocking mechanisms have been highlighted in the litera-ture (e.g., Baron & Byrne, 1991, p. 412; Bushman, 1997; see Figure 5.5).

(1) *An increase in autonomic arousal* prompted by the observation of violent media events. This increased arousal may facilitate aggression by enhancing the person's activity level and strengthen dominant responses. For example, a person confronted with a provocation is more likely to respond aggressively if he or she is already in a state of increased arousal enhancing response readi-ness. Another possibility for arousal to affect aggressive behaviour after exposure to media violence is suggested by Zillmann's "excitation transfer model" discussed in Chapter 2. This model suggests that arousal from an initially neutral source may be added to the arousal caused by a provocation and mislabelled as anger if the person is no longer aware of the source of the initial arousal, thus reinforcing an aggressive response to the provocation. This view suggests the possibility of delayed effects of media-induced

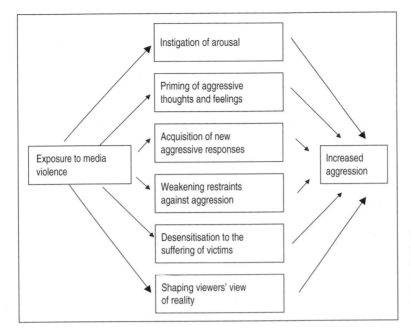

FIG. 5.5.
Psychological effects
of media violence
(based on Baron &
Byrne, 1991; and
Geen & Bushman,
1997).

arousal up to a point when the arousal is still present but is no
longer attributed to its original source.

(2) *Priming of aggressive thoughts and feelings*. Watching media
depictions of aggressive interactions increases the ease with which
the observer can access his own aggressive thoughts and feelings.
Priming is a mechanism whereby a particular external stimulus,
such as an aggressive act, guides the individual's attention to the
congruent mental constructs, such as aggressive cognitions, thus
lowering the threshold for using them to interpret social information. Asking subjects to list their thoughts following exposure to
a violent or non-violent videotape, Bushman and Geen (1990)
found that more aggressive thoughts were generated by respondents who had watched the violent videotape. In a subsequent set
of studies (Bushman, 1998), respondents who had watched a
violent videotape produced more aggressive associations to hom-
onyms with both an aggressive and a non-aggressive meaning
(such as box, punch). They were also faster in identifying letter
strings making up aggressive words than were respondents who
had seen a non-violent videotape.

The priming effect of media violence is not restricted to cognitive
associations but also extends to affective states. Anderson (1997)

showed that subjects exposed to violent film clips afterwards reported higher levels of hostility than subjects who had seen a non-violent film clip. This was true in particular for people not generally prone to feelings of hostility (those low on a measure of trait hostility). An explanation for the latter finding may be that for individuals high on trait hostility, hostile feelings are chronically accessible, so that the introduction of a short-term aggressive prime has no additional effect on them. People who are not habitually hostile require the prime to activate aggression-related affective states. However, it seems that not only do aggressive media contents prime aggressive thoughts and cognitions, but the priming of aggressive thoughts leads to a preference for violent media contents. Langley, O'Neal, Craig, and Yost (1992) first activated aggressive cognitions by asking subjects to compose short stories using words from a list of aggressive (versus non-aggressive) terms. Then, subjects were given the choice of different film clips described as varying in aggressive content. Subjects who had been asked to write aggression-related stories in the priming task expressed a greater preference for film clips containing violence than subjects who wrote a story based on the neutral words. These findings highlight the idea of a vicious cycle between media violence and aggression in that media violence fosters aggressive cognitions just as aggressive cognitions foster preferences for violent media.

(3) *Acquisition of new aggressive responses.* Exposure to aggression may instigate social learning processes which result in the acquisition of new behaviours. As we saw above, much of the aggression portrayed in the media is rewarded or at least goes unpunished. Moreover, it is often shown by attractive characters with whom viewers identify. As social learning theory suggests, learning through modelling is particularly likely under these circumstances (Bandura, 1983). The most obvious way in which aggression portrayed in the media is incorporated in the recipients' behavioural repertoire is reflected in copycat aggression. In a much publicised murder case in Germany a few years ago, a 15-year-old boy killed his aunt with an axe in exactly the same fashion as had been portrayed in a film he had watched prior to the attack. Similarly, the possibility was raised—though eventually not substantiated—that a particular violent video precipitated the actions of two 11-year-old boys who abducted and brutally killed 2-year-old James Bulger in Liverpool in 1993 (Kirby & Foster, 1993). In a more clear-cut recent case, three 16-year-old schoolboys were convicted in the UK of the murder of a 15-year-old youth in which

they re-enacted a violent scene from the film *Reservoir Dogs* in a children's playground. They launched a sustained and violent attack on their victim in which one of the boys mimicked the cult film by trying to cut off their victim's ear (*The Independent*, 26 July 2000).

Beyond such single-case evidence, studies conducted as early as the 1960s showed that children imitate the behaviours observed by attractive role models (Bandura et al., 1963). As we saw in Chapter 2, observing aggressive behaviour may lead to the *acquisition* of the observed behaviour even if the model has not been reinforced for his or her behaviour. Reinforcement of the model is important, though, for the observed behaviour to actually be *performed* spontaneously.

(4) *Weakening restraints against aggression.* Exposure to violent media contents may weaken the viewers' disinhibitions against aggression by making aggression appear as a common and accepted feature of social interactions. The widespread prevalence of aggression in the media and the fact that only a minority of violent acts are shown to lead to pain and injury in the victim may undermine the perception of violence as antisocial and harmful. For example, several studies have found that rape proclivity, i.e., the self-reported odds that a man would rape a woman provided he was not to be caught and punished (Malamuth, 1981), increases as a function of exposure to violent pornography compared to a control condition. Boeringer (1994) found correlations from .34 to .39 between exposure to pornographic material and self-reported sexual aggression, self-reported probability of using force in sexual encounters, and self-reported rape proclivity (see also Demaré et al., 1988).

(5) *Desensitisation to the suffering of victims.* Repeated exposure to media violence leads to habituation, which in turn reduces the viewer's sensitivity towards the victim's suffering. Several studies have documented a decline in physiological arousal in the course of prolonged exposure to violence (e.g., Averill, Malstrom, Koriat, & Lazarus, 1972; Cline, Croft & Courrier, 1973). In addition, it has been shown that children exposed to television violence are subsequently less sensitive toward victims of violence (e.g., Thomas, Horton, Lippencott, & Drabman, 1977). Further evidence for the desensitising role of media influences comes from a wide range of studies into the effects of pornography on sexual aggression. These studies show that subjects exposed to violent pornography rated the impact of a subsequently presented rape scenario on the victim

as significantly less severe and expressed more permissive attitudes about sexual violence than those without prior exposure to
pornographic material (e.g., Linz, Donnerstein, & Adams, 1989;
Mullin & Linz, 1995). The desensitising effect of violent pornography is not limited to men but was found to affect women as well
(Krafka, Linz, Donnerstein, & Penrod, 1997).

(6)   Finally, the effects of media presentations of violence on
viewers' perceptions of aggression and violence in the real world
should not be underestimated. As several authors have argued, the
widespread presence of aggression in the media fosters a view of
the world as a mean and violent place (e.g., Signorelli, 1990; Tyler,
1980). For example, it was shown that heavy viewers of violent
media programmes overestimate the prevalence of violent crime.
While evidence on the translation of such views into feelings of fear
for one's personal safety is inconsistent (see Comstock & Scharrer,
1999), some studies suggest that heavy exposure to media violence
leads viewers to adopt more rigorous views on crime prevention
and punishment and endorse more punitive attitudes.

Media violence and aggressive scripts

A theoretical framework that can integrate the different mechanisms
shown to be involved in both short- and long-term effects of exposure
to media violence is the concept of "aggressive scripts" discussed in
Chapter 2 (Huesmann, 1998). A script is a cognitive structure that
contains a person's stored knowledge about a particular behavioural
domain, such as *how* to act, *when* to act, and *what consequences* to
expect. Thus, scripts provide guidelines for behaviour in a particular
area. Scripts are acquired in the process of social learning, either by
direct experience or by observing and imitating the behaviour of
others acting as models. It is obvious that a host of opportunity is
provided by the different media for the latter form of social learning,
also called modelling. The formation of aggressive scripts begins as
soon as children have developed a basic understanding of the
meaning of behaviour and its consequences, and scripts are then
extended and elaborated as a function of direct or vicarious experiences. To the extent that individuals experience different responses to
their own aggressive actions or to those observed in others, they will
develop different aggressive scripts. As cognitive structures, scripts
contain abstractions and generalisations from specific instances of
direct learning or modelling. Specific experiences are stored in an
interconnected "database". This means that a particular aggressive

behaviour, such as hitting a person on the head, may elicit a variety of other aggressive behaviours stored in the script. Anderson (1997) describes the idea of an associative network of aggression-related thoughts and feelings: "Activation of one node tends to activate related nodes, which are connected. Thus, viewing a violent episode can activate a host of related nodes, and activation then spreads to other related nodes" (p. 165).

The role of media violence in priming aggressive thoughts and feelings is relevant to understanding the activation of aggressive scripts. The more individuals expose themselves to media violence, the more often they encounter stimuli relevant to their aggressive scripts. Over time, the frequent activation of aggressive scripts will make them more easily accessible, thus enhancing the likelihood that they will be used to interpret incoming stimuli. Children are particularly susceptible to this effect because their aggressive scripts are still more malleable than those of adults.

Once a script is activated, the next step is to evaluate the appropriateness of the behaviours suggested by the script. In the case of aggressive scripts, the evaluation is likely to consider the appropriateness of the observed aggressive actions. As noted above, media violence often goes unpunished or is even rewarded by success. This observation fosters the view that aggression is a useful and appropriate way of dealing with interpersonal conflict and of venting hostility or frustration. In the same vein, media violence that fails to show the effects of violence on the victims or presents violent actions as justified by a moral purpose affects the evaluation of aggressive scripts by weakening the normative beliefs that would inhibit aggressive behaviour. Finally, repeated exposure to media violence in a way "familiarises" the person with the aggressive script by reducing the affective arousal initially elicited by depictions of violence. This emotional "numbing" distracts from the adverse effects of violence and leads to a less sympathetic perception and treatment of victims.

Enactment of aggressive scripts, potentially shaped by exposure to media violence, carries immediate consequences for the actor that are important in the evaluation of the aggressive script. If children never get away with aggressive behaviour, they will eventually come to realise the inappropriateness of their aggressive scripts. However, as Huesmann (1998) points out, it is not others' reactions to aggressive behaviour as such, but the perception of those responses by the aggressive individuals that affects their scripted behaviour: "The boy who is told he is bad because he pushed others out of the way may shrug his shoulders and think, 'Nice guys finish last'" (Huesmann,

1998, p. 93). Media presentations of violence as a sign of assertiveness and dominance may well suggest such interpretations that protect the aggressive script from negative evaluation.

Mitigating the adverse effects of media violence

Given the many ways in which media presentations of aggression may affect viewers' aggressive tendencies, what can be done to mitigate these adverse effects? One conclusion suggested by the script approach is that priority should be given to interventions targeted at young viewers whose scripts are not yet consolidated and can therefore be changed more easily. Smith and Donnerstein (1998) distinguish between two broad intervention strategies which could be—and, to a limited extent, have been—adopted to counteract the detrimental effects of media violence: critical viewing and media initiatives (see also Eron, 1986). *Critical viewing* involves teaching viewers to become aware of the way in which violence is presented in the media. Important critical viewing skills are learning to distinguish between fictional and factual media presentations, identifying as unrealistic violence that fails to show the pain and injuries of victims, and developing alternatives to aggressive conflict resolution strategies. Adults viewing programmes together with children may act as role models exemplifying a critical perspective on media violence. A study by Huesmann et al. (1983) showed that even as few as two training sessions can have a mitigating effect on media violence. They selected the children who scored in the top 25% of violence viewers in the five-nation longitudinal study described above. The children were asked to develop and present statements arguing that violence as portrayed on television was a bad thing. To reinforce children's self-perception as adopting an anti-violence stance, they were videotaped while presenting their case and were later given the opportunity to watch their performance. Four months later, children who had taken part in the intervention scored significantly lower on measures of peer-nominated aggression than they had at the beginning of the study prior to the intervention.

Addressing the problem of sexual violence, Intons-Peterson et al. (1989) presented subjects with educational films about the severity of rape and the importance of concern for one's sexual partner. Following the educational films, subjects were exposed to one of three commercial films: a non-violent sex film, a non-sexual violent film, and a sexually violent film. Compared to a control group, respondents who saw the educational material showed greater rejection of rape myths and adopted a more sympathetic approach in judging a rape victim (see also Linz, Wilson, & Donnerstein, 1992, for related evidence). However, many more interventions have to be conducted and evaluated before their potential for mitigating the effects of media violence can be properly assessed.

A second approach to intervention involves the media industry itself. *Media initiatives* can take the form of self-imposed voluntary control of violence screening, both in terms of slotting violent programmes and in terms of vetting programmes for violent content. In addition, media productions can be custom tailored to educate viewers about the adverse effects of particular forms of violence, such as rape and child sexual abuse. In one such film, *Schande* (*Shame*, 1999), commissioned for German television from a well-known writer, the agony of a girl who is sexually abused by her stepfather was poignantly shown, culminating in the girl's suicide after her assailant was sentenced and sent to jail. However, in the absence of a systematic evaluation, it is impossible to decide whether or not viewing the film actually led viewers to adopt a more sympathetic attitude to victims of childhood sexual abuse. A study by Wilson, Linz, Donnerstein and Stipp (1992) is more pertinent in this context. They evaluated the effect of a film showing the traumatic impact of an acquaintance rape on the victim (*She Said No*, 1990) and found that viewing the film increased the recognition of date rape as a serious social problem. However, as the US National Television Violence Study (1997) revealed, only 4% of the sampled programmes contained an explicit anti-violence theme. This shows that there is still a long way to go in addressing the harmful effects of media violence.

Summary

- Aggression and violence are prevalent features of films, television programmes, and computer games, including those aimed at children and adolescents. A substantial proportion of time per day is spent by individuals of all age groups using these media. Studies examining the effect of media-presented aggression have provided overall support for the proposed aggression-enhancing effect of violent media contents. The link was found to be stronger in children than in adults, suggesting a "sensitive period" during which individuals are particularly susceptible to media influences.

- Violent media contents are particularly likely to affect viewers' aggressive tendencies if the violence is presented as successful or as not leading to punishment, or if it is presented as justified and not leading to any pain or harm in the victim. In addition, in line with social learning theory, aggression shown by powerful or admirable media figures is more likely to elicit aggressive behaviour. Individual differences have been observed in response to aggressive media. Habitually aggressive and hostile individuals seem to be particularly affected by media violence. At the same time, these individuals are more strongly attracted to violent media depictions, thus exposing themselves to a greater extent to an influence to which they are particularly susceptible.

- Longitudinal studies corroborate the claim that exposure to media violence can lead to long-term increases in aggressive response tendencies. There is evidence to show that differential rates of exposure to television violence at the age of 8 are associated with differences in aggressive behaviour more than 20 years later.

- Evidence examining the effect of pornography on aggression is inconclusive with regard to non-violent pornography. There are clear indications, however, that violent pornography that combines sexual and aggressive cues does lead to an increase in aggressive response tendencies. It seems that the violent aspects of such depictions are more important than the sexual content in eliciting aggression. Furthermore, violent pornography was found to affect rape-supportive attitudes, which in turn predict sexually aggressive behaviour.

- Several mechanisms have been suggested to explain the link between media violence and aggression and the formation of aggressive scripts: (1) instigation of arousal; (2) priming of aggressive thoughts and feelings; (3) acquisition of new aggressive responses; (4) weakening restraints against aggression; (5) desensitisation to the suffering of victims; and (6) shaping viewers' perception of the world as a violent place.

- To mitigate the adverse effects of media violence, two broad approaches have been proposed: (1) critical viewing, i.e., educating viewers about the antisocial and harmful nature of aggressive behaviour and helping them to imagine non-violent alternatives; and (2) media initiatives, i.e., the use of media depictions to highlight the detrimental effects of violence.

Suggested reading

Allen, M., D'Alessio, D., & Brezgel, K. (1995). A meta-analysis summarizing the effects of pornography II. Aggression after exposure. *Human Communication Research, 22,* 258–283.

Hogben, M. (1998). Factors moderating the effect of televised aggression on viewer behavior. *Communication Research, 25,* 220–247.

Paik, H., & Comstock, G. (1994). The effects of television violence on antisocial behavior. *Communication Research, 21,* 516–546.

Potter, W.J. (1999). *On media violence.* Thousand Oaks, CA: Sage.

Smith, S.L., & Donnerstein, E. (1998). Harmful effects of exposure to media violence: Learning of aggression, emotional desensitization, and fear. In R.G. Geen & E. Donnerstein (Eds.), *Human aggression: Theories, research and implications for social policy* (pp. 168–202). San Diego, CA: Academic Press.

Aggression in the public sphere 6

Up to now, we have been talking about aggression as an umbrella term covering a wide range of different manifestations. In the second part of this volume, the focus will shift towards a closer examination of specific forms of aggressive behaviour, each carrying its own unique characteristics. The media report daily about incidents of aggression from virtually all areas of social life, many of which were sparked by minor causes, yet ended in serious violence. Figure 6.1 provides a sample of such incidents from newspaper readings over just a few days.

The present chapter deals with different manifestations of aggression in public life: bullying, ethnic and politically motivated aggression, collective violence, and homicide. In the majority of cases, these forms of aggression take place outside people's own homes, in settings like schools or offices or in the streets. The next chapter will address the problems of domestic violence, focusing on the sexual, physical, and emotional abuse of children and on violence against spouses and elders (Chapter 7). Chapter 8 is devoted to sexual aggression, most notably against women, but we will also consider the problem of male sexual victimisation.

Bullying in school and at the workplace

The role of aggression in peer relationships was examined briefly in Chapter 3 in the context of the development of aggressive behaviour. In this section, we will come back to this issue by looking at a particular form of aggression among peers, i.e., bullying. Bullying has been studied with regard to two main settings: schools and the workplace. In both cases, perpetrators and victims are part of the same interacting social group.

Gang shot man dead after row over wife's parking, court told

THE INDEPENDENT, 22 January 2000

Student kidnapped and left to drown in stream

THE INDEPENDENT, 1 February 2000

Cruelty and neglect kill 1,000 children in a decade

THE INDEPENDENT, 4 February 2000

Bullying and sexual harassment rife in the workplace

THE INDEPENDENT, 15 February 2000

FIG. 6.1. Examples of aggression in everyday life (reprinted with permission from The Independent Syndication).

Bullying as a problem in schools

A widely accepted definition of *bullying* is provided by Olweus (1994): A person is bullied "when he or she is exposed, repeatedly and over time, to negative actions on the part of one or more other persons" (p. 98). In addition, bullying involves an imbalance of strength and power, leaving the victims unable to defend themselves effectively against the negative behaviour. Unlike other aggressive acts which involve one-off or short-term attacks, bullying typically occurs continuously over extended periods of time, leaving the victim in a sustained state of anxiety and intimidation. Bullying can take both direct and indirect forms, whereby direct bullying involves open, physical harassment of the victim, while indirect bullying consists of strategies leading to the exclusion and social isolation of

TABLE 6.1

Items measuring bullying from the perspectives of victim and perpetrator

Bullying items	Victimisation items
• I give weak kids a hard time. • I am part of a group that goes around teasing other kids. • I like to make other kids scared of me. • I like to show other kids I'm the boss. • I enjoy upsetting whimps. • I like to get into a fight with someone I can easily beat.	• I get called names by other kids. • Other kids leave me out of things on purpose. • I get picked on by other kids. • Other kids make fun of me. • I get hit and pushed around by other kids.

From Duncan, *Journal of Interpersonal Violence*, *14*, 871–886, copyright © 1999 by Sage Publications; reprinted by permission of Sage Publications, Inc.

the target. An example of items used to identify bullies as well as victims is presented in Table 6.1.

Bullying has been recognised as a social problem primarily among school children, and most of the research has been conducted with this group (see Schuster, 1996, for a review). Even though it does not represent a criminal offence, bullying can have highly negative effects, clearly marking it as a form of aggressive behaviour (Crick & Bigbee, 1998; Duncan, 1999). Many schools have therefore introduced anti-bullying policies, aimed at encouraging the victims of bullying to come forward and at persuading pupils to report peers that bully other school mates (Eslea & Smith, 1998). In Britain, the first privately run school was opened at the end of 1999 to give a small group of severely victimised adolescents the opportunity to learn in a protected school environment without fear of bullying.

The most extensive research programme into the causes, manifestations, and consequences of bullying has been conducted in Norway by Olweus (Olweus, 1994). According to his findings based on a sample of 130,000 Norwegian pupils aged between 8 and 16, bullying shows considerable prevalence rates. Nine per cent of his sample reported being bullied, 7% admitted bullying others "frequently" or at least "now and then". As Schuster (1996) notes in her review of 23 studies, victimisation rates for bullying show large variations across different samples, ranging from 3% to almost 90% (see Duncan, 1999, for a similar conclusion). It is clear that this variation is due in large part to methodological differences between studies, such as the time period considered, the source of data (self- versus other-reports of victimisation and perpetration), and the broadness of the operational definition of bullying (e.g., requirement of serious and lasting consequences or of a power imbalance between perpetrator and victim). The more inclusive the operational definition, the higher the prevalence rates (e.g., Branwhite, 1994). While virtually every child has probably experienced some form of upsetting treatment by older or stronger peers, the concept of bullying should be limited to those experiences that meet the criteria of frequency, persistence over time, and unequal balance of power. Studies that observe these criteria suggest a prevalence rate of victimisation between 5% and 10%, with figures for the perpetration of bullying being slightly lower (see Bernstein & Watson, 1997; Schuster, 1996, p. 299).

Apart from exploring overall prevalence rates for bullying, it is important to consider differences in the extent to which children are bullied or become bullies themselves. Age and gender have been examined as potential moderators of the risk of bullying or being bullied. Concerning age, the evidence is inconclusive, with some studies finding a decline of bullying with age (e.g., Olweus, 1994), while others failed to find an age effect. As Schuster (1996) points out, the presence or absence of an age effect varies with the reliance on self-reports versus other-reports and with the definitions of bullying presented to respondents. Studies finding an age-related decline in bullying mostly relied on self-reports and used broad definitions, whereas studies that failed to establish an age effect more often used other-reports (e.g., from teachers) and asked for specific forms of bullying behaviour. Therefore, the decline in bullying in self-report studies may be due to underreporting, with older children being more aware of the socially undesirable nature of bullying (both in terms of being a perpetrator and being a victim). An additional explanation for the age-related decline in bullying in self-reports is provided by Swain (1998), who found that younger children held broader definitions of bullying than older children. Age does seem to be important in the choice of bullying strategies: younger children's bullying primarily involves acts of physical aggression, whereas in older children it is more likely to take the form of verbal and indirect forms of aggression.

As far as gender differences are concerned, the available evidence is more conclusive: Boys feature more prominently than girls as victims as well as perpetrators of bullying (Olweus, 1994). They are also more likely to use physical aggression than girls, who rely more on verbal and relational forms of aggression, as shown consistently in a cross-national comparison involving 21 countries (Smith et al., 1999; see also Crick & Bigbee, 1998). This difference obtained for bullying reflects a general gender difference in the preferred mode of aggression (see Chapter 3).

Beyond age and gender, several studies provide clear-cut evidence as to the typical characteristics of victims and bullies, which confirms the common-sense notions about bullying (Bernstein & Watson, 1997). Victimisation is often stable over extended periods of time and across settings, e.g., after children have changed schools. The typical victim is an anxious, socially withdrawn child or adolescent, isolated from his or her peer group and likely to be physically weaker than most peers. In contrast, bullies are typically strong, dominant, and assertive, showing aggressive behaviour not just towards their victims but also towards parents, teachers, and other adults. These findings suggest that bullying is part of a more general pattern of antisocial behaviour that is associated with an increased likelihood of deviant behaviour in adolescence and adulthood. A detached parent–child relationship, parents' tolerance of aggressive behaviour by the child, and the use of aggressive child-rearing practices were found to play a crucial role in producing this antisocial behaviour pattern (Bowers, Smith, & Binney, 1994). As to the developmental prospects of bullies, Olweus (1991, p. 425) states that "youngsters who are aggressive and bully others in school run a clearly increased risk of later engaging in other problem behaviors such as criminality and alcohol abuse."

Workplace bullying

Workplace bullying, or workplace harassment, refers to a type of aggression that is highly similar to school bullying except that it takes place between adults rather than children and adolescents. Deliberate attempts at making another person's life miserable at work are at the core of this construct. In a fairly broad definition, Leymann (1993, p. 21) describes workplace bullying as "negative communicative actions, directed against an individual (by one or several others), and occurring very often and over a longer period of time, thereby characterising the relationship between victim and perpetrator." This definition includes actions such as (1) restricting communicative opportunities; (2) impairing social relationships; (3) undermining personal reputation; (4) undermining professional standing; and (5) impairing health and physical well-being. Neuman and Baron (1998, p. 393) define workplace aggression as "all forms of behavior by which individuals attempt to harm others or their organizations." These authors identify three key components of workplace aggression:

expressions of hostility, e.g., spreading rumours, holding the target person's work up to ridicule; *obstructionism*, e.g., working deliberately slowly, causing others to delay action; and *overt aggression*, such as theft of personal property, destroying mail.

Workplace bullying has only recently become the object of systematic research, and empirical evidence is still limited. The available database suggests that victimisation rates for workplace bullying are similar to those obtained for school bullying. Incidence rates covering the last 6–12 months prior to the survey range between 3% and 10% (see Hoel, Rayner, & Cooper, 1999; Randall, 1997; Schuster, 1996, for reviews). However, as with school bullying, victimisation rates increase if the time period is extended or lifetime prevalence rates are obtained. For example, in Rayner's (1997) survey of more than 1100 part-time university students, just over half of the respondents indicated that they had experienced some form of workplace bullying in their jobs.

Due to the small number of studies, conclusions about the moderating role of personal and organisational characteristics on workplace bullying remain tentative. According to Hoel et al. (1999), both the prevalence and the nature of bullying at the workplace are similar for men and women. However, women appear to be more negatively affected by bullying than men. While there is evidence that workplace bullying may be linked to post-traumatic stress disorder in both male and female victims, women generally report negative consequences, such as somatic complaints, depression, and muscular strain, to a greater extent than men. Concerning the gender constellations involved in bullying, Hoel et al. (1999) note that men are mostly bullied by other men, whereas women are bullied by men as well as women.

In terms of socio-organisational variables, Leymann (1993) suggests that power differentials within organisations play an important role. He found that 37% of all bullying incidents involved a person in a senior position bullying a subordinate, 44% involved individuals of the same hierarchical position, and only a minority of victims were bullied by somebody in a lower hierarchical position. Poor leadership quality, reflected in authoritarian management methods and communication problems, is an important organisational characteristic that allows bullying to develop and persist.

A particular form of workplace bullying that has attracted widespread attention is *sexual harassment*. Fitzgerald (1993, p. 1070) defines sexual harassment as "any deliberate or repeated sexual behavior that is unwelcome to the recipient, as well as other sex-related behaviors that are hostile, offensive, or degrading." She and her colleagues developed a self-report instrument that captures three types of sexual harassment: *gender harassment*, i.e., crude verbal, physical, and symbolic behaviours that convey degrading and hostile attitudes towards women; *unwanted sexual attention* in the form of sexually charged comments and advances; and *sexual coercion* in the form of subtle or explicit efforts to make job rewards contingent on sexual co-operation (Fitzgerald et al., 1997).

The majority of studies have focused on women as victims of sexual harassment (see O'Donohue, Downs, & Yeater, 1998, for a review). Studies including both men and women show that victimisation rates are, indeed, substantially higher for women than for men (Fitzgerald & Ormerod, 1993). Confirming this gender imbalance from the perpetrator side, Perry, Schmidtke, and Kulik (1998) found that men also had a significantly higher propensity to engage in sexually harassing behaviour than women.

As to the prevalence of sexual harassment, it is estimated that every second woman will experience sexual harassment at some point in her working life (Fitzgerald, 1993). Recent incidence studies support this estimate. For example, O'Hare and O'Donohue (1998) found that 69% of the women they surveyed reported at least one incident of gender harassment. Schneider, Swan, and Fitzgerald (1997) collected reports from women in two organisations, a private-sector company and a university. A total of 68% of respondents in the private company reported at least one incident of sexual harassment in the 2 years preceding the survey. Of these, 66% rated the experience as offensive or extremely offensive. In the university sample, 63% of respondents reported at least one experience of sexual harassment, and 48% of them rated the experience as offensive or extremely offensive.

Organisational characteristics play an important role in precipitating sexual harassment. Sexual harassment was found to be particularly prevalent in male-dominated work settings (Fitzgerald et al., 1997) and in unprofessional work environments (O'Hare & O'Donohue, 1998). Tolerance of sexist remarks and behaviour may be seen as one factor of an unprofessional work atmosphere that allows sexual harassment to develop and persist. A setting in which male dominance is combined with a strong power hierarchy is academia. Even though women account for a large proportion of students and relatively low-prestige clerical workers, men hold the majority of senior positions. Evidence of widespread sexual harassment in academic institutions has been provided by several authors (e.g., Paludi, 1990; Schneider et al., 1997). Apart from such aspects of workplace structure, gender stereotypes shared at a more general level contribute to sexual harassment. An important aspect here is the difference between men and women in perceiving sexually charged remarks and behaviours as inappropriate and offensive (Hunter & McClelland, 1991; Jones & Remland, 1992).

Just like workplace bullying in general, sexual harassment entails serious consequences, both for the victims and the institutions involved. Victims of sexual harassment experience more psychological problems and somatic complaints. They also have higher rates of absenteeism and turnover than non-victimised members of the workforce (Fitzgerald et al., 1997; Schneider et al., 1997). In trying to respond to sexual harassment, ignoring the offensive behaviour and avoiding contact with the harasser are common coping strategies. If these strategies fail to work, victims of harassment may feel forced to leave their job. Only a small proportion of harassment incidents are reported and lead to formal complaint procedures (O'Donohue et al., 1998; Welsh, 2000).

The present section examined two forms of everyday aggression in the public sphere: school bullying and workplace harassment, both found to have lasting negative effects on their victims. While a growing body of research is available addressing these social problems, the evidence is largely descriptive. The psychological processes that create and sustain bullying and harassment are still far from being properly understood (see however, Fitzgerald et al.'s, 1997, model of sexual harassment for an example of an explanatory approach). Nevertheless, the studies reviewed in this section give us an indication of how many people are affected and what kinds of characteristics are typical of perpetrators and victims. Even though the literature suggests victimisation rates of no more than 10%, these figures should not be dismissed. After all, we are talking about adverse experiences that are typically allowed to carry on for extended periods of time and are able to infuse a deep sense of terror and vulnerability in the victims. Further research is needed to illuminate the mechanisms involved in bullying in schools and at work, both at the level of the individuals involved and the level of the social system in which they operate.

Ethnic and politically motivated violence

In this section, we will examine instances of aggression in which the group membership of the *target person* motivates or triggers aggressive acts towards that person. Hostility against members of

TABLE 6.2

Number of "hate crimes" motivated by ethnic and racial bias in the United States in 1998

	Racial bias	Ethnic/national bias
Crimes against persons		
Murder and non-negligent manslaughter	8	1
Forcible rape	8	0
Aggravated assault	717	144
Simple assault	1045	194
Intimidation	2154	372
Crimes against property		
Robbery	57	9
Burglary	51	10
Larceny–theft	45	5
Motor vehicle theft	2	0
Arson	28	3
Destruction/damage/vandalism	1125	176

Source: US Department of Justice (2000) www.fbi.gov/ucr/98hate.pdf, pp. 10–11.

particular ethnic and racial groups is a widespread phenomenon all over the world, giving rise to a range of aggressive behaviour from verbal derogation to serious forms of violence. Acts of racial and ethnic violence account for a large proportion of so-called "hate crimes", i.e., crimes motivated by a bias against members of particular social groups (see however, O'Brien, 1987, on the intricacies of assessing interracial crime rates). US figures for 1998 reveal a total of 5360 racially motivated crimes and a further 919 crimes motivated by ethnic or national group membership of the victim(s). Together, these figures make up 68% of all crimes recorded under the "Hate Crimes Statistics Act" in 1998 (US Department of Justice, 2000). It is important to note that these figures include racially motivated crimes by minority members against whites. However, at 18.5% the percentage of ethnic crime against white persons is low. The scope and scale of racially and ethnically motivated crime are illustrated in Table 6.2.

Examining evidence from crime surveys on racial harassment and victimisation in Britain, Bowling (1993) concludes that racial harassment of members of ethnic minorities presents a large-scale problem. In a survey covering only those incidents that had been reported to the police, Maynard and Read (1997) identified a total of 7573 racially motivated incidents in the UK between April 1996 and March 1997. Members of ethnic minorities were found to have generally higher victimisation rates than the white majority, with a high proportion of racially motivated attacks, predominantly by groups of young white men. In Germany, dramatic incidents of ethnocentric violence, committed by perpetrators close to or part of extreme right-wing groups, have been witnessed in recent years, directed in particular against foreign refugees seeking political asylum, at the long-established Turkish community, and against Jewish institutions and memorials.

Prejudicial attitudes against members of different racial and ethnic groups have been investigated as potential predictors of heightened aggression against members of those groups. However, as Baron and Richardson (1994) point out, there is no straightforward relationship between prejudice and aggression. Whether or not prejudiced people will respond more aggressively towards members of the rejected groups depends on the influence of mediating factors, such as fear of retaliation and anonymity. If whites holding strong prejudicial attitudes towards blacks had to perform aggressive behaviour in public, they showed "reverse discrimination", i.e., acted less aggressively towards a black than towards a white target person. If their behaviour was recorded anonymously, however, they did show more aggression towards the black person (e.g., Donnerstein & Donnerstein, 1978).

Moreover, it has been demonstrated that rather than discriminating between the targets of aggression, prejudiced people show a higher tendency towards aggressive behaviour in general, that is, against targets from all kinds of social groups. According to Bar-Tal (1990), *delegitimisation* is an important process mediating between the ethnocentric devaluation of an outgroup and the performance of harmful actions against outgroup members. Delegitimisation refers to the "categorization of a group or groups into extremely negative social categories that are excluded from the realm of acceptable norms and/or values" (Bar-Tal, 1990, p. 65). If the perception of an outgroup as different and inferior is accompanied by feelings of fear, then delegitimisation is likely to occur. Its function is (a) to maximise the difference between one's own reference group and the outgroup, and (b) to provide a justification for the exploitation or other ill-treatment of the outgroup. The treatment of Jews in Nazi Germany or of black citizens under the South African apartheid regime provide extreme examples of how delegitimisation creates a basis for justifying the oppression, persecution, and killing of outgroup members (see also Bar-Tal, 1997). At an everyday level, delegitimisation strategies are frequently employed to shift responsibility for aggressive behaviour from the actor onto the target persons who are said to elicit, or at least deserve, the negative actions directed at them.

Outgroup devaluation with the aim to justify aggressive actions against members of the devalued group also plays an important role in aggressive conflicts motivated by political aims. Terrorism is one such form of politically motivated aggression, which is aimed at making an impact on the power holders within a particular country. Another form of politically motivated aggression is war, which involves the use of force against other nations or, in the case of civil wars, violent conflict between different political, religious, or ethnic groups within a nation. If the aggression is directed at the persecution and killing of entire groups for racial, political, religious, or other reasons, then it takes the form of genocide (Staub, 1989).

In defining "terrorism", Friedland (1988) points out that definitions should concentrate on *acts* rather than *persons*, because the labelling of people and groups as terrorist is ambiguous, depending on the perspective and affiliation of the person applying the label: the same group of people may be called terrorists by some and freedom fighters by others. In contrast, terrorist acts can be more easily identified according to two basic criteria. Violent acts are called terrorist if (a) they are not only used as direct means to achieve political aims, but also as instruments of publicity and intimidation; (b) they are directed at harming others than the direct opponent in the political conflict. Both criteria underline that it is not the direct physical harm that is the primary objective of terrorist acts but their psychological effects in terms of attracting public attention and undermining the authority of the state in ensuring the safety of its citizens. Despite the worldwide notoriety achieved by individual terrorists, terrorism is for the most part committed by groups, typically operating out of a position of relative weakness within their society.

To explain when and why movements directed at social change resort to violence rather than accepted forms of political participation, several authors have transferred the frustration–aggression hypothesis from the individual to the group level. Terrorist violence is seen as the result of frustrations caused by social and political deprivation. In some cases, such as the IRA or the PLO, the perceived injustice leading to the emergence of terrorist movements is immediately traceable to historical developments. Other forms of terrorism, such as the acts of the left-wing Red Army Faction in Germany in the 1970s and 1980s, are attributed to the somewhat less tangible frustration of not being able to make a significant impact on political decisions. As Baumeister et al. (1996) note, terrorists often cultivate an attitude of moral superiority over their victims from which they derive justification for their violent actions.

However, given the widespread nature of social and political injustice affecting large numbers of people without turning them into terrorists, additional factors must be assumed to explain the conditions under which frustration is channelled into terrorist activities. Friedland offers an interactionist model, arguing that terrorism is a joint function of both situational and individual factors: "The origin, in most instances, was a widespread social protest movement. Confrontations, often violent, with authorities and failure to elicit a popular response led to disillusion and deterioration of the movement. Remnants of the movement formed small, clandestine groups that maintained little external contact and a fierce ingroup loyalty and cohesion. These circumstances enhanced the status of violent individuals within the groups, elevated them to leadership positions and allowed them to establish terrorism as the groups' preferred *modus operandi*" (Friedland, 1988, p. 111).

The role of individual differences in support for aggressive strategies to resolve political conflicts was further explored by Feshbach (1994). He found that individual differences in dispositional aggressiveness failed to predict either support for nuclear armament or advocacy of military action. Instead, two more specific attitudes, nationalism and patriotism, were examined as potential candidates for predicting support for military options. While patriotism is defined in terms of pride in one's national identity, nationalism refers to feelings of national superiority and power over other nations (see also Bar-Tal & Staub, 1997). Feshbach (1994) argues that nationalism is more closely related to endorsement of military aggression than patriotism and reports a study that supports the functional distinction between the two types of attitudes. Subjects were exposed to either martial music (military marches) or patriotic music (the US National Anthem) and the effect of the music on nationalism and patriotism scores was examined. While martial music led to higher nationalism scores, but not patriotism scores compared to a control group, patriotic music had the reverse effect. Feshbach (1994, pp. 289–290) concludes that "it is possible to sustain and even reinforce patriotic attachments to one's nation while fostering internationally oriented attitudes that diminish the likelihood of war." Staub (1997) introduced the distinction between "blind" and "constructive" patriotism. The former denotes an intense identification with and uncritical acceptance of one's own nation, while the latter refers to a more critical attitude combining a positive evaluation of one's nation with a general concern for humanitarian values. In line with Feshbach's conclusion, Schatz and Staub (1997) found that individuals who scored high on blind patriotism also endorsed militaristic nationalism, while no such link was found for constructive patriotism.

Feelings of national superiority are also seen as a precipitating factor of war, along with three additional cultural preconditions conducive to the development of aggression towards other nations (Staub, 1989):

(1) the emergence of an "ideology of antagonism", triggered by an initial ingroup–outgroup differentiation, which then leads to the attribution of highly negative, often stereotype-based characteristics to the outgroup;

(2) an "ideology of national security" in which the continuous assessment of and adaptation to the dangerousness of the opponent is replaced by the unquestioned aim to dominate the enemy at all costs; and

(3) the acceptance of a world view that highlights the values fostered by war, such as companionship, loyalty, national pride, or the worthy cause. Toch refers to this aspect as the *myth of good violence*, which "earns medals, commendations, and accolades" (Toch, 1993, p. 200).

The present analysis has focused on the *psychological* mechanisms involved in politically motivated violence. Indeed, as Mays, Bullock, Rosenzweig, and Wessells (1998, p. 738) point out, interethnic conflicts are "profoundly psychological and often center around issues of identity, symbol, legitimacy, memory, and perceptions of justice." At the same time, however, it is true to say that this form of aggressive behaviour is more strongly affected than the other forms of aggression considered in this chapter by non-psychological factors, such as the historical and material dimensions of intergroup conflict (Hinde, 1997). This is highlighted, for example, in analyses of the genocide in Ruanda (Smith, 1998) and the long-standing conflicts between Catholics and Protestants in Northern Ireland (Cairns & Darby, 1998) as well as between Israelis and Palestinians in the Middle East (Rouhana & Bar-Tal, 1998). As Singer (1989) notes, *systemic conditions* (such as material resources, allegiance bonds) at the multinational level, *dyadic conditions* in the bilateral relationship between the groups involved (such as trade relationship, balance of military strength), and *national conditions* within a country (such as economic instability) interact in a complex way, creating enormous problems in the search for regular patterns explaining the outbreak of civil and international wars.

Collective violence

Politically motivated aggression is often carried out by groups rather than individuals because groups can exert greater pressure in pursuing their interests. Group membership is seen as enhancing the effectiveness of individual action, but not as changing the character of individuals' behaviour. In the present section, we will examine aggressive actions performed by groups in which the very fact that individuals are part of a larger group is thought to change the way they behave. In analysing collective aggression, an important concern is to identify the effects of being in a group on group members' behaviour. Collective violence is often directed against other social groups rather than individual targets. It includes such diverse forms as sports aggression, rioting, and gang violence.

Sports aggression

Sporting events provide a potential platform for aggressive behaviour for the athletes involved as well as the spectators. As D. Russell (1993, p. 181) notes, "outside of wartime, sport is perhaps the only setting in which acts of interpersonal aggression are not only tolerated but enthusiastically applauded by large segments of society." However, systematic research into aggression in the context of sporting competitions is scarce. Practically all the evidence reviewed by Russell in his chapter on sports aggression, while being relevant to the understanding of violence surrounding sports events, has examined aggression in other contexts. In one of the few studies assessing the impact of watching sports aggression on spectators' aggressive tendencies, Arms, Russell, and Sandilands (1979) found that respondents exposed to a wrestling competition (stylised aggression) or an ice hockey match (realistic aggression) subsequently showed greater hostility and punitiveness than spectators of a swimming contest (non-aggressive control condition). This finding directly contradicts the notion of symbolic catharsis, derived from psychoanalytic theorising, which suggests that aggressive tension may be reduced by observing aggressive sports (see also Chapter 2). Interestingly, Wann et al. (1999) showed that individuals who engaged in, or liked to watch, aggressive sports particularly adhered to the idea of symbolic sport catharsis.

Some research has been conducted on a special case of sports violence featuring prominently in Western Europe and beyond: football hooliganism. Apart from dramatic incidents like the Heysel Stadium disaster in Belgium in 1985, or the violent attack on a French policeman by German football fans during the 1998 World Cup in France, violence arising in the context of football matches has led to a tragic number of deaths and serious injuries as well as to large-scale violent exchanges between rivalling football fans and the police. A graphic illustration is provided by the cover photo of this book. To come to grips with the problem, a variety of restrictions and control mechanisms have been introduced in recent years, such as banning the sale of alcohol before matches, developing strategic seating arrangements for opposing fan groups, and segregating opposing fan clubs on their way to and from the stadium. While the success of these measures has been limited, the need for security measures surrounding matches has, in itself, proven to be a serious safety hazard by impeding escape in the case of emergencies.

In their explanation of football hooliganism, Murphy, Williams, and Dunning (1990) argue that football hooliganism is a form a aggression typically engaged in by young working-class males. They identify a subculture of aggressive masculinity, "predominantly, but not solely lower class" (p. 13), which provides the normative framework for the performance of violent behaviour by football fans. Among the factors that exacerbate the masculinity norms of aggressive spectators, alcohol and the amount of violence on the pitch seem to play an important role (Dunning, Murphy, & Williams, 1986).

The significance of violence-condoning social norms in explaining football hooliganism is also reflected in an Italian study in which violent fans cited "solidarity with the fan club" as their primary motive for participating in disturbances around football matches (Zani & Kirchler, 1991). Moreover, the assertive nature of the game itself as well as the aggression displayed by the players in the course of the match provide additional cues that may reinforce aggressive tendencies in the spectator. Simons and Taylor (1992) point out that sports requiring extensive physical contact are more likely to elicit aggressive tendencies in spectators.

Rioting

Rioting can be defined as a form of collective violence that involves "hostile collective action by a group of about 50 or more people who physically assault persons or property or coerce someone to perform an action" (Bohstedt, 1994, p. 259). Following LeBon's (1896) early work on crowd behaviour, social psychologists have explored the notion that membership of large, anonymous groups leads individuals to behave in a more aggressive and antisocial fashion than they would show on their own (Goldstein, 1994a). This notion has received considerable support through laboratory studies showing that groups do indeed show more aggressive behaviour than individuals. To explain this effect, Zimbardo (1969) introduced his theory of *de-individuation*. It claims that by becoming submerged in an anonymous group, individuals lose their sense of personal identity and responsibility and are thus less inhibited to show negative social behaviour normally suppressed by their internal standards. Subsequent research has qualified the claim that individual behaviour always becomes more negative as a result of de-individuation (Diener, 1976; Reicher, 1984). Instead, a number of laboratory experiments showed that behaviour changes in accordance with the norms prevailing in the group context: when, for example, people were de-individuated by being dressed in Ku Klux Klan outfits, their behaviour became more aggressive; when they were de-individuated by having to wear a nurse's uniform, they showed less aggression than people acting as individuals (Johnson & Downing, 1979; see Postmes & Spears, 1998, for a meta-analytic review). Thus, there is clear evidence that individual behaviour becomes more extreme as a function of group membership, but the direction of the change towards either increased or decreased aggression is determined by the norms and salient cues inherent in the situation.

Systematic analyses of naturally occurring riots also disconfirm the earlier view that crowd action is uncontrolled, disorganised, and irrational. For example, Bohstedt (1994) points out that in early modern Europe food riots were common in times of food shortages, such as when harvests were poor and crops destroyed by bad weather conditions. These riots were restrained and organised, based on the idea of a "moral economy", and usually successful in bringing down food prices.

In a detailed case study of a British riot in the St. Paul's area of Bristol in 1980, Reicher (1984) showed that the riot was confined to specific targets within a circumscribed geographical area and that the rioters had developed a sense of shared identity *vis-à-vis* their common enemy, i.e., the police. In his sociological analysis of 341 urban riots in the United States during the 1960s, McPhail (1994) rejects the view that rioting is the result of structural strains particularly affecting young black males living in socially deprived ghettos. Instead, he proposes a model in which rioting is seen as a behavioural response adopted by a person to meet a particular aim (e.g., pursuing a political goal, acting out aggressive feelings against another group). In summarising his "purposive action model", McPhail concludes that "violent actors are neither the hapless victims of structural strain nor of psychological de-individuation. Purposive actors adjust their behaviours to make their perceptions match their objectives. They bear responsibility for those violent objectives and for the violent actions in which they engage" (McPhail, 1994, p. 25).

Gang violence

In contrast to rioters and hooligans who form relatively transient social groups restricted to particular events and/or settings, (delinquent) gangs usually exist over a longer period of time, at least as far as their core members are concerned. Gangs often adopt particular visible features, such as dress, hairstyle, or insignia, which serve to reinforce cohesion within the gang and the presentation of a coherent group image to others. A gang may therefore be defined as "an age-graded peer group that exhibits some permanence, engages in criminal activity, and has some symbolic representation of membership" (Decker & van Winkle, 1996, p. 31). While gang violence is by no means confined to adolescence, research has focused primarily on juvenile gangs, not least because membership in a juvenile gang may well be the pathway into an adult criminal career. Gangs operate primarily in the neighbourhood of the gang members as well as their schools. The prevalence of gangs operating in schools is as high as 40% in some areas, and the presence of gangs in schools has been linked to increased levels of availability and use of guns (Loeber & Hay, 1997). Gang prevalence has been found to predict adolescents' fears of assault in the school setting, creating a climate of insecurity and apprehension among students (Alvarez & Bachman, 1997).

In order to explain the origins of gangs and the dynamics underlying their violent actions, Decker and van Winkle (1996) assign crucial significance to the construct of *threat*. According to this view, gangs often originate in response to perceived or genuine threats from individuals or other groups in a particular neighbourhood. This process is promoted by the failure of legal and community institutions to offer effective protection. Threats may be, or perceived to be, directed at gang members' physical safety, their territorial claims, and/or their psychological identity. To the extent that rivalling gangs adopt similar perceptions of threat and try to pre-empt their opponents' attacks, gang violence has a strong potential for escalation. Furthermore, the gang's violent actions alienate its members from legitimate social institutions. This marginalisation gives rise to feelings of vulnerability, which are likely to enhance the psychological significance of gang membership for the individual and strengthen his or her affiliation with the gang. Decker and van Winkle (1996) have presented a conceptualisation of the role of threat in gang violence, which is depicted in Figure 6.2.

By virtue of their ability to pose a threat to potential opponents, neighbourhood gangs can present themselves as attractive social groups. Group membership offers both instrumental benefits (such as protection or the opportunity for material profit through illegal gang actions) and symbolic benefits (such as participating in the power and prestige attributed to the gang). If rival gangs are present, as is typically the case, the threat emanating from the neighbourhood gang is stepped up, and the commitment of the members to their group is increased. These dynamics of gang behaviour in response to external threat are reflected in the observation that gang cohesiveness is reinforced by the arrest and incarceration of gang members.

De-individuation and substitution of their personal identity by the social identity of the group suggest themselves as crucial mechanisms to account for aggressive behaviour by gangs (Turner et al., 1987). Like the other forms of group violence considered in this section, the actions of delinquent gangs typically show a discernible pattern rather than being impulsive, uncontrolled outbursts of violent impulses in the individual: "The contemporary American juvenile gang may have a structured organisation, identifiable leadership, territorial identification, continuous association, specific purpose, and engage in illegal behavior" (Goldstein, 1994a, p. 256).

Noting the difficulties in obtaining accurate statistical evidence of gang violence, Goldstein attempts to pinpoint the characteristic features of juvenile gangs and their members. According to his review, gang membership is primarily a male phenomenon, with males outnumbering females at a rate of 20 : 1. Similar conclusions are provided by Chesney-Lind's (1997) analysis of girl gangs. Moreover, she shows that if girls are organised in gangs, they do not display violence at the same rate as male gangs. Rather than forming gangs of their own, girls' involvement in gangs is more commonly that of playing auxiliary roles in boys' gangs, as girlfriends, "little sisters", and helpers in the fight against other gangs. Furthermore, there is evidence that female gang members are exposed to physical and sexual violence by male members of the gang (Molidor, 1996).

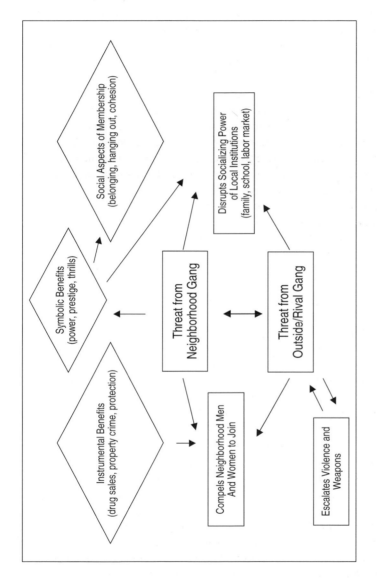

FIG. 6.2. The role of threat in gang violence (reprinted from Decker and van Winkle, 1996, p. 25, with the permission of Cambridge University Press).

According to several authors, the age range of gang membership has gone up in recent years, not least because drug-trafficking plays an increasing role in juvenile gangs (Cairns, Cadwallader, Estell, & Neckerman, 1997). In a sample of 101 gang members interviewed by Decker and van Winkle (1996), making money and selling drugs were named as the most common reasons for staying in the gang. Poor socio-economic background, preventing legitimate forms of access to material resources and status symbols, is an important factor explaining why young people are attracted to gangs. This may also explain the high proportion of juvenile gang members from ethnic minorities who are affected by both adverse socio-economic conditions and lack of acceptance by the dominant social group. Even though criminal aggression committed by gangs accounts for only a small proportion of total crimes, serious acts of violence, such as aggravated physical assault and homicide, are committed more frequently by gangs than by individual offenders.

Homicide

Taking another person's life certainly represents the most extreme form of violence conceivable. Even though homicide is rare compared to the other forms of aggression considered in this chapter, it is a pervasive feature of human societies and can hit any individual or member of a social group. A comprehensive examination of homicide as a social problem is provided by Smith and Zahn (1999). Most legal systems distinguish between different forms of criminal homicide depending on the intentionality and forseeability of the killing. While *murder* requires premeditation, intent and malice on the part of the killer, behaviour that leads to the death of another person is qualified as *manslaughter* if the lethal consequences were the result of prior provocation or caused through criminal negligence.

The scale of homicide

Incidence rates for criminal homicide are provided by official crime statistics, which also contain information about characteristics of perpetrators and victims. The US Uniform Crime Reports, published annually, reveal that 15,533 persons were murdered in 1999, corresponding to a victimisation rate of 5.7 per 100,000 inhabitants. In Germany, the most recent available crime figures for 1999 show an incidence rate for murder and manslaughter of 1.2 per 100,000 inhabitants (Bundesministerium des Inneren, 2000). In both countries, homicide rates have been declining in the course of the 1990s. US figures went down by 30% from 1995 to 1999, while the German figures went down by 13.2% from 1997 to 1999. A recent comparative analysis of homicide rates in different countries for the year 1997 was conducted by the Scottish Executive (1999). This analysis reveals incidence rates of 1.4 per 100,000 inhabitants for England and Wales, 1.8 for Scotland, 1.7 for France, 1.6 for Italy, 1.8 for Sweden, 2.6 for Spain, and 61.6 for South Africa. A comparison of homicide rates in a range of countries worldwide based on statistics by the World Health Organization (WHO) reveals large variations in national homicide rates (LaFree, 1999). Part of the variation must be attributed to differences in defining and recording homicide, but some of it probably reflects genuine differences in occurrence. However, it is as yet unclear what variables may explain why homicide seems to be more prevalent in some countries than in others. LaFree (1999) discusses various economic, political, and cultural factors, most of which turn out to be unrelated to differences in homicide rates (such as level of industrialisation, unemployment, urbanisation, and proportion of young people in the population). There are some indications, however, that the degree of economic inequality in a country and the growth rate of the population are positively related to homicide rates.

Disaggregating overall homicide figures (i.e., breaking them down by specific characteristics of the crimes) uncovers interesting variations as a function of geographical region as well as age, race, and gender of victims and perpetrators. The Uniform Crime Reports (1999) reveal that homicide rates were higher in metropolitan areas (6 per 100,000) than in rural areas and smaller cities (4 per 100,000). The same source shows that men are over-represented as both victims (76%) and perpetrators (90%) of murder. Concerning influence of race, the vast majority of murders were intra-racial killings: 94% of black murder victims were killed by black perpetrators, and 85% of white victims were murdered by a white assailant.

The gender differences in aggression that we have observed throughout this volume also apply to homicide. Men outnumber women by a wide margin on arrests for homicide and manslaughter. For example, Chesney-Lind (1997, p. 102) quotes US figures for 1994, which show an arrest rate for murder and non-negligent manslaughter of 24.2 per 100,000 men, while the rate for women was only 2.9 per 100,000. The same statistics reveal that while arrest rates for these crimes went up by 7.6% for men from 1985 to 1994, they declined by

9.4% for women. A similar "gender gap" exists with regard to homicide *victimisation*. In a large-scale study by Smith and Brewer (1995) involving data from 176 US central cities, the average proportion of female homicide victims was less than 25%. The magnitude of the gender gap was found to be inversely related to the overall number of homicides reported in a city: the higher the total number of homicides, the greater the proportion of male relative to female victims. The Uniform Crime Reports (1999) confirms the gender gap by showing that women accounted for less than a quarter of all murder victims. In 89% of the cases, female murder victims were killed by a male assailant, and 32% of female victims were killed by husbands or boyfriends. In contrast, only 3% of all male victims were killed by wives or girlfriends. A recent analysis by Browne, Williams, and Dutton (1999) confirms the long-term pattern of this gender disparity. Finally, an analysis of trends in intimate partner homicide between 1976 and 1995 by Puzone et al. (2000) contributes a further interesting finding: While rates for intimate partner homicide showed an overall decline over the 20-year period, the decrease was substantially larger for male than for female victims of partner homicide.

Explaining homicide

Berkowitz (1993) presents a detailed discussion of the psychological literature on criminal homicide. He points out that the killing of a stranger and the killing of a person known to the offender have very different dynamics and underlying motives. Killings between previously acquainted persons frequently arise from arguments that get out of hand under the influence of strong affective responses, often aggravated by alcohol (see also Chapter 9). In 1999, killings arising out of an argument accounted for 30% of all murders (Uniform Crime Reports, 1999). In these cases, the victim has typically played an active part in the cycle of violence culminating in his or her death. In terms of a distinction introduced earlier, many cases of lethal violence against a victim known to the assailant are instances of *hostile aggression*. In contrast, killings of strangers are more likely to be acts of *instrumental aggression* in that they are committed in pursuance of some other goal (e.g., covering up a criminal offence, robbery, theft). The incidence rate for these types of killings were estimated at 17% for 1996 in the United States (Uniform Crime Reports, 1999).

Across a range of studies it has been found that homicides of both types are frequently committed by individuals with a previous record of criminal violence. This observation suggests that criminal homicide may be the extreme expression of a more general tendency towards physical violence rather than an isolated outburst of intense aggressive impulses. Leaving aside aggressive tendencies resulting from psychiatric disorders, such general inclination towards violence is likely to be the result of adverse socialisation experiences (e.g., childhood abuse, association with delinquent peers) in combination with poorly developed skills for coping with these negative experiences (Blaske et al., 1989; Browne, 1994; Gresswell & Hollin, 1994). In addition, Baumeister et al. (1996) highlight the role of threatened self-esteem as precipitators of homicide. They claim that an inflated and unstable sense of self-worth is more likely to lead to violent action than low self-esteem. In support of this claim, they quote the higher homicide rates in the southern parts of the United States where a particular "culture of honour" is widely accepted (see Nisbett, Polly, & Lang, 1995; and Chapter 4). The preservation of honour is of central importance to individuals sharing this cultural norm, and retaliatory action in response to infringements of one's personal or group-related honour is obligatory.

Socio-economic stressors like low income, poor education, and poor housing are additional, frequently interrelated factors contributing to homicide (Cornell, 1993; Hsieh & Pugh, 1993). These factors have been examined by social-structural explanations that emphasise the role of particular social conditions rather than individual characteristics in understanding homicide. Messner and Rosenfeld (1999) differentiate between two aspects of social-structural facilitators of homicide: *control influences*, referring to structural conditions that lead to the breakdown of effective control systems that should prevent violent killings; and *strain influences*, which act on members of particular social groups and push them towards violent actions. Failure of social control systems, e.g., in terms of political upheaval, allows members of a community to engage in violence at a relatively low risk of apprehension and punishment. For example, LaFree's (1999) cross-national analysis reveals high homicide rates for the countries of the former Soviet Union following the collapse of communist rule in the early 1990s. Among the social strain variables, income inequality and the resulting deprivation of low-income groups have been studied widely. As noted earlier, there is evidence that nations with high income inequality also have higher homicide rates. The evidence comparing different regions within a particular country is less conclusive (Messner & Rosenfeld, 1999). In a longitudinal analysis, however, LaFree and Drass (1996) followed the co-variation of income inequality and homicide rates in the United States from 1957 to 1990. Their analysis supports the proposed impact of income inequality on homicide rates. Since members of ethnic and racial minorities are particularly affected by income inequality, this structural variable may also explain the disproportionately high rate of homicides among members of these groups (Hawkins, 1999; Martinez & Lee, 1999). In 1998, blacks were seven times more likely to commit homicide and six times more likely to be murdered than whites (US Department of Justice, 2000).

Among the immediate situational facilitators of intentional killings, the availability of firearms has received considerable research attention. It is generally assumed that gun ownership is a risk factor for lethal violence. There is ample evidence to document the prominent role of firearms in the commission of homicide. As many as 70% of murders committed in the United States in 1999 involved the use of firearms. An even higher figure was reported by Maxon (1999) for gang-related homicide. Findings such as these and similar figures on juvenile homicide (e.g., Cornell, 1993) have led to the proposition that gun ownership is a significant risk factor of homicide perpetration. However, Kleck and Hogan (1999) draw attention to the possibility that the same factors that predict homicide may also predict gun ownership, precluding any causal inferences as to the role of gun ownership in the perpetration of homicide.

An issue of particular concern is the dramatic scale of juvenile homicide in the past two decades. Comparing juvenile homicide rates in 1984 and 1991, Cornell (1993) reports that overall incidence rates more than doubled in the course of this period. From the early 1990s onwards, figures started to decline, parallel to the overall trend in homicide rates discussed earlier. However, with a rate of 22.6 per 100,000 in 1997, the incidence of juvenile homicide remains high in absolute terms as well as relative to the national average. The vast majority of juvenile homicides are committed using firearms, with a rate of 85% in 1997 (National Center for Injury Prevention and Control, 2000). This is true despite a decline in the number of adolescents carrying guns between 1991 and 1997, established in a large-scale survey by Brener, Simon, Krug, and Lowry (1999). A parallel decrease was found in this survey for the number of students involved in fights and suffering physical injuries. Despite these reductions, Brener et al. conclude that absolute levels of fighting and carrying guns are still high and give cause for concern, as does the finding that no decrease was found for carrying weapons other than guns.

The same variables proposed for adolescent aggression in general (see Chapter 3) are relevant in explaining juvenile homicide. Among the variables considered relevant are (a) adverse childhood experiences, such as abuse and witnessing violence within the family; (b) societal influences, such as lack of heroes; (c) resource availability, such as access to guns or economic deprivation; and (d) personality characteristics, such as inability to deal with strong negative feelings and prejudice (Heide, 1999).

This chapter has shown that aggression is a distressing feature of many areas of public life. The school, the workplace, the football stadium, and, not least, the street are common venues for aggressive encounters. A considerable amount of research has been conducted on the prevalence and the potential risk factors of these forms of aggression. Other public displays of aggression, of which there is also plenty of evidence to the everyday observer, have not yet attracted research attention on a larger scale. This is true, for example, for "road rage" in the form of aggressive driving, "trolley rage", i.e., aggressive interactions among shoppers, and "air rage" displayed by passengers on board an aeroplane. The limited evidence on aggressive driving suggests that the same variables that are associated with high levels of violence in the areas considered in the course of this chapter are relevant to aggression on the roads: men are far more likely to show aggressive driving than women, younger motorists are more aggressive than older drivers, and the availability of a powerful aggressive tool, in this case a high-powered car, seems to facilitate driving aggression (Krahé & Fenske, in press). Air rage has been linked to the consumption of alcohol on board planes and its intensified pharmacological effects at high altitudes. These parallels suggest that it may be possible to trace a variety of manifestations of aggression to a common core of risk factors. Clearly, additional factors specifically relevant to particular types of aggression must be taken into account. However, the possibility of a more general explanatory framework applicable to various forms of aggression has important implications for the development of strategies for preventing and curtailing violence in society (see Chapter 9).

Summary

- A large proportion of school children experience acts of aggression from their peers. A considerable minority is exposed to bullying over extended periods of time by children who are stronger and more assertive than themselves. In younger children, bullying primarily takes the form of physical attacks, whereas older children develop forms of relational bullying, such as exclusion, name calling, or gossip. Bullying is shown to have lasting negative effects on victimised pupils. Being a bully towards others is often part of a more general pattern of antisocial behaviour directed at fellow pupils as well as parents, teachers, and other adults. In recent years, the investigation of bullying has been extended to the work environment. Reports of workplace bullying, including sexual harassment, are common, with prevalence rates for long-term and serious bullying being similar to those for school bullying.

- Ethnic violence involves aggressive acts against members of ethnic or racial minorities. Prejudicial attitudes have been identified as core psychological constructs in explaining racially motivated aggression. By devaluating outgroups and questioning their legitimate rights of social participation, the basis is formed for justifying aggressive treatment of minority groups. Politically motivated aggression within nations (terrorism, civil war) and between nations (war) also involves psychological mechanisms of legitimising the ingroups' aggressive actions and attributing hostile and illegitimate intentions to the outgroup.

- Collective aggression summarises different forms of aggressive behaviour carried out by groups of individuals whose behaviour is shaped by the fact that they are acting as part of a group. Studies of riots, hooliganism, and gang violence suggest that these forms of collective violence only superficially appear unregulated and anarchic. In fact, they are often based on a normative structure evolved within the group, such as limiting aggression to specific target groups or locations. This is true in particular for the organised violence of (juvenile) gangs, which adopt a particular code of conduct and outward symbols of gang membership to reinforce ingroup cohesion.

- Homicide represents the most serious form of aggression. Even though prevalence rates have decreased continuously since the beginning of the 1990s in several Western countries, the overall levels are still high. Most homicides are carried out by men against male victims. Women account for only a small pro-portion of homicide offenders, and for about a quarter of homicide victims. Among female homicide victims, a consider-able number are killed by intimate partners, whereas spouse homicide accounts for only a marginal proportion of male homicide victims. A particularly worrying finding is the dis-proportionately high prevalence of juvenile homicide, often associated with the prominence of firearms and other weapons in this group. Homicide has been explained with reference to socio-structural variables (such as income inequality, economic deprivation), cultural variables (such as the "Southern culture of honour"), personality variables (e.g., vulnerable self-esteem, lack of impulse control), and situational facilitators (e.g., threat from rivalling gangs, firearm availability).

Suggested Reading

Goldstein, A.P. (1994a). Delinquent gangs. In L.R. Huesmann (Ed.), *Aggressive behavior: Current perspectives* (pp. 255–273). New York: Plenum Press.

National Center for Injury Prevention and Control (2000). *Youth violence in the United States.* www.cdc.gov/ncipc/dvp/fafacts.htm.

Olweus, D. (1994). Bullying at school. Long-term outcomes for the victims and an effective school-based intervention program. In L.R. Huesmann (Ed.), *Aggressive behavior: Current perspectives* (pp. 97–130). New York: Plenum Press.

Smith, M.D., & Zahn, M.A. (1999). *Homicide: A sourcebook of social research.* Thousand Oaks, CA: Sage.

US Department of Justice (2000). *Homicide trends in the U.S.* www.ojp.usdoj.gov/bjs.

Domestic violence 7

While the ideal image of family life is one of warmth, affection, and mutual respect, reality shows that a range of serious forms of aggression occur within the family setting. Physical, sexual, and emotional abuse of children, sibling aggression, marital violence, and the problem of elder abuse and neglect by relatives have all been recognised as serious social problems. As Gelles (1997, p. 1) states in the opening sentence of his book: "People are more likely to be killed, physically assaulted, hit, beat up, slapped, or spanked in their own homes by other family members than anywhere else, or by anyone else, in our society." Of all violent crimes recorded in the 1998 "National Incident-Based Reporting System" (NIBRS) in the United States, 23% involved members of the same family (Federal Bureau of Investigation, 1998).

Domestic or family violence refers to those forms of behaviour that are carried out with the intention to inflict pain or injury on a family member. A characteristic feature of these actions is that they are rarely singular events but tend to occur repeatedly, sometimes continuously, over extended periods of time (Krauss & Krauss, 1995). In addition, both suffering and watching domestic violence have been found to increase the risk of violent behaviour in the victims or witnesses themselves, often creating a transgenerational cycle of violence that is hard to break.

Because domestic violence takes place in the confined sphere of the family, it is comparatively easy to conceal from outside observers. If or when it is recognised, witnesses are frequently unwilling to take action because they do not want to get involved in what they consider to be other people's private affairs. The desire to protect the integrity of the family is not limited to external observers but is shared by many witnesses within the family as well as the victims themselves. Children abused by a family member may not disclose their experience to others because they do not want to appear as troublemakers or liars; battered women may try to cover up their partner's violent behaviour to salvage the image of an intact family; abused elders may fear to be placed into institutional care if they speak to others about the abuse. All these concerns act against the identification of victims and perpetrators of domestic violence, making it difficult to estimate true prevalence rates and to make help available to those who need it.

The present chapter provides an overview of the current state of knowledge on the manifestation, the causes and the consequences of domestic violence. Various academic disciplines have been involved in the study of domestic violence. It is, of course, impossible in the context of this chapter to do justice to the extensive specialised literature on domestic violence. Several recent sources provide comprehensive overviews of the field and will be drawn upon in the present discussion (e.g., Barnett, Miller-Perrin, & Perrin, 1997; Bergen, 1998a; Gelles, 1997; Hampton, 1999; Harway & O'Neil, 1999; Miller-Perrin & Perrin, 1999; Wiehe, 1998). According to the focus of this volume, the chapter will concentrate on psychological issues, excluding, for example, legal contributions (about how the criminal justice system deals with domestic violence; e.g., Buzawa & Buzawa, 1996), medical issues (about the physical evidence of abuse and its treatment; e.g., Veltkamp & Miller, 1994), and social services issues (about how to end domestic violence and protect the victims; e.g., Knudsen & Miller, 1991).

First, we will look at the problem of child abuse, which includes physical and sexual abuse as well as psychological maltreatment. In the second section, physical aggression occurring between spouses will be discussed. Reflecting the scope of the available evidence, the focus will be on aggression in heterosexual partnerships, but the problem of violence in gay and lesbian relationships will also be considered. The issue of *sexual violence* between spouses will be excluded from the present discussion. We shall examine this problem in Chapter 8, where it will be placed into a more general discussion of the causes and consequences of sexual aggression beyond the domestic sphere. Finally, working our way along the chronological life course, elder abuse and neglect will be examined as increasingly pressing social problems.

The following sections will present evidence addressing (a) the *scope* (or prevalence) of different forms of domestic violence, including an examination of variables associated with an increased risk of domestic violence, and (b) the *effects* of each form of domestic violence on the victims. An important issue refers to the *explanation* of domestic violence. As noted consistently throughout the literature, different forms of domestic violence are often related and/or can be traced back to a common set of underlying causes and facilitating conditions. Therefore, explanations of domestic violence will be examined in a general discussion at the end of the chapter.

Child abuse and maltreatment

Due to their status as relatively powerless members of the family system, children are particularly at risk of becoming targets of aggressive behaviour from parents and other adult relatives. As Tedeschi and Felson (1994, p. 287) note, "people who rarely if ever use coercion with others make an exception in the case of their children." In this section, we will examine the prevalence and consequences of three major forms of child abuse: physical abuse, sexual abuse, and psychological maltreatment.

Physical abuse

Corporal punishment is still practised in the vast majority of families, at least occasionally, as an accepted means of discipline. According to incidence rates reported by Straus and Gelles (1990), next to 100 per cent of parents of young children reported having hit their child at least once in the preceding year. In a nationwide survey reported by Ellison and Sherkat (1993), 80% of respondents either agreed or strongly agreed with the opinion that "it is sometimes necessary to discipline a child with a good, hard, spanking." However, if every act of physical punishment was classified as child abuse, the construct would become too broad to be useful in delineating this particularly aversive social experience. Therefore, we will restrict our discussion to what Gelles (1997, p. 15) defines as "abusive violence", denoting acts with a high potential for harming the child and including such behaviours as punches, bites, chokings, beatings, shootings, stabbings, as well as attempts to shoot or stab.

Prevalence of physical abuse. The full extent of physical violence against children is hard to establish because many acts of child abuse go unreported or undetected, and true figures are likely to be higher than those reflected in official statistics or parental self-reports of such socially undesirable behaviours. Nevertheless, these data are meaningful in that they can be seen as reflecting the lower boundary of the problem. For the United States, a nationwide database of reported abuse cases showed that, in 1994, 380 in 100,000 children were found to have been physically abused (Gelles, 1997, p. 46). Estimates of deaths per 100,000 children under 4 years of age as a result of abuse by parents or caretakers range from 5.4 to 11.6, with children being particularly at risk during their first year of life (Hegar, Zuravin, & Orme, 1994). Gelles also notes a significant increase in reported cases of child abuse, with an almost fourfold increase in the number of seriously injured children between 1986 and 1993 (see also McCurdy & Daro, 1994). In the United Kingdom, about 200 children are estimated to die every year as a result of injuries or maltreatment inflicted on them by their parents (Browne, 1989). Recent statistics from the UK Department of Health (1999) show that 7300 children in England had been on the Child Protection Register for "physical injury alone" in the year ending March 1998 and another 9300 were newly registered during that year. Taken together, the two figures amount to a rate of 148 per 100,000 children under the age of 17. In addition, another 5000 cases were recorded in which physical abuse was combined with other forms of abuse, such as neglect and sexual abuse.

Apart from official statistics, self-reports by parents are another relevant source of information. Such data were collected by Straus and Gelles (1990), who found that 23 in 1000 parents reported an act of abusive violence in the 12 months prior to the survey, and 7 in 1000 children suffered injuries as a result of a parent's violent behaviour during the same period.

Beyond looking at overall prevalence rates, researchers have tried to identify both personal and situational variables associated with an increased risk of physical abuse. As far as the sex of the abuser is concerned, several sources suggest that women are more frequently involved in child abuse than men. However, this is due to the fact that they are mostly responsible for child care, especially with young children, and are therefore much more likely to encounter problems in interacting with the child that may lead to violence. If responsibility is controlled for, e.g., by comparing women to men who are also the primary caretakers, the difference is reversed and higher abuse rates are found for men (see Featherstone, 1996). Single parents and teenaged mothers were also found in some studies to be more likely to physically abuse their children, as were parents who had problems of alcohol and drug abuse (see also Wiehe, 1998). In addition, parents who physically abuse their children were found to hold unrealistic expectancies about children's self-control and independence. However, all the links established between child abuse and individual predictor variables suffer from the problem that the predictors are often related (such as teenage motherhood and single parent status) or influenced by a third variable (such as lack of financial resources or social support), which may be the true cause of higher abuse rates. Therefore, it is difficult to assess precisely the impact of any given risk factors in the complex, multicausal pathway to abuse. We will come back to theoretical models integrating the diversity of contributing factors to physical abuse as well as other forms of domestic violence in the final section of this chapter. In a rare prospective longitudinal study, Brown, Cohen, Johnson, and Salzinger (1998) measured a number of demographic, familial, parenting, and child risk factors of childhood abuse in 1975, 1983, and 1986. Between 1991 and 1993 they collected information, through self-reports and official records, on whether or not abuse had occurred in the meantime. The findings reported by Brown et al. for physical child abuse are presented in Table 7.1. The odds ratios indicate the factor by which the likelihood of physical abuse went up if the respective risk factor had been present.

As Table 7.1 reveals, the highest risk of physical abuse was found for maternal psychopathy, which was associated with an almost fivefold increase in the probability of abuse. Among the demographic risk factors, dependency on welfare featured most prominently, with the risk of abuse being 3.74 times higher than in families not dependent on state welfare. Low paternal warmth was most prominent among parenting risk factors, while complications during pregnancy and birth were the only significant risk factors associated with the child. Because the risk factors were measured several years *prior* to establishing the occurrence of abuse, the design of this study allows researchers to examine the causal effects of the risk factors on the likelihood abuse.

Consequences of physical abuse. Clearly, suffering bodily harm at the hands of their own parents is a highly negative experience for the children concerned. Therefore, it is not surprising that many of them show serious and long-term impairments with regard to their psychological well-being, their functioning in social relationships, and their social behaviour generally. Low self-esteem, anxiety, self-destructive behaviour and the inability to engage in trusting relationships with others are commonly reported effects of physical abuse in childhood (Milner & Crouch, 1999). An up-to-date analysis of the implications of physical abuse for the development of affected children is provided by Wolfe (1999).

TABLE 7.1

Risk factors significantly associated with physical child abuse

	Odds ratio
Demographic risk factors	
Mother's low education	2.59
Low religious attendance	2.22
Mother's youth	3.52
Single parent	2.26
Welfare	3.74
Familial risk factors	
Early separation from mother	4.08
Mother's dissatisfaction	2.44
Mother's external locus of control	2.16
Mother's sociopathy	4.91
Poor marital quality	1.98
Mother's serious illness	2.06
Parenting risk factors	
Mother's low involvement	2.68
Father's low involvement	3.18
Father's low warmth	3.24
Child risk factors	
Pregnancy or birth complications	2.45

Note: The odds ratio indicates by how much the risk of physical abuse increases if the risk factor is present.

Adapted from *Child Abuse and Neglect*, *22*, Brown et al., A longitudinal analysis of risk factors for child maltreatment: Findings of a 17-year prospective study of officially recorded and self-reported child abuse and neglect, 1065–1078, copyright © 1998, with permission from Elsevier Science.

Of particular relevance in the context of this volume is the question of whether the experience of physical abuse is associated with greater likelihood of aggressive behaviour in the child. Englander (1997) reviewed evidence from both retrospective and cross-sectional studies on the link between physical punishment and aggression in children. Both data sources show that aggressive behaviour increases as a function of exposure to physical punishment. Violent and aggressive adults are more likely to have experienced physical punishment in childhood than non-aggressive comparison groups. Similarly, childhood physical punishment was found to be related cross-sectionally to higher levels of aggressive behaviour, at least from the age of 6 years onwards and particularly in boys. However, neither methodology is able to address the direction of causality: Do children become more aggressive as a consequence of being physically punished or even abused, or do they attract corporal punishment because of their aggressive behaviour? This issue can be addressed by prospective longitudinal studies that observe initially non-aggressive children over an extended period of time and look for subsequent differences in aggressive behaviour as a function of physical punishment and abuse. As Englander (1997) concluded, evidence from these studies, while not being entirely conclusive, does point towards a causal influence of parental violence on increased levels of aggression in their children.

This conclusion also receives support from a study by Prino and Peyrot (1994), who analysed the effects of physical abuse in comparison with physical neglect (failure to provide food, clothing, supervision, medical care, etc.). They found that the two types of maltreatment were associated with distinctly different effects on the children's behaviour. While the physically abused children showed high levels of aggression, the neglected children showed high levels of withdrawal (see Figure 7.1).

Both abused and neglected children scored significantly lower on the measure of prosocial behaviour than the control group. The differential effects of abuse in relation to other adverse childhood experiences were also shown by O'Keefe (1995) in a study of children who had witnessed marital violence between their parents, some of whom had additionally experienced physical abuse themselves. She found that physically abused children were more likely to develop aggressive behaviour problems than children who "only" witnessed marital violence.

A specific aspect of the link between childhood experience of abuse and subsequent aggression refers to the likelihood that abused children will themselves become abusive parents. The notion of an intergenerational transmission of abuse, leading to a "cycle of violence", features prominently in the literature (see Gelles, 1997). There is general agreement, though, that the relationship is not a deterministic one in the sense of all abused children growing up to be abusive. Instead, it is recognised that only a minority of abused children later turn into abusers (even though estimates of the size of that minority vary) and that childhood abuse should be seen as a risk factor that acts in combination with other adverse conditions (Milner & Crouch, 1999). Zuravin, McMillen, DePanfilis, and Risley-Curtiss (1996) addressed the question of whether certain characteristics of the abuse experience were differentially related to the likelihood of becoming an abuser. They found that abused women who broke the cycle of violence had

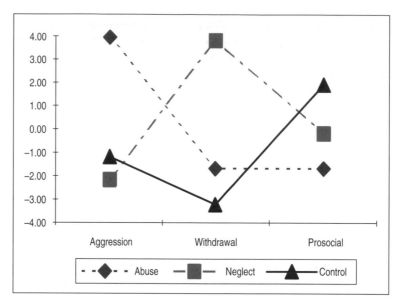

FIG. 7.1. The differential effects of physical abuse and physical neglect (reprinted from *Child Abuse and Neglect*, *18*, Prino & Reyrot, The effect of child physical abuse and neglect on aggressive, withdrawn, and prosocial behavior, 871–884, copyright © 1994, with permission from Elsevier Science).

had a better attachment relationship with their primary caretakers at the time of the abuse than those who went on to abuse their own children. Neither frequency nor severity of abuse was systematically linked to the likelihood of becoming an abusive parent.

Altogether, it seems clear that the experience of abuse has severe, often prolonged negative consequences for the affected children. Evidence is only beginning to emerge, however, on factors that account for individual differences in responding to the abuse, including the potential role of protective factors that buffer its adverse effects. While severity of the abuse, presence of more than one form of abuse, and high levels of parental stress have been named as factors associated with poorer coping, high intelligence and presence of a supportive parent figure were found to ameliorate the adverse effects of physical abuse (Barnett et al., 1997).

Sexual abuse

Childhood sexual abuse must be seen as a pervasive risk factor in children's lives: No demographic or family characteristics have as yet been identified to rule out the possibility that a child will be or has been sexually abused (Finkelhor, 1994). Sexual abuse is commonly defined as a sexual contact between a child and an adult carried out for the sexual stimulation of the perpetrator. Sexual abuse is tied to an unequal power relationship between victim and perpetrator whereby the perpetrator exploits his/her age or maturational advantage, his/her position of authority over the victim, or resorts to the use of force or trickery (Kendall-Tackett & Marshall, 1998, p. 48). Beyond this broad consensus, definitions vary as to the minimum age difference between victim and perpetrator and the nature of sexual acts considered abusive. These differences in definition clearly affect prevalence estimates. A distinction that seems to be universally accepted in the literature is that between contact abuse involving physical contact between victim and perpetrator (such as touch or penetration of the body) and non-contact abuse (such as exhibitionism, voyeurism, or use of pornography).

Prevalence and risk factors of sexual abuse. As with physical abuse, several data sources are available to estimate the prevalence of sexual abuse. Each of these data sources carries its own problems of validity. One data source is provided by reports from official agencies. These statistics only reflect the proportion of cases that have come to the attention of legal and child protective authorities and therefore underestimate the actual scale of the problem. Data from US National Incidence Studies indicate that sexual abuse occurred at a rate of 210 per 100,000 children in 1986 and at a rate of 450 per 100,000 children in 1993 (Miller-Perrin & Perrin, 1999, p. 109; see also Gelles, 1997, for related findings). Including only those cases that were reported to the police, the latest German crime report for the year 1999 shows a rate of 19 cases per 100,000 children (Bundesministerium des Inneren, 2000). Neither these nor the US figures quoted above differentiate between sexual abuse by family members and by strangers. However, they are meaningful with regard to intra-familial sex abuse given that a large proportion of sexually abusive acts is committed by members of the child's family. It is estimated that 75–80% of sexual abusers are known to their victim, with male family members accounting for a substantial proportion of perpetrators (Kendall-Tackett & Marshall, 1998). Concentrating on sexual abuse within the family, figures released by the UK Department of Health (1999) reveal that 4900 children had been on the Child Protection Register for "sexual abuse alone" in the year ending March 1998. An additional 4800 new registrations were made in the course of that year. The total of 9700 cases amounts to a prevalence rate of 87 per 100,000 children under the age of 17. A further 3000 cases were on the Register for multiple forms of abuse including sexual abuse.

A second data source is provided by self-report surveys in which respondents are asked to indicate whether or not they have experienced sexual abuse. The problem here is that these reports are typically collected retrospectively, and studies vary substantially in terms of how the critical abuse questions are phrased (see Finkelhor, 1986, Appendix 1). Nonetheless, self-report surveys are valuable because they are able to detect those cases of abuse that have not been reported by the victims. Asking a random sample of 1000 adults, Finkelhor, Moore, Hamby, and Straus (1997) found that 23% of respondents had been touched (or made to touch another person) in a sexual way against their will by an adult or older child before the age of 18. A comprehensive summary of the large number of surveys establishing prevalence rates of sexual abuse is presented by Fergusson and Mullen (1999, Tables 2.1 and 2.2). They list a total of 29 studies exploring sexual abuse rates for female victims. Prevalence rates for contact abuse ranged from around 7% to around 25%, with one study (Wyatt, Guthrie, & Notgrass, 1992) reporting a rate of 45.2%. Fergusson and Mullen (1999) also list 18 studies providing prevalence rates for male victims. This summary shows that prevalence rates for boys are generally lower than those for girls, ranging from 1% to 19.8%.

Beyond establishing overall prevalence rates, several studies have investigated factors that increase children's vulnerability to sexual abuse. Gender and age have been identified consistently in these studies: Girls are shown to be three to four times more likely to be abused than boys, especially if they live in the same household with a stepfather. Middle childhood (7–11 years) seems to be the most vulnerable age bracket. Cross, De Vos, and Whitcomb (1994) showed that the child's age is a significant predictor of the likelihood of legal proceedings following from an allegation of abuse. From the age of 7, the likelihood that a reported sexual abuse will lead to legal prosecution of the alleged offender was found to rise sharply. No link was found in the evidence reviewed by Finkelhor (1986) between low socio-economic status and risk of sexual abuse, but other studies did observe such a link (e.g., Bergner, Delgado, & Graybill, 1994; Jones & McCurdy, 1992).

The vast majority of sexual abusers are male. According to a variety of sources, men account for between 80% and 95% of child abuse perpetrators (Browne, 1994). As far as the relationship between victim and offender is concerned, the evidence points to gender as a critical moderator. Finkelhor (1986) found that about half of the female victims were abused by a member of their family, and a further third by a person they knew. Among the male victims, only 20% were abused by a family member, and 50% by a person they

TABLE 7.2

Risk factors significantly associated with child sexual abuse

	Odds ratio
Demographic risk factors	
Mother's youth	2.26
Father's death	2.62
Familial risk factors	
Mother's sociopathy	6.27
Negative life events	4.43
Presence of a stepfather	3.32
Harsh punishment	3.22
Parenting risk factors	
Unwanted pregnancy	3.10
Child risk factors	
Child gender (female)	2.44
Handicapped child	11.79

Note: The odds ratio indicates by how much the risk of physical abuse increases if the risk factor is present.

Adapted from *Child Abuse and Neglect, 22,* Brown et al., A longitudinal analysis of risk factors for child maltreatment: Findings of a 17-year prospective study of officially recorded and self-reported child abuse and neglect, 1065–1078, copyright © 1998, with permission from Elsevier Science.

knew. A comparative analysis of prevalence rates in 20 different countries corroborates this finding (Finkelhor, 1994). For both genders, sexual abuse by strangers was found to be the exception rather than the rule.

The prospective longitudinal study by Brown et al. (1998) already mentioned in the context of physical abuse also provided data on risk factors of sexual abuse. The risk factors that significantly predicted sexual abuse in their analysis are displayed in Table 7.2.

The most significant risk factors identified in this analysis were the child being handicapped (requiring special education), maternal psychopathy, negative life events, and the presence of a stepfather.

Consequences of sexual abuse. Sexual abuse is a traumatising experience that leads to both immediate and long-term consequences in many, if not most victims. A wide range of problems were found with notable consistency to be more prevalent among victims of childhood sexual abuse than in non-abused comparison groups (see reviews by Beitchman et al., 1991, 1992; Wiehe, 1998). An integrative overview of the current state of knowledge concerning the behavioural, emotional, cognitive, and physical effects of sexual abuse in childhood is presented by Barnett et al. (1997). The present section highlights some domains of psychological functioning adversely affected by the experience of sexual abuse. No justice can be done here to the impressive body of evidence that has examined potential moderators of the link between childhood sexual abuse and the magnitude of negative effects (such as the nature of the abusive act, duration and frequency of the abuse, age of victim and offender). This evidence is well covered in the reviews cited above.

Among the initial effects of sexual abuse, i.e., effects occurring within the first 2 years following the abuse, higher rates of depression, loneliness, and suicidal ideation have been identified in victim samples. Many victims show the symptomatology of post-traumatic stress disorder (PTSD) as an immediate reaction and/or as a long-term consequence of the abuse. Indeed, Kendall-Tackett, Williams, and Finkelhor (1993) conclude that PTSD is one of two core symptoms that seem to be more common in victims of abuse than in other clinical groups and carry particular diagnostic relevance (the second core symptom being sexualised behaviour; see below). Behavioural problems, such as sleep disturbances, hyperactivity, and aggression, are also common as initial responses to the trauma of sexual abuse. Victims often attempt to dissociate themselves from the experience of abuse and deny feelings of shame and anger, a coping strategy that makes them susceptible to the development of dissociative personality disorders. Furthermore, lowered self-esteem and feelings of worthlessness seem to be common reactions to the experience of sexual abuse.

Evidence from a multitude of sources suggests that the adverse effects of childhood sexual abuse frequently extend into adolescence and adulthood (see Barnett et al., 1997, p. 88). In a sample of over 1000 female adolescents, Chandy, Blum, and Resnick (1996) found that those with a history of childhood sexual abuse had significantly higher prevalence rates on 21 out of their 22 negative outcome variables. As noted above, high rates of PTSD have been found in survivors a long time after the abuse itself. The same is true for higher rates of depression, anxiety, and poor self-esteem among adults abused as children. Other long-term sequelae include health problems, substance abuse, and eating disorders, all found to be more prevalent in survivors of sexual abuse. One reason why victims of sexual abuse are vulnerable to substance abuse is that alcohol or drugs enable them to blot out painful memories of the abuse. Eating disorders, such as bulimia or anorexia, are seen as responses to the reduction in self-esteem caused by the abuse experience. At the interpersonal level, victims of child sexual abuse were found to have problems in establishing and maintaining satisfying relationships not only with sexual partners but also with their children (Banyard, 1997). Thus, sexual abuse predisposes victims to develop a wide range of emotional and behavioural problems that persist well beyond childhood and severely impair their psychological well-being and social functioning.

Childhood sexual abuse and later sexual development. Given that sexual abuse involves an infringement of the victim's sexual integrity and self-determination, sexual development is particularly likely to be affected in a negative way by the experience of abuse. In Finkelhor and Browne's (1985) "traumagenic dynamics model" of sex abuse traumatisation, "traumatic sexualisation" is identified as a key mechanism leading from sexual abuse to specific sexuality-related symptoms and adjustment problems. While many of the symptoms found in relation to sexual abuse can also be observed as a result of other forms of childhood traumatisation, sexualised behaviour seems to be a specific consequence of sexual abuse. Its prevalence is significantly higher among survivors of sexual abuse than in other clinical groups (see Kendall-Tackett et al., 1993).

Sexuality-related problems manifest themselves in different ways depending on the victim's stage of development. In childhood, evidence of inappropriate sexual behaviour has consistently been found at a higher rate among abuse victims compared to both non-abused children and children affected by other types of clinically relevant experiences. Indeed, the majority of behavioural symptoms listed by Barnett et al. (1997, p. 86) for school-age survivors of sexual abuse are sexuality related. Their list includes sexualised behaviour, sexual preoccupation, precocious sexual knowledge, seductive behaviour, excessive masturbation, sex play with others, sexual language, genital exposure, and the sexual victimisation of others.

In adolescence, preoccupation with sexuality remains characteristic for abuse survivors. Several sources suggest that childhood sexual abuse is associated with early sexualisation, manifested in an earlier age at first sexual intercourse and greater number of sexual partners (e.g., Chandy et al., 1996; Miller, Monson, & Norton, 1995). Kendall-Tackett et al. (1993) summarise findings from two studies in which 38% of adolescents abused as children were classified as promiscuous (Cahill, Llewlyn, & Pearson, 1991).

In late adolescence and adulthood, problems in initiating and maintaining intimate relationships are consistently reported in the literature. These problems are also reflected in higher divorce rates in abuse victims as compared to non-abused samples. Beyond the difficulty of establishing close emotional bonds, many survivors show problems of sexual adjustment. Victims of sexual abuse were found to be more sexually anxious, experienced more sexual guilt, had lowered sexual self-esteem, and were more likely to seek sexual therapy (Browne & Finkelhor, 1986). Furthermore, there is evidence to suggest a link between sexual abuse in childhood and prostitution.

The majority of studies have focused on female victims of childhood sexual abuse. Those studies which included male victims suggest two potential effects of the abuse experience specific to this group: Firstly, the possibility has been examined that childhood experience of abuse is linked to the development of a homosexual orientation, mediated by the victim's uncertainty about his sexual identity. However, evidence to support this link is limited (Beitchman et al., 1992; Browne & Finkelhor, 1986). Secondly, several sources have identified an increased risk for male abuse victims to become perpetrators of sexual aggression (Bagley, Wood, & Young, 1994; Barnett et al., 1997; Browne, 1994).

A particularly worrying consequence of childhood sexual abuse is termed *revictimisation*. Revictimisation refers to an increased risk for survivors of childhood sexual abuse to be victimised again in later life. In a comprehensive review, Messman and Long (1996) examined 18 studies investigating the revictimisation hypothesis. Eight of these studies investigated revictimisation in college samples. With one exception, these studies found significant links between childhood experiences of abuse and subsequent sexual victimisation. Five studies that provided data from clinical samples also lent support to the revictimisation hypothesis. The remaining five studies found evidence for the link between sexual abuse and revictimisation in unselected community samples. More recent studies corroborate this conclusion (see Krahé, 2000a, for a review of this evidence). In a study with adolescents, Krahé, Scheinberger-Olwig, Waizenhöfer, and Kolpin (1999) found significantly higher rates of victimisation for women with a history of childhood sexual abuse on the majority of items of the Sexual Experiences Survey (Koss & Oros, 1982; Koss, Gidycz, & Wisniewski, 1987). In particular, higher frequencies were found for victims of sexual abuse on sexual victimisation involving the threat or use of physical violence.

Little is known about the sexual victimisation of men generally and about the link between sexual abuse and revictimisation in particular. This issue was addressed in a recent study by Krahé, Scheinberger-Olwig, and Schütze (in press) on sexual aggression among homosexual men, in which childhood sexual abuse was included as a potential risk factor. The findings lend clear support to the revictimisation hypotheses: Homosexual men with a childhood history of contact sexual abuse were significantly more likely to report severe sexual victimisation in subsequent relationships than non-abused men. The same study also corroborated the victim-to-perpetrator cycle mentioned above in that victims of sexual abuse were found to be more likely to commit sexually aggressive acts than non-victims.

Thus, evidence from child sex abuse research and from the literature on sexual victimisation in adolescence and adulthood converge on the conclusion that women who were sexually abused as children are more likely to become victims of sexual aggression in later life than women who were not exposed to this negative childhood experience. Furthermore, there is tentative evidence to suggest a similar revictimisation pattern for male victims in subsequent homosexual relationships.

Psychological maltreatment

To denote parental behaviours that lead to the impairment of the child's psychological well-being, several terms are used in the literature. Mattaini, McGowan, and Williams (1996, p. 225) refer to *emotional maltreatment* as consisting of "acts that result in the impairment of a child's emotional or mental health, such as verbal abuse and belittlement, symbolic acts designed to terrorise a child, and lack of nurturance or emotional availability by caregivers." O'Hagan (1995, p. 456) adopted a more restricted definition of *emotional abuse* as relating to "the sustained, repetitive, inappropriate emotional response to the child's experience of emotion, and its accompanying expressive behaviour." He distinguished emotional abuse from *psychological abuse* consisting of behaviours that impair the development of mental faculties. Yet other authors include both cognitive and emotional impairments in a broad definition of *psychological maltreatment*, which denotes "the ensemble of abusive psychological acts committed by the parents and also encompasses all acts of omission that result in emotional, cognitive, or educational neglect" (Fortin & Chamberland, 1995, p. 276). Such a broad definition is adopted in the present discussion to serve as a framework for illustrating the diversity of issues involved in psychological maltreatment. According to Barnett et al. (1997, p. 123), psychological maltreatment can take a variety of forms: rejecting, degrading, terrorising, isolating, mis-socialising (i.e., permitting or encouraging antisocial or delinquent behaviour), exploiting (e.g., using a child for pornography or prostitution), ignoring the child, or restricting the child's physical movements.

Prevalence of psychological maltreatment. Official statistics reveal that psychological maltreatment is the least frequently reported and substantiated form of child abuse. Statistics from child protection agencies suggest that less than 10% of all reported cases of child abuse refer to psychological maltreatment (Miller-Perrin & Perrin, 1999, p. 182). Experts agree, however, that underreporting to official agencies is a particular problem for psychological maltreatment because (a) it is more difficult for observers to decide what exactly constitutes psychological maltreatment as compared, e.g., to physical abuse, and (b) psychological maltreatment rarely produces visible effects. Statistics based on cases reported to official agencies therefore represent the lower boundaries of the problem. Gelles (1997, p. 46) quotes figures from the US National Center on Child Abuse and Neglect for the year 1993, which show an incidence rate of 536,400 (i.e., 7.9 per 1,000) cases of emotional abuse and an additional 583,600 cases of emotional neglect. Given the difficulties in delineating and identifying psychological abuse, it is not surprising that figures restricted to substantiated cases only yield lower figures: of a total of 1,036,000 substantiated claims of child abuse, 31,080 referred to charges of emotional maltreatment (Weise & Daro, 1995). Examining the development of reported abuse cases over time, Sedlak and Broadhurst (1996) found that the rate of psychological abuse and emotional neglect increased by almost 300% from 1986 to 1993. The UK Department of Health (1999) reported 5200 children on the Child Protection Register for "emotional abuse" in the year ending March 1998 and another 4800 added to the Register during that year, which amounts to a rate of 890 per 100,000 children under the age of 17.

Prevalence rates on an even larger scale were found in self-reports of parental behaviours representing psychological maltreatment (e.g., insulting, swearing, refusing to talk). Vissing, Straus, Gelles, and Harrop (1991) showed that 63% of parents in a representative national sample reported one of these behaviours in interacting with their child over the previous 12 months. Straus et al. (1998) collected data based on the "parent child conflict tactics scale", which addresses five forms of psychological aggression: yelling, threatening to spank the child, cursing, name calling, and threatening to send the child away. They found that 856 out of 1000 parents showed one of these forms of psychological aggression toward their child in the 12 months prior to the survey. Christensen (1999) provides data from a Danish sample of 28,000 children showing that 6% of children aged between 1 and 2, 13% of children aged between 2 and 3, and 17% of children aged between 3 and 4 had been subjected to emotional abuse, defined as constant exposure to verbal insults, confinement, threats, and rejections.

As with physical abuse, the question arises whether there are any characteristics of the child that would make him or her a more likely target of psychological maltreatment. Due to the relatively low number of cases officially reported and substantiated, evidence on this issue is limited. There are indications, however, that the risk of psychological maltreatment increases with the child's age and is slightly higher for girls than for boys (Miller-Perrin & Perrin, 1999).

Consequences of psychological maltreatment. As one might expect, one area in which psychological maltreatment is shown to have detrimental effects on children is the formation of trusting relationships with others and the development of social skills. In addition, children exposed to psychological treatment were found to show deficits both in their intellectual and their affective development. Miller-Perrin and Perrin (1999, p. 185) reviewed the evidence on how psychological maltreatment affects children's development. Their summary is presented in Table 7.3.

Apart from these immediate or short-term effects, psychological maltreatment can lead to lasting psychological problems extending into adulthood. Victims of childhood psychological abuse were found to have lower self-esteem and exhibit higher levels of depression in adulthood compared to non-victimised controls (Downs & Miller, 1998; Kent & Waller, 1998). A study by Gross and Keller (1992) even found psychological maltreatment to be a stronger predictor of depression and low self-esteem than physical aggression. Additional evidence suggests that childhood psychological maltreatment may be a risk factor for subsequent victimisation, in particular sexual victimisation. In the study by Krahé, Scheinberger-Olwig, Waizenhöfer, and Kolpin (1999), women who reported that they had felt worthless in their families as children were significantly more likely to experience sexual victimisation in late adolescence. Parallel revictimisation

TABLE 7.3

Possible negative effects associated with psychological maltreatment

Interpersonal maladjustment
Insecure attachment to caregiver
Low social competence and adjustment
Few friends
Difficulties with peers

Intellectual deficits
Academic problems
Lower educational achievement
Deficits in cognitive ability
Deficits in problem solving
Deficits in creativity

Affective-behavioural problems
Aggression
Disruptive classroom behaviour
Self-abusive behaviour
Anxiety
Shame and guilt
Hostility and anger
Pessimism and negativity
Dependence on adults for help, support, and nurturance

Adapted from Miller-Perrin and Perrin, *Child maltreatment*, copyright © 1999 by Sage Publications; reprinted by permission of Sage Publications, Inc.

patterns as a function of emotional maltreatment in childhood were found for homosexual men and for heterosexual men becoming victims of female sexual aggression (Krahé, Scheinberger-Olwig, & Schütze, in press; Krahé, in prep.).

The present section has demonstrated that children are, indeed, vulnerable victims of violence within the family. Incidence rates for physical and sexual abuse as well as psychological maltreatment show that the problem can by no means be dismissed as marginal. Moreover, there can be no doubt that these adverse experiences at the hands of people they trust and depend on, happening in the very sphere that should provide protection and security, can cause lasting damage to the physical, intellectual, emotional, and social development of the affected children. It has already been pointed out that one significant negative effect of childhood experiences of family violence is to make victims more vulnerable to subsequent victimisation. In the next section, we will come back to this issue in connection with the problem of violence in close relationships.

Partner abuse and wife battering

In this section, we will look at the problem of physical aggression between partners in intimate relationships. This will include courtship as well as marital violence, but will exclude the problem of sexual aggression. Marital rape and sexual aggression in dating relationships will be examined in Chapter 8, which is devoted to a more general discussion of sexual aggression beyond the family setting.

Courtship and marital violence can be defined as "the perpetration or threat of an act of physical violence by at least one member of a dyad on the other within the context of a dating/marital relationship" (Sugarman & Hotaling, 1989, p. 5). Partner abuse is defined in a broader way to include verbal and psychological aggression towards a partner in addition to physical violence. This definition is open with regard to the gender of perpetrator and victim of partner violence. The issue of whether women are to be seen mainly as victims of partner abuse or whether they also show aggressive behaviour themselves to a significant extent has been a contentious one in past research (Currie, 1998). Studies examining the experiences of women who sought refuge in shelters for victims of partner abuse typically reveal that the vast majority of violent assaults are committed by men against their female partners. In contrast, surveys of members of the general population show that women's assaults on their male partners are about as frequent as men's. White and Koss (1991) found that 37% of male and 39% of female respondents in their representative sample of 4700 college students reported having inflicted physical aggression on a dating partner in the previous year. In a survey conducted by Stets and Henderson (1991), perpetration rates for severe physical aggression against an intimate partner were 21.9% for the male respondents and 40% for the female respondents. These figures suggest that dating aggression is one of the few areas where women are equally, if not more aggressive than men (see Archer, 2000, for a meta-analytic review).

However, it has been pointed out that descriptive incidence statistics fail to reflect the motivation underlying physical aggression as well as its effects on the victim. In particular, they ignore the fact that women more frequently engage in retaliatory as opposed to initiating acts of physical aggression, and that they suffer more serious injuries than their male counterparts. For example, Archer (2000) found that despite a slight female predominance in the number of aggressive acts committed men were more likely to inflict injuries on their partners than women, and 62% of injuries were caused by a man against a woman (see also Hamberger, Lohr, Bonge, & Tolin, 1997; Mirrlees-Black & Byron, 1999). Figures on intimate homicide, showing that more than two-thirds of intimate homicides were carried out by men against a female partner, corroborate these conclusions (Barnett et al., 1997, p. 188, and Chapter 6).

Prevalence of partner abuse

As was noted before, prevalence rates for domestic violence vary as a function of different data sources and survey methodologies (see Gelles, 2000, for a recent critical comparison). Nonetheless, they convey a picture of the upper and lower boundaries of the extent to which women are affected by violence in intimate relationships. Based on findings from the National Crime Survey, it is estimated that over 2 million women in the United States suffer physical abuse from their partners per year and that 50% of all women will be victims of battering at some point in their life (Wiehe, 1998). Eliciting self-reports of physical aggression against their female partners from a sample of over 14,500 men in the military, Pan, Neidig, and O'Leary (1994) found a prevalence rate of 24.4% for mild aggression (e.g., threw something at spouse, pushed, grabbed, or shoved spouse) and a prevalence rate of 5.6% for severe physical aggression (e.g., choked or strangled spouse, beat up spouse, kicked, bit, or hit spouse with a fist). These figures match findings obtained from civilian samples of similar demographic composition (see Pan et al., 1994, pp. 978–979). Referring to findings from the 1996 British Crime Survey, Mirrlees-Black and Byron (1999) concluded that 23% of women and 15% of men reported that they had been physically assaulted by an intimate partner at some point in their lives. Incidence rates from the same source for the last year prior to the survey showed that 4.2% of women and the same percentage of men had been victims of physical assault by an intimate partner.

The database for partner abuse in homosexual and lesbian relationships is limited, but it suggests that these relationships are by no means immune to the problem. Emphasising a cautious interpretation due to small, self-selected samples, Renzetti (1998) quoted evidence that revealed prevalence rates between 11% and 73% for domestic violence among lesbian couples. Merrill (1998) reported prevalence figures for physical aggression in bisexual and gay relationships that ranged from 18% to 47%. He noted striking similarities between same-sex and heterosexual domestic violence, concluding that "the phenomenon itself appears to be largely the same, with the most significant difference being the gender of the partners involved" (Merrill, 1998, p. 131; see also Burke & Follingstad, 1999, for a similar conclusion).

Survey data also reveal that the prevalence of heterosexual partner abuse is higher in dating as well as co-habitating couples than in married couples (Wiehe, 1998). Riggs, O'Leary, and Breslin (1990) concluded from their survey of college students that about one in four dating relationships could be classified as aggressive. On the other hand, rates of arrests for partner abuse were found to be higher for spouses than for boyfriends/girlfriends, suggesting that aggression between spouses may be more violent than aggression between dating partners (Bourg & Stock, 1994).

Searching for risk factors of partner abuse, demographic, individual, and relationship variables have been examined (Barnett et al., 1997; Wiehe, 1998). Among the demographic variables, gender has already been noted, with men being more likely to initiate severe acts of physical aggression and women being more likely to retaliate. Moreover, low socio-economic status has been linked to an increased risk of partner abuse, reflecting the impact of external stress. As far as relationship variables are concerned, evidence suggests a positive relationship between partner abuse and both duration of the partnership and partners' commitment to it. At the same time, inadequate communication patterns leading to fast escalation of hostile verbal exchanges have been identified in abusive relationships. Moreover, abuse is more likely to occur in relationships based on patriarchal attitudes and role divisions in which the man dominates the relationship and has power over his female partner, physically, materially, and in terms of decision making.

Particular attention has been devoted to the individual characteristics of men abusing their female partners (Barnett et al., 1997; Bennett & Williams, 1999; Wiehe, 1998). Low self-esteem, feelings of powerlessness originating outside the partnership, pathological jealousy, antisocial personality disorders, childhood exposure to violence, and childhood learning experiences suggesting aggression as a viable means of conflict resolution have been identified as risk factors increasing the likelihood that men will become abusive towards a partner. However, it has quickly become clear that partner abuse is a complex phenomenon that cannot be attributed to single risk factors. Therefore, several authors have tried to identify different types of batterers characterised by different risk factors and patterns of aggressive behaviour. Based on a thorough examination of previous typologies, Holtzworth-Munroe and Stuart (1994) proposed an integrative typology that distinguishes between three types of male batterers:

- *Family-only* batterers, whose violent behaviour is restricted to members of their own family, who do not show signs of psychopathological disorders, and whose violence is generally less severe and does not extend to sexual and/or psychological abuse. This group is estimated to account for about 50% of male batterers.
- *Dysphoric/borderline* batterers, whose violence is rooted in emotional instability and psychiatric disorders, whose aggression is concentrated on their family, but extrafamilial violence and criminal behaviour occur occasionally. About 25% of men abusing their partners are estimated to fall into this group.
- *Generally violent/antisocial* batterers, who show violent behaviour both within and outside their family and who engage in sexual and psychological aggression in addition to physical violence. Their general tendency towards violent behaviour makes them likely to have a criminal record. In addition, alcohol and substance abuse are found frequently in this group, which is estimated to account for 25% of male batterers.

A characteristic feature of partner abuse is the regularity with which it occurs in many relationships. Rather than remaining occasional outbursts of aggression, violent acts against the partner tend to be used as a habitual strategy of conflict resolution. Walker (1984) proposed a "cycle of violence", which integrates abuse into a couple's continuous interaction patterns.

Walker's model, depicted in Figure 7.2, describes how tension within a relationship builds up, then leads to the eruption of violence, which in turn is followed by a more harmonious period in which the abuser shows his affection for the partner. This pattern can help to explain why victims remain in abusive relationships and/or fail to seek help, at least as long as Phase 3 stages occur with sufficient frequency and duration to counterbalance the abusive periods. It may lead to the development of "learned hopefulness", i.e., the hope that despite one's own inability to control the abusive situation the abuse will come to an end and a non-violent relationship may be resumed. Just as learned hopefulness leads women to remain in an abusive relationship, so does the experience of "learned helplessness" (the construct from which learned hopefulness was derived). Learned

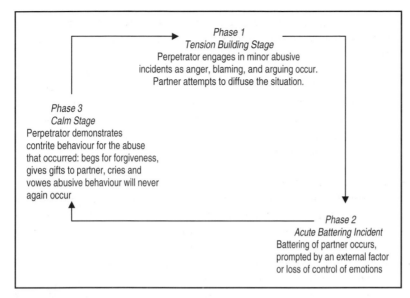

Phase 1
Tension Building Stage
Perpetrator engages in minor abusive
incidents as anger, blaming, and arguing occur.
Partner attempts to diffuse the situation.

Phase 3
Calm Stage
Perpetrator demonstrates
contrite behaviour for the abuse
that occurred: begs for forgiveness,
gives gifts to partner, cries and
vowes abusive behaviour will never
again occur

Phase 2
Acute Battering Incident
Battering of partner occurs,
prompted by an external factor
or loss of control of emotions

FIG. 7.2. The cycle of violence in partner abuse (based on Walker, 1984; from Wiehe, 1998 *Understanding family violence*, copyright © 1998 by Sage Publications; reprinted by permission of Sage Publications, Inc.).

helplessness refers to the experience that an adverse event cannot be averted or prevented despite the person's best efforts (Seligman, 1975). This experience undermines a victim's sense of personal control, giving rise to emotional distress, passivity, and poor problem-solving attempts. It creates a frame of mind in which the victim feels unable to end, or escape from, a violent relationship (Walker, 1984).

Consequences of partner abuse

The present section focuses on the psychological impact of partner abuse on the victim, but it should be noted that abuse also entails physical consequences (serious injuries, higher incidence of stress-related physical illnesses) and economic effects (material deprivation as a result of leaving an abusive relationship). Among the psychological effects of partner abuse, depression, anxiety, and negative self-esteem have been identified as common responses. In addition, partner abuse has an adverse effect on victims' interpersonal relationships in general: Fear of closeness and lack of interpersonal trust are commonly reported in the literature as being more prevalent in victims of partner abuse than in non-victimised controls or in victims of other forms of interpersonal violence. However, a word of methodological caution is in order here, because comparisons of victims and non-victims are typically made *after* the victims were abused, and this design cannot rule out the possibility that differences in depression, self-esteem, and other psychological variables may have existed prior to the abuse, potentially enhancing victims' vulnerability.

Especially since partner abuse tends to continue over time, many victims are traumatised by the experience, showing symptoms of PTSD. Kemp, Green, Hovanitz, and Rawlings (1995) found that PTSD was more common in women who experienced more severe physical abuse involving injuries, but that even among women who reported verbal abuse only, 63% met the criteria for PTSD. There is some disagreement in the literature as to whether the post-traumatic symptoms shown by victims of partner abuse are sufficiently distinctive to constitute a "battered woman syndrome" (BWS; Walker, 1984) as a subcategory of PTSD. There is consensus, however, that partner abuse may lead to long-term psychological distress. To ameliorate these adverse effects, a critical first step is to stop the continuation of abuse. As we saw above, the cycle of violence acts against women leaving abusive relationships over and above the fact that economic dependency makes it hard for many victims to establish an independent life away from the abuser. Being entrapped in abusive relationships because of psychological mechanisms, such as denial, self-blame, and adaptation to violence, is a common fate of victims of partner abuse. Even of those who make an attempt at breaking away and seek refuge in shelters for battered women, about a third eventually return to their abusive partners, with some studies suggesting even higher figures (see Barnett et al., 1997, p. 224). Thus, empowering women to gain independence from abusive partners, both psychologically and in terms of managing their everyday lives, must be a key objective of intervention work with victims of partner abuse.

Elder abuse and neglect

When people think or hear about family violence, images of abused children or battered partners easily come to mind as prototypical examples of this type of aggression. Another form of domestic violence is less prominent in public consciousness as well as in research: the abuse of elderly people by their caregivers. As the average life expectancy continues to rise throughout the Western world, a growing number of people become dependent on the care of younger relatives, mostly their children, or of professional caregivers. Providing care for dependent elders can be a highly demanding and strenuous task, sometimes leading to abusive behaviour of the caregiver towards the old person in his or her care. In this section, we will summarise the evidence on elder abuse that has been accumulated since the problem of elder abuse first attracted research attention about 20 years ago.

Forms and prevalence of elder abuse

In order to study elder abuse, the two terms involved need to be properly defined. This obvious requirement turns out to be problematic with respect to the term "elder". Unlike children, wives, or siblings, who can be identified with relative ease, there is no clear-cut criterion as to when a person becomes an elder. As Griffin (1999, p. 267) points out, entrance age into the category varies from 50 to 70 years of age, depending on the criteria required by different institutions as well as legal entitlements. Variations in defining the target group for elder abuse not only affects prevalence estimates, it also hampers comparisons of prevalence figures across different studies. Despite the ambiguity as to the lower limit of the category, there seems to be a consensus among researchers to regard individuals over the age of 65 as "elders".

As far as the second term, "abuse", is concerned, definitions are more consistent. Generally, four forms of elder abuse are distinguished in the literature (Gelles, 1997; Griffin, 1999):

- *Physical abuse*, which involves the infliction of physical pain or injury on an elderly person, such as battering, restraining, or bruising. Some authors also include *sexual abuse*, i.e., the enforcement of sexual contacts against the elderly person's will, in this category (Gelles, 1997), while others list it as a separate form (Wiehe, 1998).
- *Psychological* or *emotional abuse*, which is defined as the "dehumanisation of the victim through fear of violence or other consequences of angering the perpetrator" (Griffin, 1999, p. 267). It includes verbal assaults, threats, name calling and infantilising (using baby talk, limiting the victim's freedom of decision).
- *Financial* abuse, which involves the "illegal and improper exploitation of the elderly's property or assets" (Gelles, 1997, p. 116). Since many elderly people are unable to handle their own

financial interests for physical or mental reasons, they have to trust their caregivers to look after their financial affairs.

- *Neglect*, i.e., the withholding of adequate care to meet a dependent elder's physical, medical, and psychological needs. While the previous forms of elder abuse referred to acts of *commission*, neglect represents a form of elder abuse through *omission*. Refusal to meet the elderly person's physical needs (such as regular provision of food, personal hygiene), respect, or financial support are forms of abuse that can be equally damaging to the victim as the active commitment of abusive acts.

Prevalence rates are even harder to establish for elder abuse than for the other forms of domestic violence. One reason is that victims are usually confined to the domestic setting with limited contact to people in the outside world who might be alerted to their situation. In addition, the very fact that they are dependent on the care provided by the abuser often makes victims reluctant to disclose the abuse to a third party. Furthermore, elders abused by their children may be embarrassed or even feel guilty about having brought up children who turn against their parents in this way. Therefore, elder abuse is regarded as a "hidden" form of domestic violence, and established prevalence rates reflect the lower limits rather than the full scale of the problem. Official statistics suggest that between 5% and 10% of individuals over the age of 65 experience some form of abuse (Gelles, 1997). In a ground-breaking study eliciting self-reports of victimisation from a random sample of over 2000 respondents aged 65 or above, Pillemer and Finkelhor (1988) identified a rate of abuse of 32 per 1000 individuals in that age bracket. Physical abuse was the most common form of abuse. Abuse was committed most frequently by spouses, who accounted for almost 60% of all perpetrators. Pillemer and Finkelhor also established that only 1 in 14 incidents elicited through their survey had been reported by the victims.

Risk factors of elder abuse

As with other forms of domestic violence, a central task for researchers has been to identify characteristics associated with an increased likelihood of becoming the victim of elder abuse as well as to establish risk factors for perpetrating elder abuse. Few factors have been identified with some consistency as increasing the likelihood for an elderly person to become a victim of abuse (see Barnett et al., 1997; Griffin, 1999; Wiehe, 1998):

- social isolation (i.e., few contacts within their own family and beyond);
- higher age;
- poorer state of physical as well as mental health; and
- living in the same household with the caregiver.

The evidence is inconsistent with regard to victim gender. While some statistics suggest that women are at higher risk of elder abuse (Tatara, 1993), others report higher victimisation rate for men (e.g., Pillemer & Finkelhor, 1988).

On the perpetrator side, a number of risk factors contribute to the likelihood of becoming abusive towards a dependent elder:

- Psychopathology of the abuser: Abusers were found to be more likely to have a history of mental illness and psychiatric hospitalisation (Pillemer & Suitor, 1988).
- Substance abuse: Anetzberger, Korbin, and Austin (1994), for example, found that compared to a non-abusive control group, individuals who physically abused elderly parents in their care reported higher alcohol consumption and were more likely to have been identified with a drinking problem.
- Dependency of the abuser on the victim, both financially and emotionally (Pillemer & Suitor, 1988). It has been suggested that abuse may be a response to deal with the sense of powerlessness experienced by grown-up children who are dependent on their parents (Gelles, 1997).
- Transgenerational transmission of violent behaviour. The "victim-to-perpetrator" cycle that has been identified with respect to both child abuse and partner abuse has also been invoked as an explanation for elder abuse. Evidence, albeit limited, suggests that elder abuse is more frequently committed by individuals who were themselves victims of family violence (e.g., Steinmetz, 1978).
- External stress, i.e., life stress that originates outside the family context: Unemployment and financial difficulties have been identified as external stressors more prevalent in abusive than non-abusive carers (e.g., Bendik, 1992).
- Gender: Men were found to be over-represented among abusers, especially in the perpetration of physical abuse. This finding is due, at least in part, to the fact that men abusing their female spouses account for a relatively large proportion of abuse cases (Barnett et al., 1997).

It is important to bear in mind, however, that these risk factors may well be present in many caregiving relationships, only a small number of which will turn abusive. How different risk factors add up or interact to produce abusive behaviour or whether there are protective factors buffering the negative impact of risk factors still remains to be investigated.

Consequences of elder abuse

The adverse effects of abuse on elderly victims have been shown to be serious and affect different aspects of physical, psychological, and social functioning: Compared to non-abused older persons, victims were found to have higher levels of depression, to show symptoms of learned helplessness, and to experience feelings of shame and guilt about the behaviour of their children or partners. These feelings are closely related to denial, which is another way for victims to cope with the trauma of abuse (Wolf, 1997). A review of the problems experienced by elderly victims of abuse was presented by Anetzberger (1997). Her summary is shown in Table 7.4.

TABLE 7.4
Effects of elder abuse

Physical effects	Behavioural effects
Sleep disturbances	Mental confusion
Eating problems	Anger
Headaches	Suicidal actions
	Helplessness
Psychological effects	Reduced coping
Denial	
Resignation	Social effects
Fear	Fewer contacts
Anxiety	Violent actions
Depression	Dependence
Embarrassment	Withdrawal
Self-blame	
Phobias	Intervening variables
Hopelessness	Age at onset
Dissociation	Relationship to perpetrator
	Nature of family functioning

From Anetzberger, *Violence Against Women, 3*, 499–514, copyright © 1997 by Sage Publications; reprinted by permission of Sage Publications, Inc.

Considering the evidence discussed in the previous sections, Table 7.4 illustrates that the adverse consequences of elder abuse show a high degree of similarity to the negative effects of other forms of domestic violence. Similar parallels can be observed with respect to the precipitating factors of abuse. Therefore, it is not surprising that many of the causes and mechanisms invoked to explain abuse can be applied to different forms of violence in the family. The main explanatory frameworks offered to account for the problem of family violence are introduced in the next section.

Explaining domestic violence

Despite the variety of forms that domestic violence can take, it is possible to identify a set of interlocking factors common to the different types of abuse discussed in this chapter:

- inequality of power between perpetrator and victim, substantiated by economic factors, enabling the dominant person to enforce his or her needs through the use of aggression and get away with it;
- a normative structure that condones the use of violence as a strategy of conflict resolution, leading to the transmission of aggressive response styles from one generation to the next;
- the presence of external stressors, such as unemployment and poor housing conditions;
- childhood experiences of family violence by the abusive adults;
- characteristics of the abuser, such as individual psychopathology or inadequate conflict resolution skills; and finally
- both short-term and enduring behaviour patterns of the target persons, such as difficult behaviour of the child or dependent elder.

In the present section, we will briefly review the main theoretical explanations for domestic violence, which may help in understanding how the above factors operate, and interact with each other, in leading to aggression in the family (see also Barnett et al., 1997; Heise, 1998; Wolf, 1997). Most theoretical accounts of family violence can be allocated to one of three levels of explanation:

- the macro level of the society, or social group, in which domestic violence occurs;

- the micro level of family functioning; and
- the level of individual characteristics of victims and perpetrators.

Macro-level theories

Theories in this group look for the causes of domestic violence in the social structure and value systems of a society or a particular social group. The extent to which violence is culturally accepted in a society is thought to affect the prevalence of violence against family members. For example, if there is a general consensus that spanking is an accepted, even necessary way of disciplining children, this consensus presents the use of corporal punishment as a legitimate child-rearing practice. Another social consensus that lowers the threshold for domestic violence is the view that the way in which parents treat their children, or husbands treat their wives, is nothing but their own business and that it is inappropriate for outside observers to intervene in domestic conflicts. In addition, the patriarchal structure of most societies has been identified as promoting domestic violence, not least in feminist accounts of violence against women (Marin & Russo, 1999). Patriarchal societies are characterised by a clear-cut power differential between men and women, with men dominating women in most areas of public and private life. Male dominance is linked to a positive evaluation of male assertiveness and aggressiveness. Social institutions are dominated by men, making it hard for women to be acknowledged as victims of male violence, to secure help, and to enforce the legal prosecution of perpetrators.

In addition to cultural values condoning the use of aggression towards family members, economic conditions are variables at the macro level that may affect domestic violence. External stress (i.e., stress originating outside the family), such as poverty, unemployment, or crammed housing conditions, may make families vulnerable to domestic violence.

Macro-level theories describe the societal conditions under which domestic violence can emerge and develop. They do not address the issue of why domestic violence occurs in some families but not others, and is performed by some individuals and not others.

Micro-level theories

These theories look at the family as the unit of analysis and try to identify features of family functioning that enhance the probability of domestic aggression. Intra-familial stress, resulting from marital conflict, inadequate communication skills, and reciprocal provocation (e.g., between a difficult child and a punitive parent), has been proposed as a risk factor for domestic violence. Moreover, it has been argued that members of a family may learn aggressive behaviour patterns through reinforcement and modelling. If the abuser learns that his violent acts lead to the intended consequences and the victim learns that the violence can be stopped by complying with the perpetrator's demands, interaction routines develop that reinforce the performance of aggressive behaviour. Moreover, abusers may serve as role models for other family members, suggesting that aggression is an adequate—and perhaps the only—strategy to resolve conflicts within the family.

From the point of view of *social exchange theory*, satisfaction with family life is based on a cost–benefit analysis in which family members set their investments (e.g., emotional input, time, money) in the relationship against the perceived benefits (e.g., emotional gratification, material goods, social status). If the investments are perceived as outweighing the benefits, e.g., when expectations about the partner are not fulfilled or when children's demands are perceived as unacceptable, the theory predicts that dissatisfaction will arise and alternative relationships will be explored. Given that marital relationships are not easily dissolved and parent–child relationships are practically impossible to dissolve, violence has been explained as a response to the dissatisfaction resulting from inequitable relationships.

Individual-level theories

A third group of theories looks for potential causes of domestic violence in the *individual perpetrator*. One theoretical perspective looks at family violence as a learned behaviour. Social learning theory as well as learning through reinforcement (instrumental conditioning) have been invoked to explain why childhood experiences of abuse and the witnessing of parental violence may turn victims into perpetrators. In abusive families, children learn that aggressive behaviour is rewarded in that the abuser usually achieves his/her objective and they may incorporate aggression into their own patterns of behaviour. Another explanation has focused on psychopathology to explain abusive behaviour. From this perspective, individuals suffering from personality disorders or mental illness are at increased risk of abusing family members, not least because, among other things, they are less capable of controlling hostile feelings and aggressive impulses. In a related vein, personality characteristics such as low self-esteem, insecurity, and feelings of vulnerability have been proposed to explain why perpetrators turn to domestic violence, which typically involves victims less powerful than themselves (see, however, Baumeister & Boden, 1998, for a critical analysis of the role of low self-esteem). Finally, socio-cognitive explanations have stressed the importance of cognitions in predicting domestic violence. In particular, misperceptions and misguided expectations have been shown to play a role in both child abuse and partner abuse. For example, misinformed expectations of children's behaviour and abilities at different ages can lead parents to perceive their child's behaviour as unreasonable and inadequate, leading to excessive punitive reactions. In child sexual abuse, the abuser may misperceive the child's lack of resistance as an indication of consent. Misperceptions also occur frequently in heterosexual relationships, with men interpreting women's friendly behaviour as suggesting sexual interest (Abbey, 1991). This misperception gives rise to frustrations and feelings of anger, which have been shown to precipitate aggression.

The theoretical perspectives presented in this section all address different aspects involved in explaining domestic violence. None of them can aspire, nor, indeed, claims, to predict exactly who will show abusive behaviour and who will not. Not every man growing up in a patriarchal society turns into an abuser, nor does everyone exposed to external stress or aggressive role models within the family. It is the combination and interaction of these different risk factors that eventually determines individual behaviour. Gelles (1997, p. 65) has presented a social psychological model of child abuse that integrates the different levels of explanation and specifies the way in which different risk factors interact to produce physical abuse. His model, adapted to refer to domestic violence in general, is presented in Figure 7.3.

The model depicted in Figure 7.3 illustrates that the precursors of a particular episode of domestic violence involve both distal factors and proximal factors. Distal factors, such as cultural norms and the abuser's social position, socialisation history or personality structure, are relatively stable and continuously present. They provide the platform on which an aggressive response may be carried out. Proximal factors, such as distressed family relationships, external stress, and, most notably, target-produced stress, are less stable and have a more immediate impact on the aggressive episode. For example, children going through the temper tantrum stage or elders losing

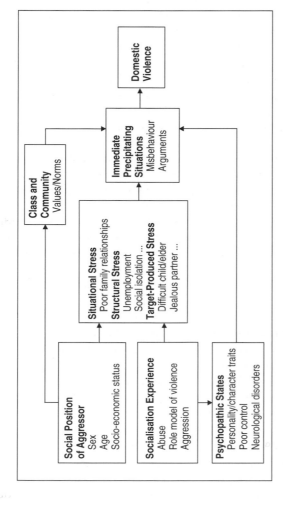

FIG. 7.3. A social psychological model of domestic violence (adapted from Gelles, 1997, *Intimate violence in families* (3rd ed.), copyright © 1997 by Sage Publications; reprinted by permission of Sage Publications, Inc.).

The diagram contains the following boxes:

Social Position of Aggressor
Sex
Age
Socio-economic status

Socialisation Experience
Abuse
Role model of violence
Aggression

Psychopathic States
Personality/character traits
Poor control
Neurological disorders

Situational Stress
Poor family relationships
Structural Stress
Unemployment
Social isolation ...
Target-Produced Stress
Difficult child/elder
Jealous partner ...

Class and Community
Values/Norms

Immediate Precipitating Situations
Misbehaviour
Arguments

Domestic Violence

control over vital faculties and needing full-time care may create tension within the family and frustration within the individual carer, both increasing the likelihood of aggressive behaviour. The effects of both distal and proximal factors combine in the immediate precipitating situation and enhance the probability that a particular stimulus, such as misbehaviour from the child or a disagreement with the partner, will elicit an aggressive response. While it will undoubtedly be difficult to examine the full model within a single analytical design, it outlines a framework for conceptualising the complex interactions of factors ultimately precipitating violent interactions within families.

Summary

- The present chapter reviewed evidence on the prevalence, risk factors, and consequences of three major forms of domestic violence: child abuse (physical, sexual, and emotional), partner abuse, and elder abuse.
- Since domestic violence is shielded from outside detection by the widespread belief in family privacy, under-reporting is a particular problem in trying to establish the scale of domestic violence. Nonetheless, the available sources (official reports, survey data, and clinical studies) present substantial prevalence rates for each form of domestic abuse. Nowhere are women and children more at risk of suffering violence and abuse than in their immediate family.
- Factors that contribute to the problem of domestic violence operate at the societal level (e.g., patriarchal value systems, acceptance of interpersonal aggression, and adverse economic conditions resulting in external stress), at the level of the family system (e.g., poor communication skills of family members, unrealistic expectations of parents about their children's behaviour, economic dependency of abusive carers on dependent elders), and at the level of the individual perpetrator (e.g., psychopathology, childhood victimisation, dysfunctional learning experiences).
- The consequences of domestic violence on the victims show a high degree of similarity across different types of abuse. Depressive symptoms, low self-esteem, stress-related physical complaints and post-traumatic stress disorders are commonly identified in child and adult victims of domestic violence.

Suggested reading

Barnett, O.W., Miller-Perrin, C.L., & Perrin, R.D. (1997). *Family violence across the lifespan*. Thousand Oaks, CA: Sage.

Gelles, R.J. (1997). *Intimate violence in families* (3rd ed.). Thousand Oaks, CA: Sage.

Harway, M., & O'Neil, J.M. (Eds.) (1999). *What causes men's violence against women?* Thousand Oaks, CA: Sage.

Wiehe, V.R. (1998). *Understanding family violence*. Thousand Oaks, CA: Sage.

Sexual aggression 8

Sexual aggression against women is one of the most prominent issues both in academic research and in public debate on aggression (Koss et al., 1994). Within the psychological literature on sexual aggression, social psychologists have explored the scale, antecedents, and consequences of sexual violence in the context of social norms, gender roles, and the history of evolution (Allison & Wrightsman, 1993). In contrast, clinical psychologists have been concerned primarily with the immediate and long-term effects of sexual violence on the victim and with the development of appropriate intervention strategies to mitigate the trauma of rape (Koss & Harvey, 1991).

A comprehensive review of the research literature on sexual aggression is well beyond the scope of this chapter. Instead, the aim is to highlight the major findings from this literature and to refer the reader to sources offering more in-depth coverage. The chapter starts with a brief review of definitions and prevalence rates of different forms of sexual aggression. The sections that follow examine the most prominent explanations of sexual aggression, explore so-called risk factors of sexual victimisation, i.e., variables associated with an increased risk of suffering sexual aggression, and examine the effects of sexual aggression on the victims. The vast majority of studies addressing these issues have looked at heterosexual aggression involving male perpetrators and female victims. However, the problem of male-on-male rape is gradually becoming recognised as a form of sexual aggression not to be underestimated and will also be dealt with. The final section of the chapter is devoted to an issue that has only recently emerged on the agenda of sexual aggression research: women's use of coercive strategies against male partners.

Definition and prevalence of sexual aggression

Sexual aggression includes a range of forced sexual activities, such as sexual intercourse, oral sex, kissing, and petting, using a range of coercive strategies, such as threat or use of physical force, exploitation of the victim's inability to resist, or verbal pressure (see Abbey, McAuslan, & Ross, 1998). It also includes unwanted sexual attention in the form of sexual harassment, stalking, and obscene phone calls (Belknap, Fisher, & Cullen, 1999; Sheffield, 1993; see Chapter 6 for a discussion of sexual harassment in the context of workplace bullying). Despite a consensus about the general meaning of sexual aggression, there is a great diversity of specific definitions. There are at least three levels at which definitions of sexual aggression are proposed and used as a basis for decision making: (1) the level of *legal definitions*, determining which behaviours represent sexual offences; (2) the level of *research definitions*, guiding conceptual and empirical work on the prevalence and causation of sexual aggression; and (3) the level of *everyday discourse* deciding whether or not a particular incident is accepted as an account of sexual violence and the roles of victims and perpetrators are assigned to the individuals involved.

Defining sexual aggression

Legal definitions vary as to the type of sexual acts and coercive strategies constituting rape. As Koss and Cook (1998) note, the FBI adopts a definition of rape restricted to forcible actual or attempted vaginal intercourse with a woman without her consent, by force or threat of force. In contrast, most states in the United States have adopted legislation in which rape is defined more broadly in terms of oral, anal, or vaginal penetration through threat, force, or intentional incapacitation. Moreover, definitions are now gender neutral, allowing for both women and men to be victims (and perpetrators) of sexual violence. The restriction of legal definitions to extramarital acts of sexual aggression was removed in all US states in 1993, thereby instituting "marital rape" as a criminal offence (Bergen, 1996). However, as Bergen noted, a substantial number of states grant exemption from rape prosecution to husbands under particular circumstances. "Ironically, in most of these states, a husband is exempt when he does not have to use force because his wife is vulnerable (e.g., mentally or physically impaired, unconscious) and is legally unable to consent" (Bergen, 1996, p. 150).

In Britain, rape is legally defined as sexual intercourse with a person without consent where the defendant knows that the other person does not consent or is reckless as to whether that person is consenting or not. Sexual intercourse is defined as vaginal or anal penetration with the penis. This definition of rape covers both marital rape and rape of male victims. In Germany, rape was legally defined until 1997 as the use or threat of violence against a woman to force her into extramarital sexual intercourse. In a subsequent revision, a broader definition was adopted, which removed the restriction to female victims and non-marital intercourse. This current legal definition includes the use or threat of violence or the exploitation of the victim's incapacitated state to force another *person* into sexual activities. Forced sexual activities qualify as rape if the act involves penetration of the victim's body, which is no longer restricted to vaginal intercourse.

Considerable ambiguity exists in definitions of rape used as a basis for research on sexual aggression. Muehlenhard, Powch, Phelps, and Giusti (1992) highlight the diversity of definitions employed in empirical studies of sexual aggression. This diversity makes it difficult to compare findings across different studies and to gain an overall impression of the prevalence and risk factors of sexual aggression. For example, Wiehe and Richards (1995, p. 5) define rape as "any sexual activity that one experiences without giving consent." In contrast, Koss et al. (1987) distinguish between sexual contact, sexual coercion, and rape (see below), the latter referring only to penetrative sexual acts obtained through the use of threat of force or the deliberate incapacitation of the victim. It is obvious that prevalence estimates of sexual aggression are strongly influenced by such differences in defining the constructs under investigation.

Unlike crime statistics, which do not record the relationship between victim and perpetrator, victimisation surveys frequently distinguish between different subtypes of rape, varying with regard to the victim–offender relationship: *stranger rape*, committed against a victim unknown to the offender; *acquaintance rape*, referring to assaults committed by anyone who is not a complete stranger; *date rape*, occurring between individuals engaged in some form of romantic relationship, and *wife rape* (or more generally, partner rape) committed against a spouse or cohabiting partner.

Finally, in addition to formal definitions in legal and research contexts, everyday discourse represents a third level at which sexual aggression is defined. Unlike the first two levels of definition, everyday discourse is less concerned with the nature of the sexual acts enforced and with the specific strategies employed to force a non-consenting person into sexual contacts. Instead, particular importance is attached to the circumstances of the incident. In everyday understanding, rape is commonly seen as an attack in the dark by a stranger on an unsuspecting victim who puts up physical resistance against her attacker (Rozee, 1999). The more a specific incident differs from this prototypical representation of the "real rape", the smaller the number of people prepared to consider it as rape (Burt & Albin, 1981; Krahé, 1991).

This reduction of the "real rape" stereotype to stranger assaults affects the way in which people evaluate and respond to the fate of rape victims. Victims whose experiences deviate from the real rape stereotype, e.g., because they were assaulted by an acquaintance, in their own homes or while under the influence of alcohol, are more likely to be blamed for the assault and less likely to receive sympathetic treatment from others. Moreover, the real rape stereotype affects women's self-identification as victims of rape. Kahn, Mathie, and Torgler (1994) asked women to describe a typical rape situation. One group of women had previously reported forced sexual experiences on a behavioural measure *and* identified themselves as rape victims on a direct question (acknowledged victims). A second group of women reported forced sexual experiences but answered "no" to the direct question of whether or not they had been raped (unacknowledged victims). Kahn et al. found that rape descriptions provided by the acknowledged victims depicted the typical acquaintance rape scenario, involving a previously known assailant, an indoor location, and verbal protest rather than physical struggle on the victim's part. In contrast, the scripts generated by the unacknowledged victims corresponded to the typical "blitz rape scenario", involving an unknown assailant, the use of weapons, and an outdoor location. It is important to note that the personal victimisation experiences of all but one of the respondents had been acquaintance rapes. This suggests that unacknowledged victims failed to identify themselves as rape victims because their rape scripts were restricted to the stranger rape scenario and thus did not cover the particular events that had happened to them.

Prevalence of sexual aggression

The task of establishing prevalence rates for sexual aggression is impeded by the same problem of widespread under-reporting that was noted with regard to domestic violence. Including only rape cases that came to the attention of the police, US crime figures for 1999 revealed a total number of 89,107 forcible rapes, which corresponds to a rate of 64 of every 100,000 female members of the population (Uniform Crime Reports, 1999). These figures represent a decline of 5% against the previous year and are in line with a continuous decrease in reported rapes since the early 1990s. In Britain, 7139 rapes and 19,463 indecent assaults against female victims were recorded in official crime statistics for England and Wales between April 1998 and April 1999; 353 rapes and 3672 indecent assaults were reported during the same period against male victims (Criminal Statistics in England and Wales, 1999). In contrast to the United States, no comparable decline in rape cases has been observed in the United Kingdom. Instead, the number of reported rapes has shown an almost threefold increase between 1985 and 1995. Interestingly, the number of cases leading to convictions showed a drop from 23% to 11% during the same period (Temkin, 1999). German figures for 1999 show a total of 7565 reported rapes and serious indecent assaults, corresponding to a rate of 9.2 per 100,000 female citizens (Bundesministerium des Inneren, 2000). Similar to the United Kingdom, no consistent decline in rape figures comparable to US developments is apparent in Germany.

Since official crime figures only include those cases that have been reported to the police, they seriously underestimate the true scale of sexual aggression. Derogatory attitudes towards victims and the widespread acceptance of rape myths (see below) create a climate in which women may be unwilling to identify themselves as victims of sexual aggression (Williams, 1984). In a nationwide telephone survey including a representative sample of women, Kilpatrick, Edmunds, and Seymour (1992) found that 84% of the women who identified themselves as victims of forcible rape had *not* reported the offence to the police. Moreover, there is evidence that a sizeable proportion of women respond "no" to the question of whether they have ever been raped despite reporting experiences that meet the defining features of sexual assault (Koss, 1985). Therefore, Koss and co-workers developed a survey instrument (the "Sexual Experiences Survey" [*SES*]; Koss & Oros, 1982; Koss et al., 1987) that uses behavioural descriptions of sexually aggressive behaviour rather than categorical labels, such as rape. For example, instead of asking "Have you ever been raped?" the *SES* presents potential victims with the following item: "Have you ever had sexual intercourse with a man when you didn't want to because he used some degree of physical force (twisting your

TABLE 8.1

Prevalence rates (%) of sexual aggression against women: victim
and perpetrator reports

Victimisation or aggression level	Women (n = 3187)	Men (n = 2972)
No victimisation/aggression	46.3	74.8
Sexual contact	11.4	10.2
Sexual coercion	11.9	7.2
Attempted rape	12.1	3.3
Rape	15.4	4.4

Adapted with permission from Koss, Gidycz, & Wisniewski (1987, p. 168); copyright © 1987 by the American Psychological Association.

arm, holding you down etc.)?" The *SES* or similar measures derived from it have been used widely to elicit prevalence rates of sexual aggression (Belknap et al., 1999).

Self-report surveys are an important data source to come closer to the full extent of sexual aggression and victimisation. These surveys typically produce far higher prevalence rates than official crime statistics, in some cases more than 100 times higher than official figures (Koss, 1992). In a large-scale survey of college students using the *SES*, Koss et al. (1987) found that more than 50% of female students reported some form of sexual victimisation since the age of 14. More than 25% of the male students indicated that they forced a woman to engage in sexual acts at some point after the age of 14. The distribution of prevalence rates for different forms of sexual victimisation and aggression obtained by Koss et al. (1987) is presented in Table 8.1.

In Table 8.1, attempted rape and rape referred to penetrative sexual acts through the use or threat of force or the deliberate incapacitation of the victim (e.g., via alcohol or other drugs). Sexual coercion comprises sexual intercourse against the woman's will through menacing verbal pressure or misuse of authority. Sexual contact refers to sexual behaviour other than penetrative sex against the woman's will through the use of verbal pressure, physical force (or threat thereof), or misuse of authority. It is important to note that even though multiple responses were possible in the survey, the figures in Table 8.1 are based on each respondent's most serious form of sexual victimisation or aggression. Thus, they present a conservative picture of the scale of sexual aggression. Koss et al. also asked their respondents about sexual victimisation and aggression that occurred during the 6 months prior to the survey and found an incidence rate of 83 per 1000 women for rape victimisation and an incidence rate of 34 per 1000 men for the perpetration of rape.

Later studies eliciting self-reports of sexual victimisation provide similar findings. Abbey, Ross, McDuffie, and McAuslan (1996) established a prevalence rate of 59% for any sexual victimisation and 23% for rape. In a parallel study with male respondents, Abbey et al. (1998) found that 26% of men reported some form of sexual aggression, and 9% reported completed rape. In a study by Testa and Dermen (1999), 67% of women reported some form of sexual experience against their will (see also Gidycz, Coble, Latham, & Layman, 1993; Himelein, 1995; Tyler, Hoyt, & Whitbeck, 1998; Ullman, Karabatsos, & Koss, 1999, for comparable findings).

Using the same instrument as Koss et al. (1987), highly similar prevalence rates were found in a German study. Of a sample of 189 female adolescents aged between 17 and 20 years, 54% reported some form of sexual victimisation, and 11% reported unwanted sexual intercourse through use or threat of force or following incapacitation by alcohol or drugs (Krahé, 1998). A follow-up study with a new sample found a corresponding victimisation rate for unwanted sexual intercourse of 12.2% (Krahé, Scheinberger-Olwig, & Waizenhöfer, 1999). These figures tie in with Belknap and Erez's (1995) review of the North American evidence, which revealed a prevalence of 8–14% of forced sexual intercourse for college women.

The majority of sexual assaults take place between individuals who previously knew each other, contradicting the notion of stranger rape as the "real rape". Prevalence estimates for these sexual assaults are particularly affected by the problem of under-reporting. Several studies suggest that victims of acquaintance rape or date rape are even less likely to report the assault to the police than are victims of stranger rape (Pino & Meier, 1999; Rozee, 1999). Moreover, as noted above, victims who were sexually assaulted by assailants they previously knew may be less likely to identify themselves as victims in self-report surveys. The US National Crime Victimization Survey indicates that for 1992–1993 about half of all rapes and sexual assaults against women were committed by friends and acquaintances, and 26% were committed by intimate partners (Bachman & Saltzman, 1995). Other surveys support the conclusion that only about a third of all rapes were committed by men who were strangers to the victims (Craig, 1990; Stermac, Du Mont, & Dunn, 1998). Prevalence estimates in the North American literature for marital rape suggest that between 14% and 25% of women are forced by their husbands to engage in sexual acts (Russell, 1990; Bergen, 1998b). Contributing

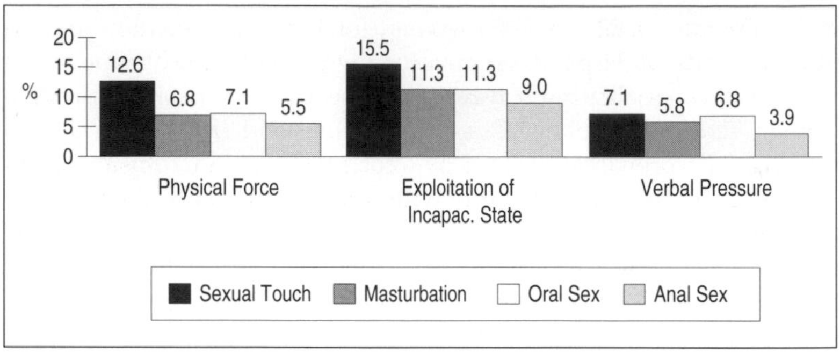

FIG. 8.1. Prevalence rates of male sexual victimisation in homosexual relationships (adapted from Krahé, Schütze, Fritsche, & Waizenhöfer, 2000).

data from a British survey, Painter and Farrington (1998) reported that 13% of a sample of over 1000 wives were forced to have sexual intercourse by their husbands. They also corroborate previous evidence that marital rape is particularly likely to occur in relationships characterised by physical violence between the partners (see also Chapter 7).

Little evidence is available on the prevalence of male sexual victimisation. In a survey of 310 homosexual men, Krahé, Schütze, Fritsche, and Waizenhöfer (2000) obtained prevalence rates for sexual aggression and victimisation, using an adapted version of the *SES*. The victimisation rates obtained for different forms of sexual acts are presented in Figure 8.1.

A total of 16.1% of respondents reported victimisation experiences meeting the legal definition of rape (i.e., oral and anal sex involving the use of force or the exploitation of the victim's incapacitation following the consumption of alcohol or drugs). The overall prevalence rate for any sexual victimisation was 44.5% (Krahé, Scheinberger-Olwig, & Schütze, in press).

Parallel to victimisation rates, Krahé, Schütze, Fritsche, and Waizenhöfer (2000) elicited self-reports of the perpetration of sexually aggressive acts. Prevalence rates were lower than the corresponding victimisation figures. Nevertheless, more than 5% of respondents indicated that they had used, or threatened to use, physical force to make an unwilling man comply with their sexual demands, over 16% reported exploiting a person's inability to resist their advances, and over 6% admitted to the use of verbal coercion. A total of 11.3% of respondents reported the perpetration of acts that meet the legal definition of rape.

Altogether, the figures presented in this section make it abundantly clear that sexual aggression is a reality in the lives of many women and also—even though much less researched—in the lives of men. What is particularly worrying is the consistent finding that the majority of sexual assaults take place between people who are known to each other—as casual acquaintances, dating partners, or spouses. This finding brings home the threat of rape to the private sphere, making it more pervasive than is implied in the "real rape" stereotype of the stranger attacking in the dark. Trying to understand why men commit acts of sexual aggression has been a prime objective of psychological research, not least because a better understanding of the causes that lead to sexual assault may provide directions for the development of prevention strategies.

Causal explanations of sexual aggression

Explanations of sexual aggression can be broadly divided into two groups. The first group will be called "macro-level" explanations because they locate the causes of sexual aggression in general processes of societal functioning or evolutionary development. The second group will be called "individual-level" explanations because they focus on the individual perpetrator and look at biographical, cognitive, and affective variables precipitating sexually aggressive behaviour. Rather than being mutually exclusive, the two sets of approaches represent complementary levels of analysis and jointly contribute to the task of clarifying the underlying mechanisms of sexual aggression.

Macro-level explanations

In this section, two models of sexual aggression are discussed that propose very different processes leading to sexual aggression: the sociocultural approach and the evolutionary approach. The sociocultural approach highlights societal features that create the breeding ground for sexual aggression and allow it to persist. In contrast, the evolutionary approach suggests a biological explanation of sexual aggression by placing modern-day sexual aggression in the developmental history of the human species. What the two approaches have in common is their emphasis on general conditions (either societal or biological) that promote sexual aggression.

   The sociocultural approach. According to the sociocultural approach, the roots of sexual aggression are to be found in the fabric of a society, most notably in the way in which gender relations are defined (see White & Kowalski, 1998, for a review). This perspective has been advanced in particular by feminist authors arguing that the built-in power differential between men and women in many societies fosters the emergence of sexual aggression. By virtue of their greater social power, men claim the right to seek sexual satisfaction regardless of the woman's wishes. Moreover, sexual aggression is instrumental in perpetuating male dominance by instilling a sense of fear and vulnerability in women.

Support for the proposition that sexual aggression is the product of sociostructural characteristics that may vary between societies comes from cross-cultural evidence of societies in which sexual aggression is far less frequent or even non-existent compared to Western countries. For example, Sanday (1981) conducted an ethnographic study of 95 tribal societies, about half of which (47%) she identified as "rape free", i.e., showing no or only a minimal prevalence of sexual aggression. In contrast, 18% of societies were classified as "rape prone", with a high prevalence of sexual aggression. In the remaining societies, there were reports of rape, but no frequency information was available. In the rape-prone societies, sexual aggression served a ceremonial function (e.g., as a rite of passage for adolescent males) and/or functioned as a means of domination and punishment of women. Rape-free societies were found to have low levels of aggression overall and to place a high value on the contribution of women to the reproduction and continuity of the society.

Cross-cultural analyses such as Sanday's (1981) suggest that sexual aggression is not an isolated phenomenon but must be seen in the context of general patterns of gender interaction within a society (see also Rozee, 1993). Compatible with this view is the stipulation that sexual behaviour is regulated to a large extent by cognitive scripts, furnished by the norms and values of a given society. "Sexual scripts" provide culturally shared cognitive frameworks for evaluating, planning, and executing sexual behaviour (Krahé, 2000b). Rape is seen as a variant of sexual behaviour accommodated within the normal sexual script, which is based on the notions of male initiative and female receptivity: "Sexual relationships are built around sexual inequalities, are scripted for actors whose roles have been predefined as subordinate and superordinate, and hence involve the exercise of power which may be manifested in the sexual act itself. [. . .] Rape, then, is simply an extreme manifestation of our culturally accepted patterns of male–female relationships" (Jackson, 1978, p. 37; see also Herman, 1984).

Crucial elements of a sexual script that condones aggressive tactics are stereotypical beliefs about victims, perpetrators and circumstances of rape that have no foundation in reality. Such "rape myths" include the idea that women secretly desire to be raped, that rapes only happen between strangers, and that no woman can be raped if she puts up genuine resistance (Burt, 1980; Ward, 1995). They foster an atmosphere of suspicion and hostility against victims of sexual violence, which has been consistently shown to affect the social perception of rape victims in an adverse way. For example, the stronger people's endorsement of rape myths, the less they are likely to label a forced sexual contact as rape and the more they are likely to attribute blame to the victim (e.g., Burt & Albin, 1981; Krahé, 1988). Moreover, acceptance of rape myths was found to be related to more general sexist attitudes and the acceptance of violence in interpersonal relationships (Costin, 1985; Hall, Howard, & Boezio, 1986).

Among the social forces considered influential in fostering rape-supportive sexual scripts, the availability of pornography has been highlighted by several authors. As we saw in Chapter 5, there is indeed evidence that exposure to pornography promotes rape myth acceptance even after short-term exposure. While there is some ambiguity as to the effects of non-violent pornography (see Allen, D'Alessio, & Brezgel, 1995; Linz, 1989), conclusive support was found for the adverse impact of violent pornography on rape-supportive attitudes.

The sociocultural view outlines conditions that impinge on the members of a particular society and create a platform for the development of rape-supportive attitudes and sexual scripts. It seeks to explain how socially shared conceptions such as rape myths and gender stereotypes of male dominance and female subordination are fed into the socialisation experiences of individual members of the society. Clearly, not all men exposed to the same sociostructural influences turn into sexual aggressors. Why it is that some men seem to be more strongly affected by those influences than others is a question addressed by individual difference approaches considered later in this section.

The sociobiological approach. At the core of the sociobiological approach is the assumption that the male propensity to use force in order to obtain sexual contacts has evolved in the course of the development of the human species. The general rationale of the sociobiological approach to human aggression was outlined in Chapter 2. The question guiding the evolutionary analysis of social behaviour refers to the *function* that a particular behaviour has for the survival of an individual member of a species and/or for the species as a whole. With regard to sexual aggression, the answer to this question has been that for some men and under certain circumstances rape may be an adaptive strategy that enhances the genetic "fitness" of the aggressor, i.e., increases his chances of passing on his genes to future generations. A less prominent variant of the sociobiologist approach is the idea that sexual aggression has evolved as a by-product of a strong male sex drive—rather than being an adaptive mechanism to enhance reproductive fitness.

The mainstream sociobiological argument holds that rape is a facultative form of sexual behaviour that enhances the reproductive fitness of those men who have difficulties securing the transmission of their genes through non-aggressive means. Such reproductive disadvantage may result from low status, lack of financial resources, or lack of physical attractiveness, which makes these men undesirable mating partners (Thornhill & Thornhill, 1991; see Thornhill & Palmer, 2000, for a recent much-debated presentation of the sociobiological argument). According to this view, rape is a potential option in the reproductive behaviour of all men. However, it represents a high-cost mating strategy because most societies impose sanctions on sexually aggressive behaviour, such as prison sentences and social stigma, which ultimately restrict a man's reproductive opportunities even further. Moreover, the chances of conception from a single sexual act are low compared to repeated sexual contacts with a consenting partner. Therefore, sexual aggression will be used only if less risky options are not available.

To support this evolutionary hypothesis, two main data sources are quoted: (1) findings from animal studies provide observational data on forced copulation in various species (such as the panorpa fly and the elephant seal). Harding (1985) and Ellis (1989) list a number of studies demonstrating that forced copulation is part of the reproductive repertoire of several animal species. (2) A second data source drawn upon by sociobiologists is that of statistical reports on the prevalence of rape in different demographic groups. For example, the over-representation of women of reproductive age among victims and of low-status men among perpetrators is quoted in support of the sociobiological model (Shields & Shields, 1983).

However, both data sources are limited in terms of promoting the understanding of human sexual aggression. As noted by Harding (1985), the operational definition of what constitutes rape in animal behaviour is inconsistent across studies. In addition, the very use of the term of rape, which implies constructs such as "without consent" or "against the female's will", to describe animal behaviour is problematic. Relying on statistical information about rape prevalence is inconclusive because these sources represent a distorted picture of the true prevalence of sexual aggression. For example, the fact that low-status men and men from ethnic minorities feature more prominently in official statistics on sexual violence than high-status or majority group members of society may reflect the operation of social class stereotyping and ethnic bias as much as they may be a result of evolutionary processes (see Lenington, 1985; Sunday & Tobach, 1985, for detailed criticisms of the sociobiological approach).

Furthermore, the "mate deprivation hypothesis" arguing that rape is a reproductive strategy adopted by men barred from consensual sexual contacts is contradicted by the consistent finding that sexually aggressive men are more sexually active in terms of taking up sexual activity at an earlier age and having a greater number of sexual partners (e.g., Kanin, 1985; Malamuth, Sockloskie, Koss, & Tanaka, 1991). If anything, this finding is more compatible with the notion of rape as a by-product of male reproductive fitness.

Finally, the sociobiological approach fails to account for several manifestations of sexual aggression which, taken together, are too widespread to be dismissed as marginal: sexual assault on children, on post-menopausal women, on men, and on individuals genetically related to the assailant. None of these forms of sexual aggression are functional in enhancing the reproductive fitness of the aggressor.

While the sociocultural approach emphasises "proximate" causes of sexual aggression affecting members of a given society, the sociobiological approach claims to elucidate its "ultimate" causes going back to the evolutionary history of the human species. Both approaches are limited to explaining heterosexual aggression by male perpetrators against female victims, which is without doubt the most prevalent form of sexual aggression. However, the reality of male-on-male sexual aggression and the fact that women use aggressive strategies against male victims cannot be denied.

Individual-level explanations

The sociocultural approach and the sociobiological approach outline general conditions that promote sexual aggression. In order to understand why only some members of the species or of a given society perform sexually aggressive behaviours, different types of models are required that focus on sexually aggressive and non-aggressive individuals and try to identify variables that are able to differentiate between aggressors and non-aggressors. Hall and Hirschman (1991) proposed a complex model in which sexually aggressive men are supposed to differ from non-aggressive men with regard to four central aspects: (a) the extent to which they are physiologically aroused by sexual stimuli; (b) the way they perceive and process stimuli pertinent to sexual behaviour in general and sexual aggression in particular; (c) the extent to which they are able to control their affective responses; and (d) their socialisation experiences and personality characteristics. These aspects may be used as a framework for summarising the available evidence on individual differences in sexual aggression.

Physiological arousal. Several studies looked for differences between known sexual aggressors and non-aggressive comparison groups in terms of sexual arousal following sexually explicit stimuli (Barbaree & Marshall, 1991). Sexual arousal is typically measured by phallometry, which indicates changes in penile erection following exposure to sexual stimuli. Two processes have been examined: *stimulus control*, i.e., the extent to which different types of sexual stimuli (consensual versus coercive) elicit different patterns of physiological arousal; and *response control*, i.e., the extent to which sexual arousal can be suppressed in response to sexually aggressive stimuli. In terms of stimulus control, the question is whether sexually aggressive men respond with higher sexual arousal to depictions of coercive as compared to consensual sexual contacts. A meta-analysis by Hall, Shondrick, and Hirschman (1993) suggests an affirmative answer to this question. When sexual stimuli are combined with aggressive cues, for instance by exposing respondents to violent pornography, non-aggressive men show a *decrease* in sexual arousal not apparent in the arousal patterns of sexually aggressive men. In terms of response control, sexually aggressive men were less able to deliberately suppress sexual arousal. Moreover, the inability to experience sexual arousal and aggressive arousal simultaneously, characteristic of non-aggressive men, was not found in sexual aggressors. Thus, there are indications that sexual aggressors exhibit distinctive patterns of sexual arousal, most notably in response to sexually aggressive stimuli.

Cognitive processes. Cognitive processes also play an important role in differentiating between sexually aggressive and non-aggressive men. Drieschner and Lange (1999) recently reviewed evidence concerning differences between sexually aggressive and non-aggressive men in terms of a range of cognitive variables. Sexually aggressive men were found to show higher acceptance of rape myths, to be more likely to attribute blame to victims of sexual assault, and to endorse right-wing authoritarian attitudes (see also Bohner et al., 1998). They also display more hostile attitudes towards women and greater acceptance of violence in interpersonal relationships. Moreover, sexually aggressive men are more likely to misperceive women's friendly behaviour as sexually suggestive (Abbey, 1991; McDonel & McFall, 1991). A study by Bargh, Raymond, Pryor, and Strack (1995) suggests that sexual aggressors have developed a cognitive association between sex and power that is not apparent in non-aggressors. They conducted two reaction time experiments in which men high or low on rape proclivity (i.e., self-reported likelihood of raping a woman if certain not to be caught and punished; Malamuth, 1981) were exposed to subliminal prime words that referred to power or sex or were neutral with regard to the two domains. They then had to pronounce a target word that was either sex related or power related or neutral. Shorter reaction times in pronouncing a sex-related word following the presentation of a power-related prime (compared to reaction times for neutral words following a power-related prime or for sex-related words following a neutral prime) were taken as an indication of an automatic cognitive association of power and sex. As predicted by the authors, such shorter reaction times for the power-prime/sex-target combination were only found for respondents who scored high on rape proclivity.

Lack of impulse control. Sexually aggressive men frequently display strong feelings of hostility and anger towards women (Lisak & Roth, 1990). The stronger these negative feelings, the greater the likelihood that they will override inhibitory factors against sexual aggression, such as moral standards or fear of sanctions. According to Kanin (1985), sexual frustration resulting from exaggerated, "hypersexual" needs is a primary cause of date rape. Lack of impulse control leads to spontaneous and particularly violent sexual assaults, and it is also seen as playing a role in sexual transgressions against children (Browne, 1994).

Socialisation experiences and personality traits. In the search for variables that predict sexual aggression, particular attention has been paid to adverse childhood experiences. Childhood experiences of abuse and the quality of the parent–child relationship have been examined most thoroughly in this line of research. Several studies demonstrate that victims of childhood sexual abuse are over-represented among sexually aggressive men (Hall & Hirschman, 1991). Negative relationships with the parents, in particular with the father, are also linked to an increased likelihood of subsequent sexual aggression (Lisak, 1994). Furthermore, negative family relationships are seen to be at the root of social isolation, social skills deficits, and a general tendency towards delinquency characteristic of many sexual aggressors (Blaske et al., 1989; Marshall, 1989).

Several authors have proposed typologies capturing differences between sexual aggressors in terms of their pathways into sexual aggression, the processes triggering their sexually aggressive behaviour, and their predominant *modus operandi*. Such typological classifications of sexually aggressive men, if empirically supported, would be useful for assessing the risk of recidivism and selecting appropriate treatment approaches. For example, Prentky and Knight (1991) suggest a broad distinction between sexual aggressors who are motivated by sexual desire and those who are motivated by hostility towards women or show sexual aggression as part of a general pattern of antisocial behaviour. Seto and Barbaree (1997) differentiate between persistent and opportunistic sexual aggressors. Persistent sexual aggressors show an early onset and long-term persistence of a range of antisocial behaviours, of which sexual aggression is just one facet. In contrast, opportunistic sexual aggressors exhibit sexual aggression in the absence of other deviant behaviours, predominantly against easily accessible targets, such as acquaintances and dating partners, and only during adolescence and early adulthood. Persistent sexual aggressors are assumed to be more likely to use force, whereas opportunistic aggressors are considered more likely to use verbal pressure or intoxication of their victim as coercive strategies. One of the most elaborate and well-tested typological models is the "confluence model" presented by Malamuth and co-workers (Malamuth, 1998; Malamuth et al., 1991). This model seeks to recon-cile the evolutionary explanation of sexual aggression in terms of the reproductive advantage of having high numbers of sexual contacts and the feminist account of sexual aggression as an expression of male dominance. The confluence model is presented in Figure 8.2.

Two pathways are described in the confluence model as leading to sexual aggression: a promiscuous/impersonal sexual orientation, which induces men to seek as many sexual contacts as possible without forming a personal relationship with the sexual partner; and an orientation of hostile masculinity in which the motivation for

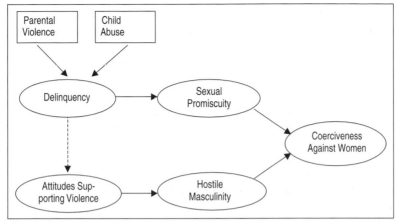

FIG. 8.2. Malamuth's "confluence model" of sexual aggression (adapted with permission from Malamuth, 1998, p. 535).

sexual aggression lies in the desire to hurt and dominate women. Either path may lead to sexual aggression independently, but the model assumes that the probability of sexual aggression is higher in men who are both promiscuous and hostile towards women. In a large-scale study involving 3000 men, the two paths differentiated well between aggressive and non-aggressive men, explaining 78% of the variance in coerciveness against women (Malamuth et al., 1991). In terms of discriminant validity, men who were sexually aggressive against women showed elevated levels of both sexual promiscuity and hostile masculinity, whereas men who showed physical aggression against women only scored higher on hostile masculinity and not on sexual promiscuity. Furthermore, a longitudinal study by Malamuth et al. (1995) showed that the two paths predicted sexual aggression across an interval of 10 years. The confluence model also specifies antecedent conditions that are assumed to promote a promiscuous orientation and hostile masculinity. Sexual promiscuity is seen as deriving from a general tendency towards delinquent behaviour, which is in turn promoted by childhood experiences of harsh parental punishment and abuse. In contrast, hostile masculinity is influenced by attitudes supporting the use of violence, including rape myth acceptance.

In addition to the relatively stable differences between aggressors and non-aggressors, situational factors have been identified as micro-level influences affecting sexual aggression. A powerful situational precipitator of sexual aggression is alcohol consumption. As we saw in Chapter 4, alcohol is generally associated with a greater likelihood of aggression, and sexual aggression is part of this general pattern. A large proportion of sexual assaults take place under the influence of alcohol, and alcohol consumption is a reliable predictor of sexual aggression. Moreover, the reduction in information-processing capacities induced by alcohol consumption ("alcohol myopia") makes it more likely for men to misperceive women's sexual intentions. Abbey et al. (1998) showed that alcohol consumption affected sexual aggression both directly and indirectly through its effect on the misperception of sexual intent.

The present section has shown that men who are sexually aggressive differ from non-aggressive men in systematic and predictable ways. The available evidence provides a basis for identifying groups of men particularly susceptible to sexual aggression and may ultimately prove useful for prevention and intervention.

Risk factors of sexual victimisation

To complement the evidence on factors that put men at risk of committing acts of sexual aggression, a number of recent studies have been concerned with identifying risk factors of *sexual victimisation* on the part of women. It is important to note that this research is directed at identifying variables linked to an increased risk of victimisation without thereby suggesting in any way that the victim herself might be to blame. Rather than implying victim blame, accumulating evidence on risk factors of victimisation may help women to develop a realistic perception of potentially dangerous situations and behaviours and to protect themselves against sexual victimisation.

Evidence is available to date concerning two groups of risk factors of sexual victimisation: behavioural variables and biographical experiences. For both sets of variables, remarkably consistent findings have emerged across a range of studies. Among the behavioural variables, level of sexual activity (defined by age of onset of sexual activity and number of sexual partners), alcohol consumption in the context of sexual encounters, and the ambiguous communication of sexual intentions have been identified as risk factors of sexual victimisation.

High levels of sexual activity put women at risk of sexual victimisation because they entail an increased likelihood of encountering aggressive men. Abbey et al. (1996) found that both lifetime number of sexual partners and number of times a woman had consensual sex discriminated between victims and non-victims of sexual coercion as well as attempted or completed rape. In Gidycz, Hanson, and

Layman's (1995) prospective study, number of sexual partners at initial assessment was significantly related to victimisation in the subsequent 3 months. In another longitudinal study, Himelein (1995) used a combined index of consensual sexual activity, which comprised both age at first intercourse and number of partners. She found that high scores on this index were associated with an increased risk of sexual victimisation over a period of 32 months. In addition, the importance of sexual activity as a risk factor of sexual victimisation has been supported by many other studies (e.g., Gidycz et al., 1993; Mandoki & Burkhart, 1989; Miller et al., 1995; Testa & Dermen, 1999; Tyler et al., 1998; Vicary, Klingaman, & Harkness, 1995; Wyatt, Newcomb, & Riederle, 1993). Alcohol consumption is the second behavioural factor consistently associated with an increased likelihood of sexual victimisation. Several studies show that alcohol consumption generally, alcohol consumption in connection with consensual sex, and intoxication in the situation of the sexual assault each contributed to the prediction of sexual victimisation (Abbey et al., 1996; Testa & Dermen, 1999; Tyler et al., 1998). The strongest influence was found for the most proximal involvement of alcohol, i.e., pre-assault alcohol consumption (Ullman et al., 1999). One way in which alcohol affects the risk of victimisation is by impairing the victim's judgement of potentially dangerous behaviour by the perpetrator. In addition, a woman's consumption of alcohol may be misperceived by men as a sexual cue: A woman's friendliness is more likely to be interpreted as sexual intent when she has been drinking alcohol than when she has not been drinking (Abbey et al., 1996).

Finally, the ambiguous communication of sexual intentions was found to be a risky strategy with regard to sexual victimisation. In particular, this is true for "token resistance", i.e., the apparent rejection of sexual advances despite being willing to engage in sexual contacts ("saying 'no' when you mean 'yes'"; Muehlenhard & Hollabaugh, 1988). Several studies showed (a) that more than a third of men and women report the use of token resistance (e.g., Sprecher et al., 1994), and (b) women who use token resistance are more likely to report sexual victimisation (Krahé, 1998; Krahé, Scheinberger-Olwig, & Kolpin, 2000; Shotland & Hunter, 1995). Muehlenhard and Hollabaugh (1988) argued that token resistance is likely to imply negative consequences: it discourages honest communication, it makes women appear manipulative, and it encourages men to ignore women's refusals.

Among the biographical experiences linked to sexual victimisation, sexual abuse in childhood stands out consistently as a risk factor of subsequent revictimisation (see Krahé, 2000a; and Messman & Long, 1996, for reviews). Support for the revictimisation hypothesis from the literature on childhood sexual abuse was reviewed in some detail in Chapter 7. This evidence is corroborated by studies concerned with adolescent and adult sexual victimisation that look at childhood abuse as a potential antecedent (e.g., Gidycz et al., 1993, 1995; Krahé, Scheinberger-Olwig, Waizenhöfer, & Kolpin, 1999) and by evidence for revictimisation among homosexual men (Krahé, Scheinberger-Olwig, & Schütze, in press).

In addition, several authors have claimed that other adverse childhood experiences, such as physical abuse and emotional neglect, are also associated with an increased risk of subsequent sexual victimisation (e.g., Becker-Lausen, Sanders, & Chinsky, 1995; Moeller, Bachmann, & Moeller, 1993; Mullen et al., 1993). Sanders and Moore (1999) showed that date rape victims had significantly higher scores on a measure of negative home environment and neglect than a non-victimised control group, even though no corresponding difference was found with respect to sexual abuse in childhood. Furthermore, Schaaf and McCanne (1998) reported that sexual victimisation in adults with a history of childhood physical abuse was higher than for adults with a history of sexual abuse. These findings suggest that the search for childhood-based risk factors of sexual victimisation in adolescence and adulthood should look beyond sexual abuse to include physical abuse, emotional neglect, and other indicators of poor family environment to identify individuals at risk of revictimisation.

Addressing the question of how childhood abuse paves the way for subsequent sexual victimisation, abuse victims were found to have different patterns of adolescent and adult sexual behaviour compared to non-abused individuals. In particular—and perhaps counterintuitively—victims of childhood sexual abuse were shown to be more sexually active in terms of earlier onset of sexual activity and greater number of sexual partners (e.g., Chandy et al., 1996; Mayall & Gold, 1995; Vicary et al., 1995). Given the link between high sexual activity and sexual victimisation described earlier in this section, abuse victims' higher levels of sexual activity may be seen as a mediator of the link between childhood abuse and later revictimisation.

In terms of the prevention of sexual victimisation, the findings discussed in this section may serve two important purposes. First, evidence suggesting that behaviours such as high sexual activity and alcohol consumption are associated with an increased risk of victimisation can be incorporated into rape awareness programmes enabling women to make informed behavioural choices. Second, the evidence on revictimisation points to victims of childhood abuse as a particular risk group for subsequent victimisation that should be specifically targeted by rape prevention programmes.

Consequences of sexual victimisation

Becoming the victim of a sexual assault is a devastating experience. Many rape victims show symptoms that meet the defining criteria of "post-traumatic stress disorder" (PTSD; Resnick, Kilpatrick, & Lipovsky, 1991). Burgess and Holmstrom (1985) introduced the concept of "rape trauma syndrome" to describe a pattern of psychological and physical symptoms characteristic of victims of sexual assault. The rape trauma syndrome comprises three stages which have been well documented in victims' responses to rape: (1) an *acute phase* immediately following the assault, in which victims are plagued by intense fear, shame, and often guilt about having finally succumbed to the assailant; (2) a phase of *superficial readjustment* in which victims adjust their daily lives to the experience of assault, e.g., by increasing security measures in their homes, moving to a different area, or no longer going out on their own. Trying to deny the assault experience to themselves and others, victims in this phase appear relatively unaffected. At the same time, feelings of vulnerability prevail, and many victims find it difficult to resume sexual relationships and settle back into everyday routines; (3) a phase of *long-term readjustment*, which enables the victim to gradually overcome the fear, depression, and anger elicited by the assault. According to several studies, the psychological aftermath of sexual assault persists over extended periods of time, often over years rather than months, and affects the victim in many domains of psychological functioning, such as partnership, work, and leisure activities (Koss & Harvey, 1991).

In the process of coping with sexual victimisation, many victims require therapeutic help. Such help is available both in the form of short-term crisis intervention, e.g., through rape help lines, and in terms of extended psychotherapy. Therapeutic interventions for victims of sexual assault are described by Calhoun and Atkeson (1991), Koss and Harvey (1991), and Resick and Schnicke (1993).

Several factors have been identified that impede the process of coping with sexual assault. One such impeding factor is the extent to which victims blame themselves for their victimisation (Arata &

TABLE 8.2

The role of victims' self-blame in coping with sexual victimisation

	Asymptomatic victims	Symptomatic victims
Characterological self-blame*	−8.17	−1.92
Behavioural self-blame*	1.60	3.24
Societal blame	−3.00	−0.08

Scores could range from −18 to +18. Negative scores indicate rejection of blame, positive scores indicate endorsement of blame.

* $p < .05$.

Based on Arata and Burkhart (1998, p. 232).

Burkhart, 1998; Frazier, 1990; Meyer & Taylor, 1986). Arata and Burkhart studied victims who showed severe psychological symptoms following sexual victimisation and victims who did not show any symptoms, and compared them with regard to their attributions of characterological self-blame, behavioural self-blame, and societal blame. Characterological self-blame measures the extent to which victims regard aspects of their personalities as having contributed to the fact that they were assaulted. Behavioural blame refers to aspects of the victim's behaviour she feels have facilitated the assault. Societal blame refers to the role of society in allowing sexual violence to happen. The main findings from this study are presented in Table 8.2.

Table 8.2 shows that victims in the symptomatic group, who showed severe psychological adjustment problems, were significantly more likely to accept characterological self-blame and behavioural blame than victims who had adjusted better to the assault. No difference was found between the two victim groups in terms of attributing societal blame.

In addition to self-blame, other factors have been identified as preventing victims from coping with the assault. Women who were sexually abused in childhood (Arata, 1999) and who experienced negative responses of important others following the assault (Davis, Brickman, & Baker, 1991) find it more difficult to cope with sexual victimisation. No difference was found in coping with sexual victimisation between victims of stranger versus acquaintance rape (Koss, Dinero, Seibel, & Cox, 1988).

Beyond the impact of the assault itself, victims have to come to terms with the responses of their social environment, often perceived as a form of *second assault*. Women who decide to report the assault to the police often complain about unsympathetic treatment and feel they are treated with suspicion or disbelief (e.g., Temkin, 1999). Women who do not report their assault to the police still have to face the responses of partners, friends, or colleagues. These responses often contain doubts about the victim's causal role in the attack, suggesting some degree of victim precipitation and, accordingly, blame. The tendency to attribute blame to victims of sexual aggression has been studied widely (see Krahé, 1991; and Pollard, 1992, for reviews). It was shown that certain victim characteristics, such as low social status, higher number of sexual partners, and pre-rape behaviour that is at odds with female role requirements, are linked with higher attributions of responsibility to the victim (and often with correspondingly lower responsibility attributions to the attacker). At the same time, individual differences between observers have been found in the sense that individuals with a more traditional sex role orientation or with a greater rape myth acceptance assign more responsibility to victims of rape (Anderson, Cooper, & Okamura, 1997; Lonsway & Fitzgerald, 1994).

Sexually aggressive women

As a recent addition to the agenda of sexual aggression research, several authors have begun to explore the prevalence, antecedents, and consequences of women's sexual aggression against men (Anderson & Struckman-Johnson, 1998). Whether or not women's sexual aggression needs to and should be investigated as part of the psychological study of sexual aggression has been a controversial issue, particularly among feminist researchers. A balanced assessment of the benefits and potential drawbacks of devoting greater attention to sexually aggressive women and male victims is provided by Muehlenhard (1998). She sees the study of women's sexual aggression as important to avoid research bias, to challenge gender stereotypes and to acknowledge the reality of men's victimisation experiences. At the same time, she warns about taking a gender-neutral approach, arguing that sexual violence is not a gender-neutral problem. Victim and perpetrator roles are not evenly distributed between men and women. Moreover, as we shall see, men and women differ with regard to the coercive strategies they predominantly use, the types of coercion they are subjected to by their assailants, and the extent to which they are traumatised by the experience of victimisation.

Even though prevalence rates for male sexual victimisation by women are consistently lower than rates of female victimisation by men, they are still of a magnitude that must be taken seriously. Evidence is available from men's report of victimisation and from women's reports of the commitment of sexually aggressive behaviour (see Byers & O'Sullivan, 1998, for a comprehensive summary of available studies). Surveying a sample of over 3000 Los Angeles residents, Sorenson et al. (1987) found prevalence rates of adult sexual victimisation of 9.4% for men and 16.7% for women. A greater proportion of assaulted men were victimised by friends, compared to women, who were more likely to have experienced stranger assault. In a study by Poppen and Segal (1988), 14% of women (compared to 56% of men) reported committing sexually aggressive acts; 44% of men reported victimisation (compared to 74% of women). Struck-man-Johnson (1988) found that 16% of men and 22% of women reported sexual victimisation by a dating partner, and that 2% of women, compared with 10% of men, had perpetrated sexual aggression. In a subsequent interview study with men, 34% reported at least one incident of sexual victimisation since the age of 16 (Struckman-Johnson and Struckman-Johnson, 1994). Again, sexual assaults by acquaintances or intimate friends were far more frequent (77%) than assaults by strangers (7%). Finally, Larimer, Lydum, Anderson, and Turner (1999) found that 20.7% of men—compared to 27.5% of women—reported experiences of unwanted sexual contacts during the year prior to the survey. The substantial variation in female sexual aggression and male sexual victimisation across different studies is due in large part to differences in methodology and in the operational definition of sexual aggression. Nevertheless, the findings show that women's sexual aggression occurs, and does so at a rate that warrants closer research attention. Moreover, the difference between male and female victimisation rates shows a high degree of consistency across studies.

Looking at specific coercive tactics used by men and women, consistent gender differences emerge. Women are more likely than men to use verbal pressure to coerce a man into sexual activities, whereas men are more likely than women to use physical force. In Anderson's (1996) study, 28.5% of women showed verbal coercion, and 7.1% reported use or threat of physical force (see also Larimer et al., 1999; Poppen & Segal, 1988; Struckman-Johnson, 1988; Struck-man-Johnson & Struckman-Johnson, 1994). Moreover, Waldner-Haugrud and Magruder (1995) showed that male and female victim-isation differed with regard to the sexual acts in which the victims were made to engage. When men reported sexual victimisation, they were more likely to have experienced kissing or unwanted touch than penetrative sex.

As to the risk factors of female sexual aggression, parallels have been found to male sexual aggression. Research on women sexually aggressive towards adult men and on female child molesters shows that prior victimisation and deviant sexual arousal are more common among sexually aggressive than among non-aggressive women (Anderson, 1996; Green, 1999). In addition, alcohol consumption was shown to be a risk factor of male sexual victimisation in the same way as it was shown for female victims (Larimer et al., 1999), and ambiguous communication of sexual intentions was found to be related to an increased risk of male victimisation by Krahé (2000c).

In terms of the consequences of sexual victimisation, it seems that men are less adversely affected than women. In Struckman-Johnson's (1988) sample, only 27% of the male victims said they had felt "bad" or "very bad" about the experience, while the corresponding figure for female victims was 88%. A subsequent study including only male respondents confirmed the finding that men generally do not report strong negative reactions following sexual coercion by a woman (Struckman-Johnson & Struckman-Johnson, 1994; see also Krahé, in prep.). However, it would be premature to conclude from these findings that male victims are genuinely less affected by sexual assault than female victims. For one, evidence that men are left severely traumatised by the experience of sexual victimisation can be found in the literature (e.g., Sarrel & Masters, 1982). Moreover, the possibility must be considered that men may be reluctant to admit a negative impact of being sexually assaulted by a woman, which would be tantamount to acknowledging their vulnerability. Sarrel and Masters (1982, p. 121) quote one of their male victims who was terrified that if his friends found out about his "disgrace" they would think him "less than a man" because he had been "raped by a woman". Parallel tendencies of denying the trauma of sexual assault in male victims were found in research with sexually abused boys (e.g., Friedrich, Berliner, Urquiza, & Beilke, 1988). Current evidence on the adverse effects of sexual victimisation on men rests entirely on self-reports of the extent to which the incident was experienced as aversive. In order to clarify whether these responses reflect a genuine lack of impact or the unwillingness to acknowledge a negative impact, self-reports must be complemented by other indicators of distress, such as physical and psychological symptoms.

Summary

- Legal definitions of sexual assault specify those forms of sexual aggression which constitute criminal offences (such as rape and attempted rape), whereas research definitions cover a wider range of coercive strategies as well as sexual acts. In everyday discourse, sexual assault is defined primarily in terms of the "real rape stereotype", characterising rape as an attack by a stranger who uses physical violence to force the victim into sexual acts.

- Prevalence studies demonstrate that sexual assault is a widespread problem. Crime statistics, reflecting only reported cases, seriously under-represent the true scale of women's sexual victimisation, as evidenced in much higher prevalence rates established in surveys of victims and perpetrators. The majority of sexual assaults is committed by perpetrators known to the victims, such as acquaintances, dating partners, and spouses, contradicting the real rape stereotype, which designates stranger rape as the prototypical form of sexual assault.

- One group of causal explanations of sexual aggression refers to macro-level processes, such as sociocultural patterns of male–female power relationships or the evolution of sexual aggression as a strategy enhancing male reproductive fitness. A second group concentrates on individual-level mechanisms in the perpetrator. Sexual aggressors were found to differ from non-aggressors in terms of sexual arousal patterns, rape-supportive attitudes, lack of impulse control, and childhood experience of violence and poor parent–child relationships.

- Without questioning that the responsibility for sexual aggression lies with the attacker, one line of research has identified risk factors associated with an increased likelihood of sexual victimisation for women. High levels of sexual activity, alcohol consumption in the context of sexual encounters, and the ambiguous communication of sexual intentions were shown to be behavioural risk factors of sexual victimisation. In addition, there is consistent evidence that childhood experiences of sexual abuse are linked to an increased risk of subsequent revictimisation.

- Sexual victimisation has a profoundly negative impact on most victims. A "rape trauma syndrome" has been acknowledged as a special form of post-traumatic stress response frequently observed in victims of sexual assault. Victims who blame themselves for being assaulted have greater problems coping with the assault. Moreover, responses by others to the disclosure of the assault are often experienced as a "second assault", reflecting victim-derogatory attitudes widely shared by laypersons, police, and legal professionals.

- It has been documented that women also commit sexually aggressive behaviour against male victims, albeit with lower prevalence rates. Female sexual aggressors differ from male assailants in their use of verbal pressure rather than physical force as the predominant coercive strategy. Most men are victimised by women they know. Even though the evidence shows that men rate their victimisation experiences as less distressing than women, this does not necessarily mean they are less affected. Acknowledging that he has been sexually victimised by a woman may be highly damaging to a man's self-esteem, undermining his sense of masculinity and making him reluctant to describe the experience as distressing.

Suggested reading

Anderson, P.B., & Struckman-Johnson, C. (Eds.) (1998). *Sexually aggressive women*. New York: Guilford Press.

Krahé, B., Schütze, S., Fritsche, I., & Waizenhöfer, E. (2000). The prevalence of sexual aggression and victimization among homosexual men. *Journal of Sex Research, 37*, 142–150.

Malamuth, N.M. (1998). The confluence model as an organizing framework for research on sexually aggressive men: Risk moderators, imagined aggression, and pornography consumption. In R.G. Geen & E. Donnerstein (Eds.), *Human aggression: Theories, research and implications for social policy* (pp. 229–245). San Diego, CA: Academic Press.

White, J.W., & Kowalski, R.M. (1998). Male violence toward women: An integrated perspective. In R.G. Geen & E. Donnerstein (Eds.), *Human aggression: Theories, research and implications for social policy* (pp. 203–228). San Diego, CA: Academic Press.

Controlling and preventing aggressive behaviour 9

In the course of the preceding chapters, is has become abundantly clear that aggressive behaviour occurs on a grand scale in many areas of social life and brings misery and suffering to large numbers of victims and their families. Therefore, exploring effective ways of preventing and reducing aggressive behaviour is a pressing task for psychological research on aggression. Unfortunately, the development of strategies to prevent aggression is hampered by the fact that the causes and moderating variables leading to the manifestation of aggressive behaviour are still far from being fully understood. As long as our knowledge is limited as to why and when aggressive behaviour occurs and to what extent different forms of aggressive behaviours share the same underlying mechanisms, interventions directed at the roots rather than the symptoms will be difficult.

As Lore and Schultz (1993) point out, another fundamental obstacle impeding the development of effective strategies for dealing with aggression is a public attitude that all too readily accepts aggression and violence as inherent and inevitable features of human nature. These authors argue that by resigning to the inevitability of aggression, the potential contribution of research on aggression to the development of intervention strategies remains unrealised. They quote evidence from animal studies and behavioural observations of children to support their claim that aggressive behaviour shows high variability within the individual across situations and settings. This variability demonstrates, as Lore and Schultz point out, that aggression is not an inevitable, but an optional strategy for humans, which should lead researchers as well as political decision-makers to devote greater attention to the mechanisms by which the inhibitory forces against aggression can be strengthened.

In the present chapter, a range of approaches will be presented that are designed to tackle the problem of reducing aggression and violence. Some of these approaches are general in nature in that they specify mechanisms that are potentially applicable to diverse forms of aggressive behaviour. Other approaches are domain specific, addressing particular forms of aggressive behaviour. Flannery and Williams (1999) refer to this distinction as *universal* versus *targeted* approaches. The first section of the present chapter is devoted to a review of universal approaches to the prevention of aggression. The potential effectiveness of catharsis, punishment, and anger management training are examined as approaches targeting the individual aggressor. Furthermore, societal responses to aggression, including legal regulations and community-based interventions, are considered in terms of their potential in reducing the scale of aggressive behaviour. The second part of the chapter is devoted to strategies of prevention and intervention targeting particular forms of aggression: bullying and gang violence, domestic violence, and sexual aggression. While drawing upon general principles of aggression reduction, intervention strategies in these areas are custom tailored to address the unique characteristics of different forms of aggression.

General strategies for reducing aggression

Assumptions about the processes and mechanisms by which aggressive behaviour is elicited are an integral part of theories seeking to explain aggression (see Chapter 2). These assumptions can also be used for conceptualising strategies for preventing and modifying aggressive behaviour. For example, the view that aggression is the result of anger arousal points to the potential effectiveness of programmes aimed at promoting anger control. Explaining aggression as a response to aggressive situational cues suggests that limiting the availability of firearms and violent media contents may be effective in reducing aggression. In the present section, general prevention strategies such as these are discussed that are applicable to a range of aggressive behaviours. We begin by looking at strategies targeting the individual and then move on to measures implemented at the community or societal level.

Measures directed at the individual

Aggressive behaviour is ultimately performed by individual actors. Therefore, the majority of intervention efforts are directed at reducing the probability that individuals will show aggressive behaviour. Three main mechanisms have been explored by which aggressive behaviour may be prevented: catharsis, punishment, and anger management.

Catharsis. According to a widely accepted notion, bottling up one's aggressive feelings leads to problems of adjustment, carrying the risk of uncontrolled outbursts of aggression. This idea of *catharsis*, endorsed by both Freud (1920) and Lorenz (1974), suggests that the ventilation of hostile feelings can lead to a discharge of aggressive impulses that temporarily reduces the likelihood of aggressive behaviour (see Chapter 2). A more general version of the catharsis hypothesis claims that any expression of aggressive feelings reduces the likelihood of subsequent aggression.

However, empirical evidence on the effectiveness of catharsis shows it is not just ineffective but even counterproductive for reducing aggression (Baron & Richardson, 1994). Several studies indicate that the imaginary performance of aggressive behaviour, such as in pretend play or aggressive games, is more likely to enhance aggression than to reduce it. The same is true for the effects of watching violent actions in the media (see Berkowitz, 1993). In a recent test of the catharsis hypothesis, Bushman, Baumeister, and Stack (1999) exposed their respondents to either a pro-catharsis message (advocating attacking an inanimate object to release aggressive tension) or an anti-catharsis message (arguing against the effectiveness of such behaviour and recommending relaxation techniques). Following the message, respondents had to write an essay, and anger was induced in half of the respondents by an allegedly negative feedback on their essays. In the final part of the experiment, respondents were presented with a list of activities, one of which they were asked to choose for performance later in the experiment. Among the list of activities was "hitting a punching bag", which represented the critical dependent variable. The findings showed that among the angered respondents, those who had read the pro-catharsis message were significantly more likely to choose to hit the punching bag than respondents who had received the anti-catharsis or control messages. No effect of message on preference for hitting the punching bag was found in the non-angered group.

In a follow-up study, Bushman et al. (1999) examined the proposition that engaging in catharsis would enhance rather than reduce respondents' tendencies to behave aggressively towards a human target. As in the previous study, respondents received a pro-catharsis or an anti-catharsis message, wrote an essay, and were angered by negative feedback on their essays. They then either chose to hit the punching bag spontaneously from a list of activities or, if they had failed to do so, were asked by the experimenter whether they would like to hit the bag. In this way, all participants eventually hit the punching bag for 2 minutes. In the final stage of the study, respondents participated in a competitive reaction time task (see Chapter 1), which involved punishing an opponent by aversive blasts of noise if his/her reactions were slower than those of the respondent. Half of the respondents were led to believe that their opponent was the person who had given them negative feedback about their essays, while the other half thought their opponent was a person unrelated to their essay feedback.

As in the previous study, respondents who read the pro-catharsis message expressed a stronger preference for hitting the punching bag than those who had received the anti-catharsis message. More importantly, respondents in the pro-catharsis condition acted more aggressively towards their opponent in the reaction time task by setting more aversive noise levels than those in the anti-catharsis condition. Whether the opponent was responsible for the negative feedback on their essay (direct target) or unrelated to it (displaced target) did not make any difference to the strength of the aggressive response. A significant, albeit small correlation ($r = .11$) was found between enjoyment of hitting the punching bag and subsequent aggression: The more people enjoyed hitting the punching bag, the more aggressive they were later on. Bushman et al. (1999, p. 373) conclude: "Thus, even the people who were led to believe in catharsis failed to show any signs of it." On the contrary, believing and engaging in catharsis increased subsequent aggressive behaviour. It is worth noting that venting aggressive feelings has other detrimental effects beyond enhancing aggressive tendencies. There is evidence to show that acting out anger in interpersonal conflict situations increases the likelihood of high blood pressure and heart disease as well as being more common in the so-called Type A coronary-prone behaviour pattern (e.g., Diamond, 1982; Harburg, Blakelock, & Roeper, 1979; see also Guijarro & Hallet, 1996, for a meta-analysis).

Given the effects of aggressive cues in the cognitive priming of aggression, discussed in Chapter 4, it is not surprising that engaging in imaginary or innocuous forms of aggression or watching others' violent behaviour serves as an instigator for subsequent behavioural aggression. Overt expression of aggression in verbal or physical form has, indeed, been found to reduce negative affective arousal. Yet rather than acting against the subsequent performance of further aggression, the experience that negative feelings can be reduced through aggressive behaviour is likely to promote rather than inhibit future aggression.

Punishment. Explanations of aggression as a result of learning processes stress the role of reinforcement and punishment in regulating the performance of aggressive behaviour. Aggression is thought to be promoted to the extent that actors (or others observed by them) experience positive consequences as a result of their aggressive actions. Conversely, aggressive behaviour followed by adverse consequences, such as punishment, should become less frequent. The effectiveness of punishment as a control mechanism for aggression is viewed with scepticism by most reviewers (e.g., Baron & Richardson, 1994; Berkowitz, 1993). There is general consensus that punishment can only be expected to suppress aggressive behaviour if several conditions are met: (1) Anticipated punishment must be sufficiently adverse; (2) it must have a high probability of being imposed; (3) it can only exert a deterrent function if the individual's negative arousal is not too strong to impede his or her assessment of the severity and likelihood of sanctions and (4) it will only be effective if attractive behavioural alternatives are available to the actor in the situation; (5) finally, actual punishment must follow immediately upon the transgression so that it is perceived as contingent upon the aggressive behaviour.

Apart from the fact that the co-occurrence of these factors is relatively rare, critics have argued that punitive responses are in themselves instances of aggression. As such, they convey the message that the use of aggression is a viable strategy of conflict resolution. Moreover, they are likely to elicit negative affect in the target which, in turn, may instigate further aggressive acts. If punishment is to produce any desirable consequences, it needs to be embedded into a more general approach towards instrumental learning in which the primary aim is to reward desirable rather than penalising undesirable behaviour (e.g., Patterson, Reid, Jones, & Conger, 1975). As stated in the research agenda for reducing violence drawn up by the American Psychological Society (1997, p. 18), "punishment may suppress antisocial behavior briefly, but more lasting behavior modification comes only after alternative ways of coping with social problems are learned." Based on this line of reasoning, programmes directed at preventing aggressive conduct disorders in children have focused on teaching parents non-violent discipline strategies (Coie & Dodge, 1998). *Parent management training* is aimed at teaching parents to interact with their children in a way that reinforces prosocial behaviour. It involves the development of new parenting behaviours, such as providing positive reinforcement for appropriate behaviour, delivering mild forms of punishment and negotiating compromises (Kazdin, 1987). Parent management training was shown in a wide range of studies to be successful in changing children's antisocial behaviour patterns. As Kazdin (1987) notes, improvements were shown to remain stable over long periods after the end of treatment.

Anger management. Compared to catharsis and punishment, approaches aimed at promoting new skills, enabling the individual to engage in behavioural alternatives to aggression, have generally been more successful. Anger and negative affective arousal play a key role in many expressions of aggressive behaviour (see Chapter 2). Therefore, enabling the person to control his or her anger should prove to be effective in reducing hostile aggression. The focus of anger management approaches is on conveying to the aggressive individual "an understandable model of anger and its relationship to triggering events, thoughts, and violent behaviour itself" (Howells, 1989, p. 166). Anger management approaches draw heavily on the principles of cognitive-behavioural therapy, in particular on Meichenbaum's (1975) "stress inoculation training" (SIT), which was adapted to anger management by Novaco (1975). The central features of the anger-related SIT, as summarised by Beck and Fernandez (1998), are presented in Table 9.1.

A meta-analysis of anger management studies based on the stress inoculation approach was conducted by Beck and Fernandez (1998).

TABLE 9.1

The "Stress Inoculation Training" approach to anger management

Phase 1	• Identification of situational triggers that precipitate the onset of the anger response
	• Rehearsal of self-statements intended to reframe the situation and facilitate healthy responses (e.g., I can handle this. It isn't important enough to blow up over this)
Phase 2	• Acquisition of relaxation skills
	• Coupling cognitive self-statements with relaxation after exposure to anger triggers with clients attempting to mentally and physically soothe themselves
Phase 3	• Rehearsal phase
	• Exposure to trigger utilising imagery or role play
	• Practising cognitive and relaxation techniques until the mental and physical responses can be achieved automatically and on cue

Based on Beck and Fernandez (1998, p. 64).

Their analysis included a total of 50 studies, the majority of which used self-reported anger as the dependent variable. The remaining studies used behavioural observation of aggression as the criterion. Forty studies compared differences in anger or aggressive behaviour between an anger management group and a control group, while 10 studies explored intra-individual changes in the critical variable (anger or aggression) from a pre-test to a post-test subsequent to the anger management training. The meta-analysis yielded a large effect size across the set of studies (average weighted $d = .70$), suggesting that anger management is an effective strategy for the reduction of anger-related aggression. In another recent meta-analysis of school-based interventions using cognitive behaviour modification to reduce aggressive behaviour, Robinson, Smith, Miller, and Brownell (1999) supported this finding. They obtained an overall weighted effect size of $d = .64$, demonstrating the effectiveness of the anger management approach with school populations.

However, recent research suggests a less optimistic appraisal of the anger management approach when applied to populations with a history of violence or known to be at high risk for violent action. Studies evaluating anger management training for violent offenders (Watt and Howells, 1999), juvenile male offenders (St. Lawrence et al., 1999) and high-risk adolescents (McWhirter & Page, 1999) failed to support the effectiveness of these interventions.

As Howells (1989) argues, anger management methods can only be expected to work with individuals who are aware of the fact that their aggressive behaviour results from a failure to control their aggressive impulses and who are motivated to change their inadequate handling of these impulses. Moreover, anger control can be improved by training individuals to consider the potential causes and mitigating circumstances for the other person's frustrating or negative behaviour. Here, evidence from several experimental studies shows that aggression can be reduced to the extent that the other's behaviour is interpreted as unavoidable or unintentional.

While anger management strategies require the full cooperation of the individual, a less obvious means of suppressing aggressive behaviour is to induce responses incompatible with the simultaneous performance of aggressive acts (Tyson, 1998). *Empathy* with the target of an aggressive act may lead to a reduction in aggression, provided that the aggressor is not emotionally aroused to an extent that he or she perceives the victim's suffering as a positive reinforcement. Similarly, inducing *humour* may block aggressive tendencies, unless the humorous material itself contains aggressive or hostile cues.

Finally, *mild sexual arousal* seems to generate an affective state which is incompatible with the expression of aggressive impulses (Baron & Bell, 1977). However, each of these effects is restricted to the immediate context and will not result in decreased aggression over time and across situations.

Observational learning. Exposure to non-violent role models is directed at the acquisition of new behavioural repertoires by which aggressive response patterns can be replaced in a more lasting way. Observing people behaving in a non-aggressive fashion has been found to decrease the performance of aggressive acts in the observers (Baron & Richardson, 1994). However, as Eron (1986) points out with respect to role models on the TV screen, the mere observation of non-aggressive models is less effective in changing aggressive response patterns than an integrated approach in which observation is combined with strategies for implementing the observed behaviour, such as role playing and performance feedback.

Societal-level approaches

Every society is under the obligation to offer its members the best possible protection against aggression and violence. Despite the fact that aggressive behaviour must ultimately be changed at the level of the individual, the societal norms and practices to which people are exposed can have a profound effect on the scale of aggression displayed by individual members. A case in point is the relationship between the availability of pornographic material and sexual violence rates identified by Scott and Schwalm (1988). In Chapter 5, we discussed media initiatives limiting the extent and accessibility of violent programming in an attempt to reduce aggression in viewers. However, the self-regulation efforts by the media industry itself are unlikely to go far enough, given that violent programmes attract large audiences irrespective or rather because of their aggressive content and the aim of protecting viewers from high levels of violence clashes with economic interests. Therefore, it is important that independent bodies, operating on a well-defined legal basis, take charge of controlling the availability of violent media contents.

From an ecological perspective, Goldstein (1994b) presents a crime prevention approach based on creating a physical and social environment that restricts the opportunities for aggressive behaviour. Making it harder for the criminal offender to reach his or her target (through physical barriers or access control), controlling facilitators (e.g., banning the sale of alcohol at sports events), implementing formal or informal surveillance systems (e.g., CCTV cameras, neighbourhood watch schemes) and identifying property (e.g., through labels or electronic codes) are measures to reduce criminal opportunity. A crucial question, though, is whether these strategies can reduce the overall level of criminal behaviour or simply lead to a "displacement" of criminal activities towards less protected targets. Fritsch, Caeti, and Taylor (1999) evaluated the effects of policing measures to bring down gang violence. They found that imposing a curfew and truancy enforcement significantly reduced gang violence, whereas merely increasing the presence of police patrols had no effect. A more effective way of preventing aggression may be to remove stressors known to enhance aggressive tendencies via elicitation of negative affect, such as high temperature, noise, and crowded living conditions (see Chapter 4). This could be achieved, for example, by installing air conditioning systems in schools or by reducing spatial density in prisons.

Legal sanctions and gun control legislation

A further important mechanism to control aggression and violence at the societal level is the imposition of legal sanctions. Over and above the penalisation of the individual offender once he or she has committed a criminal act of violence, the punishment of aggressive behaviour is designed to act as a deterrent of further violence. In his detailed review, Berkowitz (1993) concludes that there is little evidence to support the deterrent effect of legal sanctions. While some studies have found a short-term effect of more severe punishment (e.g., Sherman & Berk, 1984), overall support for the deterrence hypothesis is weak.

The role of legal sanctions in preventing violence has received particular attention with respect to the deterrent function of *capital punishment*. Deterrence theory assumes that "preventing crime requires the development of a system of punishment that will teach the lesson that 'crime does not pay'" (Bailey & Peterson, 1999, p. 258). Furthermore, it stipulates that criminal acts are preceded by a rational decision-making process in which the potential offender weighs the presumed benefits of the criminal act against the cost of punishment. With few exceptions, studies examining the deterrent effect of capital punishment on homicides are limited to the United States as the only western nation to retain the death penalty. In this research, reviewed by Bailey and Peterson (1999), two main strategies have been employed: comparing homicide rates between US states with and without capital punishment and comparing homicide rates before and after the abolition of capital punishment within a state. Findings from both paradigms converge to contradict the deterrence hypothesis by failing to find evidence of lower homicide rates in states with capital punishment and increases in states that abolished capital punishment. Further disconfirmation of the deterrence hypothesis comes from findings showing that neither the certainty nor the speed with which the death penalty is imposed was related to homicide rates. Even when enforced swiftly and with high certainty, capital punishment failed to act as a deterrent against future crimes. This was true for different types of murder, including police killings and homicides committed by female perpetrators. In view of this overwhelmingly negative evidence for the deterrent effect of capital punishment, Bailey and Peterson (1999, p. 274) conclude "that policy makers would do well to consider means *other* than capital punishment to significantly reduce the rate of homicide in the United States." This conclusion also sends a clear message to those countries that have abolished capital punishment but in which public opinion calls for its reintroduction at regular intervals following high-profile murder cases.

Another controversial issue with regard to aggression prevention by legal regulations refers to the effectiveness of *gun control legislation*. This issue has been the object of intense controversy between policymakers and representatives of the gun lobby. On the day this paragraph was written, the papers reported an acrimonious attack by the National Rifle Association on US President Clinton's campaign for tighter gun control laws, culminating in the accusation of Clinton lying about the extent to which guns pose a danger to the public (e.g., [Charlton] "Heston accuses Clinton of lying in guns dispute"; *The Independent*, 15 March 2000).

Isolating the effects of gun control legislation from the complex network of variables associated with the role of firearms in American society is an extremely difficult task. Nonetheless, there is considerable consensus on the conclusion that gun control restrictions can reduce the fatal effects of violent assaults (Berkowitz, 1993). Even if gun control legislation does not bring down violence rates, as some authors claim (e.g., Kleck and Patterson, 1993; Kleck & Hogan, 1999), there is clear evidence that it has a positive effect on reducing fatality rates. Cook and Moore (1999) provide a comprehensive review of the evidence showing that gun control reduces the likelihood that violent assaults will lead to lethal consequences. In particular, they quote two lines of evidence, addressing the issues of gun instrumentality and gun availability. In terms of instrumentality, crimes that involve the use of firearms are more likely to lead to the victim's death than instances of the same crime that do not involve a firearm. For example, the fatality rate in robberies in which a firearm is used is three times higher than in robberies involving a knife and 10 times higher than in robberies involving another weapon (Cook, 1987). In terms of availability, the ease with which firearms and licences to carry them in public can be acquired is related to the seriousness of violent assaults. For example, a cross-national study including 11 countries found a highly significant correlation of $r = .72$ between a country's rate of gun ownership and the rate of homicides committed with a gun (Killias, 1993).

Legal regulations designed to impose stricter gun control fall into three categories: (1) reducing overall supply and availability by raising prices and taxation of guns—a measure compromised by existing high rates of gun ownership; (2) restricting access by denying certain groups of individuals (e.g., youths, convicted criminals, or substance abusers) the right to acquire a firearm—a measure hard to enforce through rigorous control mechanisms; and (3) controlling the way in which guns are used by those who own them, e.g., by increasing prison sentences if a firearm is used in committing an offence or prohibiting the carrying of guns in certain locations. However, it is clear that in order to have long-term effects gun control measures must be complemented by attempts to change public attitudes towards firearms and to enhance citizens' sense of personal security in their communities so that guns are no longer seen as vital means of self-protection.

Looking back at the general approaches to violence prevention discussed in this section, the impression is that the majority of overarching strategies for reducing aggression have so far had limited success. In the case of catharsis and the punishment of individual aggressive actions, there are indications that they may be counter-productive, i.e., enhance rather than reduce the likelihood of aggressive behaviour. In the case of gun control legislation, the evidence of effectiveness of tighter legislation in reducing fatal out-comes of violent actions seems to be there, but the implementation of tighter control is impeded by conflicting interests. The remainder of this chapter is devoted to prevention approaches that are directed at specific forms of aggressive behaviour.

Tackling bullying and gang violence

Children and adolescents are prime target groups for programmes designed to prevent aggression for at least two reasons: (1) Aggressive behaviour begins to emerge early in individual development and, if left unaddressed, is likely to become consolidated or escalate as the individual gets older (see Chapter 3). Therefore, the sooner aggressive behaviour patterns and their cognitive and affective foundations are targeted, the greater the chances of halting an individual's pathway into an aggressive career; (2) serious forms of aggressive behaviour, such as bullying and gang violence, show high prevalence rates among children and adolescents and cause pain and misery to large numbers of victims.

Many acts of bullying and gang violence take place in and around school settings where children and adolescents spend a large proportion of their time and conduct many of their social relationships. Therefore, schools are aggression hot spots and at the same time suggest themselves as settings for the implementation of anti-violence programmes (Hilton et al., 1998). An example of a school-based approach is Olweus' (1994) anti-bullying programme, which consists of several interconnected layers of intervention (see Table 9.2).

The programme makes it quite clear that a combination of strategies is required to tackle bullying in schools. A school climate must be established in which:

- both teachers and pupils recognise acts of bullying as such rather than trivialising them;
- the occurrence of bullying is regularly monitored; and
- bullying behaviour is unanimously rejected as unacceptable by the pupils.

In addition, parents need to share the school's policy on bullying to reinforce its central ideas in interactions with their children at home.

Similar multi-layer frameworks have been proposed for interventions directed at reducing gang violence. Kodluboy (1997) describes four important components of gang-oriented intervention programmes:

(1) *Staff training and protocol*. Teachers need to be informed about the psychological and social factors facilitating gang

TABLE 9.2

Interlocking measures for dealing with the problem of bullying in schools

General prerequisites
Awareness and involvement on the part of adults (parents, teachers)

Measures at the school level
Questionnaire survey
School conference day
Better supervision during recess
Parent–staff meetings (PTA meeting)

Measures at the class level
Class rules against bullying
Class meetings

Measures at the individual level
Serious talks with bullies and victims
Serious talks with parents of involved students
Teacher and parent use of imagination

Reprinted from Olweus (1994), in Huesmann (Ed.), *Aggressive behavior: Current perspectives* (pp. 97–130) by permission of Plenum Publishers.

membership, about gang structure and mode of operation, basic gang identification signals and local gang-related activity. Schools should develop a gang prevention protocol that describes the school's anti-gang policy, contains sample letters to be sent out to parents to inform them about their child's involvement in gang-related activities, and provide gang prevention education materials as well as contact addresses and safety procedures within the school.

(2) *Student educational approaches.* Among the measures directed at students as potential gang members, peer education, i.e., reports by former gang members about the detrimental effects of gang membership, are used widely, but there is a lack of systematic evaluations of the effectiveness of this measure. Several custom-tailored intervention programmes are available, often simulta-neously directed at preventing drug abuse, such as the Gang Resistance Education and Training (GREAT) and the Gang Risk Intervention Pilot Program (GRIPP). The focus of these programmes is on strengthening resistance to gang affiliation and on reducing gang members' involvement in criminal activities (see Kodluboy, 1997, for more detailed descriptions). In addition, conflict mediation programmes are widely used as semi-formal procedures for

negotiating solutions to episodes of interpersonal and intergroup conflict. Mediators need to be familiar with the local gang culture and ensure that any compromise they negotiate, while being acceptable to the gang or its individual members, does not enhance the status of the gang or undermine a "zero tolerance" policy towards gang violence.

(3) *Dress and behaviour codes.* Imposing restriction on the ways students dress and behave is another common element of gang prevention measures. Gangs often develop elaborate systems of symbolic communication that serve to reinforce cohesion within the group and to signal hostility towards outsiders. For example, wearing white shoe laces in heavy leather boots is used by right-wing "skinhead" gangs in Germany to signal their readiness for physically aggressive clashes with resented outgroups, such as young Turks or other foreigners. By banning such gang insignia and prohibiting certain types of language, gang presence may be made less visible in schools, and opportunities for interactions based on gang membership are reduced. However, care must be taken to enforce only the minimum amount of control over students' gang-related dress and speech that is necessary to avoid disruption of normal interactions in the school.

(4) *School safety plans.* The aim of these measures is to ensure the protection of both students and staff from gang-related violence within and around the school. School safety plans outline a sequence of increasing and proportional responses to perceived threats to school safety from gang activities. They involve practical measures, such as the installation of CCTV surveillance systems, visitor admission procedures to prevent violent intruders from entering the school premises, and offering protection to students arriving and departing on school buses. In addition, school safety plans need to be overseen by a standing committee responsible for monitoring the extent of gang-related activity in and around the school and for disseminating relevant information to staff, parents, and students.

As Kodluboy (1997, pp. 211–212) concludes, "the social structures of gangs teach, reinforce, and reward antisocial behavior; as such, gangs always present a risk to their members, other students, and school staff." The measures described in this section clearly show the scale of the institutional costs incurred in trying to prevent bullying and gang violence and the distress caused to the victims of these aggressive behaviours.

Preventing domestic violence

The experience of domestic violence entails a host of negative consequences that are likely to affect the victim's future development in many ways. Therefore, a primary concern of practitioners and researchers alike must be to develop strategies for preventing the occurrence of abuse and for minimising its detrimental effects. Just as the theories of domestic violence were classified as pertaining to the macro level, the micro level or the individual level (see Chapter 7), strategies designed to stop and prevent domestic violence are directed at these different levels. As various forms of domestic violence are often related and can be traced back to a common set of underlying causes and facilitating conditions, measures suggested to tackle domestic violence show a high degree of similarity across different types of abuse. Therefore, the approaches presented in this section are relevant to the prevention of different forms of domestic violence rather than being specific to just one particular manifestation.

Societal-level interventions

Three main approaches have been advocated to tackle domestic violence at the macro level of society: (a) changing the social climate that allows domestic violence to thrive; (b) creating a legal framework that helps to uncover and then prosecute domestic violence; and (c) improving protective services that enable victims to escape from abusive home environments.

Changing the foundations of domestic violence at the societal level requires, first and foremost, to create a consensus that violence is unacceptable. As Gelles (1997, p. 166) puts it, "we need to cancel the hitting license in society." This involves measures directly related to domestic violence, such as creating an awareness that corporal punishment is not an adequate child-rearing technique, but also includes wider issues, such as restricting the availability of guns and other weapons and campaigning against media presentations of violence as masculine, entertaining, and ultimately rewarding. It also involves the removal of the traditional gender gap in the distribution of power, both within relationships and in society at large. To the extent that social structures become more egalitarian, e.g., by providing equal pay and job opportunities, women will gain influence in society, and patriarchal attitudes will become less influential.

Another way in which domestic violence can be tackled at the societal level is by means of the legal system. Two aspects are of primary significance here: (a) the introduction of mandatory reporting, which requires professionals who suspect a case of domestic violence to report it to the authorities; and (b) the enforcement of stricter prosecution of domestic violence once it has been reported. *Mandatory reporting* laws have been implemented in the United States to increase the detection rate for several forms of domestic violence. These laws put professionals dealing with the respective target groups, such as social workers, medical doctors, and mental health professionals, under a legal obligation to report suspected cases of abuse. The introduction of mandatory reporting of childhood abuse as well as elder abuse has led to a substantial increase in recorded cases of alleged abuse (see Gelles, 1997; Pillemer & Suitor, 1988). However, if mandatory reporting is to expose cases of abuse that would otherwise have gone unrecognised, it is essential that the professionals mandated to report abuse are sufficiently well educated about the different forms of abuse to read the warning signs. The second way in which the legal system can be used to combat the problem of domestic violence is to implement a more rigorous prosecution of perpetrators. Given the widespread belief that violence within the family is not a matter for outside intervention, it is not surprising that rates of arrest and conviction for domestic violence have traditionally been low. Police officers called in to deal with domestic assault have been found to often trivialise the attacks or to be unwilling to intervene. Bourg and Stock (1994) examined more than 1800 complaints of domestic violence and found that only 28.8% of all cases and 37.4% of the cases involving serious injury resulted in arrest. As a consequence, many abusers are never held responsible for their actions, and fear of prosecution does not act as a deterrent against domestic violence. This problem has been particularly acute with regard to partner abuse, and many US states have adopted *mandatory arrest policies* to overcome police reluctance to arrest. However, it yet remains to be seen whether these policies will actually be followed at grass-roots level and whether they will effectively deter potential perpetrators from carrying out abusive behaviour (see Barnett et al., 1997, p. 204).

The third approach to dealing with domestic violence as a society consists in improving *protective services* offering support to the victims. Measures include the provision of sheltered accommodation for women and children who suffered domestic violence, regular visits by social workers to families identified as "at risk" to pre-empt the development of abusive situations, provisions for placing abused children and elders into high-quality care, and providing treatment programmes for the perpetrators of abuse.

Family-level interventions

Interventions directed at influencing the micro system of the family to prevent abuse have to start by identifying interaction patterns in the family associated with an increased likelihood of abuse. The factors linked to differential prevalence rates of abuse, such as lack of financial resources and social support, provide only rough indications of which families might be at risk. Standardised instruments have been developed to measure parent characteristics, aspects of the parent–child relationship, and typical interaction patterns that have been identified as predictors of child abuse (see Blau, Dall, & Anderson, 1993). For example, Milner and Wimberly (1980) developed the Child Abuse Potential Inventory (CAPI), which measures three risk factors of abuse in parents: rigidity, unhappiness, and problems with child and self. They showed that scores on the CAPI were able to discriminate between abusive and non-abusive parents. Apart from using the scale to identify parents who are particularly at risk for abuse, it can also be employed to identify variables that give rise to these risk factors and which may potentially be targeted by intervention measures. For example, Moncher (1996) found that single mothers' scores on the CAPI could be predicted by insecure attachment styles in romantic relationships.

Once families have been identified as abusive or being at risk of abuse, a micro-level strategy for stopping or preventing the abuse is *community-based intervention* (see Blau et al., 1993). Community-based intervention is directed at providing help to abusive families in their own homes, both in response to an acute crisis and as a more long-term form of social support. Trained helpers teach parenting and anger management skills, act as role models in dealing with conflict situations in a non-abusive way, and assist the families in securing material resources and support from social services (e.g., Fetsch, Schultz, & Wahler, 1999). The aim of this approach is to create a non-violent family environment to enable the child to stay within the family. As critics point out, however, "some families cannot be preserved, and others should not be preserved" (Gelles, 1997, p. 154). Therefore, any decision about offering community-based intervention requires a careful judgement of the chances of changing an abusive environment into a non-violent one without exposing the victim to the risk of further violence and abuse.

Individual-level interventions

At this level, the focus of interventions is on the individual person who commits aggressive acts towards a family member. The main response here is to offer *psychological treatment for abusers* in the form of individual or group therapy. Such treatment is directed at (a) breaking habitual patterns of reacting abusively to the target (the child, partner or elderly dependant) and learning alternative, non-abusive responses, (b) changing the cognitive appraisal of the target's behaviour in abuse-eliciting situations and learning to control feelings of anger towards the target, and (c) promoting empathy for the victims and changing normative beliefs so that abusive behaviour is no longer regarded as acceptable. For example, several types of programmes, based on different theoretical understandings of the causes of partner abuse, have been developed to treat male batterers (see Wiehe, 1998). Studies evaluating the outcome of such treatments suggest they are able to lower men's acceptance of interpersonal violence and to reduce the proportion of men who reoffend in comparison to men who did not participate in treatment. However, success rates are qualified by relatively high drop-out figures (i.e., failures to complete the treatment) and recidivism rates, especially by men who take part in the treatment on the basis of a court order.

Rather than treating the offenders, an alternative strategy for tackling domestic violence at the individual level has been to target potential victims of abuse to enable them to successfully counter the risk of abuse. This approach has been most prominent with regard to the prevention of childhood sexual abuse. Educational programmes have been designed to empower children to resist sexual exploitation, e.g., by teaching them to enforce their right to privacy, to be assertive in rejecting unwanted touch and in eliciting support from other adults. The outcome measure in most of the studies evaluating these prevention programmes is the extent to which children understand and remember the contents of the programme, not—for obvious methodological reasons—whether or not they become sexually abused. Concerns that the programmes might have detrimental side effects, such as frightening or upsetting children, were not supported by systematic research (e.g., Finkelhor & Dziuba-Leatherman, 1995).

Preventing sexual aggression

Given the widespread occurrence of sexual aggression and the devastating effects it has on the victims, it is clear that the development of measures for preventing sexual aggression is a key challenge for researchers and policy-makers alike. Existing strategies aimed at reducing the risk of sexual aggression can be broadly categorised into four groups:

(1) *Changing men's cognitive and affective predispositions to sexual aggression.* Measures in this category are directed at changing men's rape-supportive attitudes, such as rape myth acceptance, and promoting information about the adverse effects of sexual assault on the victims. For example, Hamilton and Yee (1990) demonstrated that greater knowledge about rape, in particular about the rape trauma syndrome, was associated with men's lower likelihood of committing sexually aggressive acts. A meta-analysis conducted by Flores and Hartlaub (1998) indicates that human sexuality courses, workshops, video interventions, and other formats all have short-term success in reducing rape myth acceptance. However, in order to prevent men from acting out rape myths in sexually aggressive behaviour, such intervention effects need to persist over a longer period. In addition to preventing first-time sexual assault by supplementing rape-supportive attitudes by greater victim empathy, programmes need to focus on sexually aggressive men to prevent them from reoffending. Abbey et al. (1998) found that of those men in their sample who reported sexual aggression, 71% had committed multiple assaults. These men are a prime target group for intervention efforts. One approach is to train men to discriminate between their arousal by consensual and non-consensual sexual stimuli and to teach them to activate inhibitory self-persuasion (Porter & Critelli, 1994).

(2) *Alerting women to potentially dangerous situations and behaviours to reduce the risk of victimisation.* This category comprises measures directed at the potential victims of sexual assault. As we saw in Chapter 8, high levels of sexual activity, alcohol consumption in the context of sexual encounters, and the ambiguous communication of sexual intentions were linked to an increased risk of sexual victimisation across a range of studies. Women should be informed about the risks involved in these behaviours to give them the opportunity to adjust themselves to the threat of rape. As Abbey et al. (1996, p. 165) note, "perpetrators are responsible for their actions; however information about risk factors such as misperception and alcohol consumption empowers women." Programmes teaching self-defence skills and strengthening women's assertiveness are aimed at reducing women's feelings of

vulnerability and increasing their self-confidence when faced with a potentially dangerous situation (Koss & Harvey, 1991). However, systematic evaluations of rape prevention programmes suggest their success may be limited. For example, Hanson and Gidycz (1993) found that their rape prevention programme reduced the incidence of first-time assaults on women, but was ineffective at reducing the risk of revictimisation in women who had experienced a prior sexual assault. Using a modified programme to address the risk of revictimisation, Breitenbecher and Gidycz (1998) failed to find any differences between the intervention group and a control group in terms of changes in the attitudes and behaviours targeted by the programme. Finally, the intricacies of victim-directed rape prevention efforts are illustrated by Breitenbecher and Scarce's (1999) finding that their sexual assault education programme increased participants' knowledge about rape, but failed to affect the incidence of sexual victimisation compared to a control group.

Whether or not women are willing to take behavioural precautions against the risk of sexual assault depends to a large extent on their "rape prevention beliefs", i.e., their perceptions of the effectiveness of different preventive strategies. Furby, Fischhoff, and Morgan (1990) showed that the rape prevention beliefs of most women are restricted to the stranger rape scenario and fail to cover the risk of acquaintance rape. A recent review by Nurius (2000) confirms that women generally perceive a low personal risk of acquaintance rape and thus do not see a great need to engage in protective behaviours against this form of threat. Moreover, Furby et al. found that rape prevention beliefs were primarily concerned with responding to a sexual attack so as to minimise harm rather than with avoiding an assault in the first place.

(3) *Promoting women's reflection about potential protective responses in an assault situation.* This approach deals with the issue of self-protection once an assault situation has arisen. The crucial issue here is whether active resistance from the victim is more likely to enhance the chances of escaping the assault or to increase the risk of injury and escalation of violence. The available evidence suggests that fighting back is more likely to succeed in avoiding rape than to lead to greater injury (e.g., Kleck & Sayles, 1990; Ullman & Knight, 1992; Zoucha-Jensen & Coyne, 1993). Analysing rape complaints reported to the police, Zoucha-Jensen and Coyne (1993) found that only 6.5% of women who showed no resistance avoided rape. In contrast, 54.5% of women who physically resisted

TABLE 9.3

Positive aspects of victim self-defence against sexual assault

Current research on self-defence concludes unequivocally that:

1. Women who fight back immediately are less likely to be raped than women who do not.
2. Women who fight back are no more likely to be injured than women who do not fight back.
   In fact, it has been shown that victim resistance often occurred *in response* to physical attack.
3. Pleading, begging, and reasoning are ineffective in preventing rape or physical injury.
4. Women who fight back experience less postassault symptomatology due to avoiding rape.
5. Women who fought back had faster psychological recoveries whether or not they were raped.
6. Fighting back strengthens the physical evidence should the victim decide to prosecute for rape or attempted rape.

Adapted from Rozee (1999, p. 110).

their attacker were able to avoid rape. Drawing on evidence from numerous studies, Rozee (1999, p. 110) concludes that self-defence is an advisable response to a sexual attack. In support of this view, she lists six positive aspects of active resistance, as displayed in Table 9.3.

However, it is important to bear in mind that the positive evaluation of active resistance is based on probability estimates for *samples* of assault victims and does not guarantee that resistance is the best strategy in any single case. Therefore, authors are careful to stress that the decision for or against physically fighting back in an attack must be based, in the final instance, on an assessment of the particular circumstances of the attack. For example, putting up resistance against an assailant who is far stronger than the victim or in a remote place where it is unlikely that others will come to the victim's aid may well be counter-productive. Recommendations on how to respond to a sexual attack can therefore only be guidelines enabling women to think about adequate responses to an attack in advance rather than being faced with the need to make an instantaneous decision under the stress of an assault situation (Fischhoff, 1992).

(4) *Societal measures designed at reducing sexual aggression.* Measures in this category reach beyond the individual perpetrator or victim and try to change the social context in which sexual violence occurs. One measure is to impose stricter regulations on the accessibility of violent pornography to ensure that such material remains (or becomes) unavailable to children and adolescents. Moreover, education campaigns should inform the public about the negative aspects of violent pornography with regard to

promoting aggressive behaviour. Linz et al. (1992) consider the following aspects to be important elements of such programmes: (a) information about the desensitising effect of repeated exposure to violent pornography in terms of decreasing empathy for victims of sexual assault; (b) a comparative appraisal of media depictions of sexual aggression (often suggesting victim enjoyment of coercive actions) with real-life experiences of victims; (c) self-persuasion techniques in which participants have to generate arguments to support the detrimental effects of pornography; and (d) the use of influential communicators (e.g., peer educators) to convey the programme messages. Other measures are directed at increasing reporting rates for sexual assault to make sure a greater number of sexual aggressors come to the attention of the legal authorities. In order to encourage victims of rape to come forward, confidence must be established in the treatment victims expect to receive from police, medical professionals, and legal institutions.

Ultimately, a reduction in the prevalence of sexual aggression is the criterion of success by which prevention efforts must be measured. However, no substantive database is available to date that demonstrates the effectiveness of rape prevention programmes in reducing incidence rates of sexual assault (see Yeater & O'Donohue, 1999, for a critical review). Moreover, the large-scale under-reporting of sexual victimisation turns out to be problematic again. As long as the true scale of the problem of sexual assault can neither be accurately measured nor reliably estimated, the ultimate success of rape reduction measures will remain hard to assess. For the time being, most prevention measures are judged on the basis of whether or not they are successful in changing those aspects which they have targeted as antecedent conditions of sexual aggression.

The research reviewed in this chapter has illustrated once more how very difficult it is to come to terms with the problem of aggression between individuals and groups. While several firmly entrenched beliefs about effective control mechanisms, such as the role of cathartic release of aggressive feelings or the deterrent function of punishment, need to be revised on the basis of this research, support for alternative courses of action is limited and far from conclusive. Progress towards reducing and preventing aggression is most likely to be achieved by focusing on specific types (e.g., sexual violence, bullying) and mediators (e.g., frustration, media consumption) of aggression. Given the diversity and complexity of aggressive behaviours, general strategies for intervention need to be complemented by domain-specific approaches to prevent the occurrence of particular forms of aggression. Mercy and Hammond (1999) have presented such an integrative framework for violence prevention that illustrates how different subsystems interact in the emergence of violence and how effective prevention measures need to target each of these subsystems. Their model is presented in Table 9.4.

Many of the strategies discussed in the course of this chapter appear in this model and are placed into the perspective of a broader prevention framework. Mercy and Hammond (1999) point out that their model simplifies the task of violence prevention ignoring the distinction between the prevention of violent *behaviour* and the prevention of violent *victimisation*. Even as it is, though, the model clearly conveys the challenges involved in conceptualising a comprehensive approach aimed at a substantial reduction in aggression and violence.

The present volume has focused on the contribution of social psychological research to understanding the causes and consequences of aggression between individuals and groups. It is important to stress that this focus does not in any way imply that the aggression-related problems of today's world can be comprehensively addressed and fully understood within the perspective of a single psychological discipline nor, for that matter, by psychology as a whole. Aggression and violence are the products not only of cognitions, emotions, and actions of individual persons, acting alone or in groups, but also of historical developments (as in the case of conflicts between nations and ethnic groups), predominant value systems (such as pitting the role of civil liberties against gun control and media restrictions), and cultural traditions (as in the much-quoted "Southern culture of honour"). Approaches from a variety of disciplines need to be brought together to a greater extent than is currently discernible to arrive at a comprehensive analysis of aggression including the historical and cultural roots of this antisocial behaviour.

In terms of its standing within social psychology, the large number of recent studies reviewed in this volume indicates that aggression research is alive and well. This impression, which would be seen as an unreservedly positive development in most other fields of research, has a sad side to it in the case of aggression: It underlines the pressing need to find answers to the questions of causation and prevention of aggression and violence, which cause immeasurable suffering to victims and their families and pose one of the greatest challenges to societies in securing the safety of their citizens. Therefore, developing a better understanding of the processes that lead individuals and groups to engage in aggressive, often lethal actions

TABLE 9.4

An integrative framework for violence prevention

System Influencing violence	Type of preventive measure		
	Universal	Selective	Indicated
Individual factors	• Provide violent risk education for all students • Teach children to recognize and report sexual abuse • Provide enriched pre-school education for all children	• Provide therapy for children who witness violence • Teach convenience store clerks techniques to avoid injury during robberies	• Treat sex offenders • Provide psychotherapy for violent offenders • Use former perpetrators to influence non-conforming peers through social marketing programmes
Close interpersonal relationships	• Provide parenting education for all new parents • Teach adolescents how to form healthy relationships with the opposite sex	• Use peer mediation to resolve disputes in schools • Increase adult mentoring of high-risk youth • Visit families at high risk of child abuse	• Improve parent management strategies and parent–child bonding in the families of violent children
Proximal social contexts	• Use metal detectors to keep weapons out of schools • Initiate after-school programmes to extend adult supervision of youths	• Create safe havens for children in homes and businesses on high-risk routes to and from school • Establish violence prevention coalitions in high-risk neighbourhoods	• Provide adequate shelter space for battered women • Disrupt illegal gun markets in communities • Train health care professionals in identification and referral of family violence victims
Social macrosystems	• Reduce violence in the media • Reduce income inequality	• Deconcentrate lower-income housing • Establish meaningful job creation programmes for inner-city youths	• Increase severity of penalties for violent crimes • Reduce illegal interstate transfer of firearms by limiting purchases to one gun a month

From Mercy and Hammond, in Smith and Zahn (Eds.), *Homicide: A sourcebook of social research* (pp. 297–310), copyright © 1999 by Sage Publications; reprinted by permission of Sage Publications, Inc.).

against each other and using this understanding to develop strategies for their prevention and control remains one of the greatest challenges for both basic and applied research in psychology.

Summary

- Measures designed to reduce the scale of aggression and violence may be classified into two groups: strategies that specify general mechanisms likely to prevent aggression and those which target specific forms of aggression. General principles examined for changing aggressive responses in the individual aggressor include the cathartic release of aggressive tension, the punishment of aggressive behaviour, the training of anger management skills, and the provision of non-aggressive role models showing non-aggressive modes of responding to aggression-eliciting situations.

- Catharsis has been found not only to be ineffective in reducing aggressive response tendencies but even to be counter-productive. Engaging in the cathartic expression of aggressive feelings was found to enhance rather than reduce the probability of subsequent aggressive behaviour. The effectiveness of punishment in extinguishing aggressive responses is at best limited. At worst, because of its inherently aggressive nature, punishment reinforces aggressive behaviour by presenting aggression as a socially acceptable mode of conflict resolution. Anger management and observational learning are more successful strategies for the modification of aggressive behaviour. Rather than suppressing aggression, they substitute aggressive responses by more adequate ways of dealing with frustration and provocation.

- At the societal level, reducing the opportunity for crime by increasing police presence and other means of surveillance are general measures by which the rate of criminal activities may be reduced. However, it is unclear whether such measures lead to a genuine decrease in crime or only to a "displacement" of criminal activity towards less well-protected areas and targets. Legal regulations represent further instruments used by society to reduce the level of aggression and violence. The deterrent effect of punishment and the tightening of gun control laws have received widespread research attention. Evidence on the effects of capital punishment on homicide rates provides little support for the deterrence hypothesis. In contrast, limiting the availability and use of firearms is likely to reduce the fatal effects of violent attacks.

- To tackle bullying and gang violence as major forms of youth aggression, approaches are required that combine interventions directed at the individual perpetrator with measures located at the organisational level of the school, the intergroup level of classes and gangs, and the interpersonal level of dyadic conflict.

- Strategies for the prevention of domestic violence are located at three levels. At the societal level, creating more egalitarian gender relationships, changing the endorsement of family aggression as acceptable or inevitable, using legal institutions to uncover and prosecute abuse, and providing public services to support victims represent major ways of addressing domestic violence. At the family level, breaking up inadequate patterns of conflict resolution and improving communication skills among the family members are of prime importance. Finally, at the individual level, programmes of offender treatment are essential to change offenders' perceptions of their own actions as acceptable and teach alternative strategies of resolving conflicts with children and partners. In addition, preventive measures are important that target the potential victims of family abuse and empower them to successfully defend their physical, sexual, and emotional integrity.

- Strategies for preventing sexual assault are directed at changing men's rape-supportive attitudes and strengthening empathy for rape victims. Moreover, intervention measures have been developed to educate women about potentially risky behaviours and situations to enable them to protect themselves against victimisation. Finally, measures taken at a societal level, such as restricting violent pornography and improving the treatment of rape victims by police and courts, are required to create a social climate in which the seriousness of sexual assault is recognised and victims are treated with sympathy and respect.

Suggested reading

Barnett, O.W., Miller-Perrin, C.L., & Perrin, R.D. (1997). *Family violence across the lifespan*. Thousand Oaks, CA: Sage.

Cook, P.J., & Moore, M.H. (1999). Guns, gun control, and homicide. In M.D. Smith & M.A. Zahn (Eds.), *Homicide: A sourcebook of social research* (pp. 277–296). Thousand Oaks, CA: Sage.

Kodluboy, D.W. (1997). Gang-oriented interventions. In A.P. Goldstein & J.C. Conoly (Eds.), *School violence intervention* (pp. 189–214). New York: Guilford Press.

Yeater, E.A., & O'Donohue, W. (1999). Sexual assault prevention programs. *Clinical Psychology Review, 19*, 739–771.

References

Abbey, A. (1991). Misperception as an antecedent of acquaintance rape: A consequence of ambiguity in communication between women and men. In A. Parrot & L. Bechhofer (Eds.), *Acquaintance rape: The hidden crime* (pp. 96–111). New York: Wiley.

Abbey, A.A., McAuslan, P., & Ross, L.T. (1998). Sexual assault perpetration by college men: The role of alcohol, misperception of sexual intent, and sexual beliefs and experiences. *Journal of Social and Clinical Psychology, 17,* 167–195.

Abbey, A.A., Ross, L.T., McDuffie, D., & McAuslan, P. (1996). Alcohol and dating risk factors for sexual assault among college women. *Psychology of Women Quarterly, 20,* 147–169.

Allen, M., D'Alessio, D., & Brezgel, K. (1995). A meta-analysis summarizing the effects of pornography II. Aggression after exposure. *Human Communication Research, 22,* 258–283.

Allen, M., Emmers, T., Gebhardt, L., & Giery, M.A. (1995). Exposure to pornography and acceptance of rape myths. *Journal of Communication, 45,* 5–26.

Allison, J.A., & Wrightsman, L.S. (1993). *Rape: The misunderstood crime.* Newbury Park, CA: Sage.

Alvarez, A., & Bachman, R. (1997). Predicting the fear of assault at school and while going to and from school in an adolescent population. *Violence and Victims, 12,* 69–86.

American Psychological Society (Ed.) (1997). Reducing violence: A behavioral science research plan for violence. *APS Observer Special Issue.*

Anderson, C.A. (1989). Temperature and aggression: Ubiquitous effects of heat on occurrence of human violence. *Psychological Bulletin, 106,* 74–96.

Anderson, C.A. (1997). Effects of violent movies and trait hostility on hostile feelings and aggressive thoughts. *Aggressive Behavior, 23,* 161–178.

Anderson, C.A., & Anderson, K.B. (1996). Violent crime rate studies in philosophical context: A destructive testing approach to heat and southern culture of violence effects. *Journal of Personality and Social Psychology, 70,* 740–756.

Anderson, C.A., & Anderson, K.B. (1998). Temperature and aggression: Paradox, controversy, and a (fairly) clear picture. In R.G. Geen & E. Donnerstein (Eds.), *Human aggression: Theories, research and implications for social policy* (pp. 247–298). San Diego, CA: Academic Press.

Anderson, C.A., Anderson, K.B., & Deuser, W.E. (1996). Examining an affective aggression framework: Weapon and temperature effects on aggressive thoughts, affect, and attitudes. *Personality and Social Psychology Bulletin, 22,* 366–377.

Anderson, C.A., Benjamin, A.L., & Bartholow, B.D. (1998). Does the gun pull the trigger? Automatic priming effects of weapon pictures and weapon names. *Psychological Science, 9*, 308–314.

Anderson, C.A., & Bushman, B.J. (1997). External validity of "trivial" experiments: The case of laboratory aggression. *Review of General Psychology, 1*, 19–41.

Anderson, C.A., Bushman, B.J., & Groom, R.W. (1997). Hot years and serious and deadly assaults: Empirical tests of the heat hypothesis. *Journal of Personality and Social Psychology, 73*, 1213–1223.

Anderson, C.A., & Dill, K.E. (2000). Video games and aggressive thoughts, feelings, and behavior in the laboratory and in life. *Journal of Personality and Social Psychology, 78*, 772–790.

Anderson, K.B., Cooper, H., & Okamura, L. (1997). Individual differences and attitudes toward rape: A meta-analytic review. *Personality and Social Psychology Bulletin, 23*, 295–315.

Anderson, P.B. (1996). Correlates of college women's self-reports of heterosexual aggression. *Sexual Abuse, 8*, 121–131.

Anderson, P.B., & Struckman-Johnson, C. (Eds.) (1998). *Sexually aggressive women.* New York: Guilford Press.

Anetzberger, G.L. (1997). Elderly adult survivors of family violence. *Violence Against Women, 3*, 499–514.

Anetzberger, G.L., Korbin, J.E., & Austin, C. (1994). Alcoholism and elder abuse. *Journal of Interpersonal Violence, 9*, 184–193.

Arata, C.M. (1999). Coping with rape: The roles of prior sexual abuse and attributions of blame. *Journal of Interpersonal Violence, 14*, 62–78.

Arata, C.M., & Burkhart, B.M. (1998). Coping appraisals and adjustment to nonstranger sexual assault. *Violence Against Women, 4*, 224–239.

Archer, D., & McDaniel, P. (1995). Violence and gender: Differences and similarities across societies. In B.R. Ruback & N.A. Weiner (Eds.), *Interpersonal violent behaviors* (pp. 63–87). New York: Springer.

Archer, J. (1988). *The behavioural biology of aggression.* Cambridge, UK: Cambridge University Press.

Archer, J. (1991). The influence of testosterone on human aggression. *British Journal of Psychology, 8*, 1–28.

Archer, J. (1995). What can ethology offer the psychological study of human aggression? *Aggressive Behavior, 21*, 243–255.

Archer, J. (1999). Assessment of the reliability of the Conflict Tactics Scale: A meta-analytic review. *Journal of Interpersonal Violence, 14*, 1263–1289.

Archer, J. (2000). Sex differences in aggression between heterosexual partners: A meta-analytic review. *Psychological Bulletin, 126*, 697–702.

Archer, J., Birring, S.S., & Wu, F.C.W. (1998). The association between testosterone and aggression among young men: Empirical findings and a meta-analysis. *Aggressive Behavior, 24*, 411–420.

Archer, J., & Browne, K. (1989). Concepts and approaches to the study of aggression. In J. Archer & K. Browne (Eds.), *Human aggression: Naturalistic approaches* (pp. 3–24). London: Routledge.

Archer, J., Holloway, R., & McLoughlin, K. (1995). Self-reported physical aggression among young men. *Aggressive Behavior, 21*, 325–342.

Archer, J., Kilpatrick, G., & Bramwell, R. (1995). Comparison of two aggression inventories. *Aggressive Behavior, 21*, 371–380.

Archer, J., & Lloyd, B.B. (in press). *Sex and gender* (3rd ed.). New York: Cambridge University Press.

Arms, R.L., Russell, G.W., & Sandilands, M.L. (1979). Effects on the hostility of spectators of viewing aggressive sports. *Social Psychology Quarterly, 42,* 275–279.

Averill, J.R., Malstrom, E.J., Koriat, A., & Lazarus, R.S. (1972). Habituation to complex emotional stimuli. *Journal of Abnormal Psychology, 80,* 20–28.

Azar, B. (1998). APA launches "Decade of Behavior". *APA Monitor, 29,* 1 and 23.

Bachman, R. & Saltzman, L.E. (1995). *Violence against women: Estimates from the redesigned survey.* Washington, DC: US Department of Justice.

Bagley, C., Wood, M., & Young, L. (1994). Victim to abuser: Mental health and behavioral sequels of child sexual abuse in a community survey of young adult males. *Child Abuse and Neglect, 18,* 683–697.

Bailey, W.C., & Peterson, R.D. (1999). Capital punishment, homicide, and deterrence. In M.D. Smith & M.A. Zahn (Eds.), *Homicide. A sourcebook of social research* (pp. 257–276). Thousand Oaks, CA: Sage.

Ballard, M.E., & Lineberger, R. (1999). Video game violence and confederate gender: Effects on reward and punishment given by college males. *Sex Roles, 41,* 541–558.

Bandura, A. (1983). Psychological mechanisms of aggression. In R.G. Geen & E.I. Donnerstein (Eds.), *Aggression: Theoretical and empirical reviews* (Vol. 1, pp. 1–40). New York: Academic Press.

Bandura, A., Ross, D., & Ross, S.A. (1963). Imitation of film-mediated aggressive models. *Journal of Abnormal and Social Psychology, 66,* 3–11.

Banyard, V.L. (1997). The impact of child sexual abuse and family functioning on four dimensions of women's later parenting. *Child Abuse and Neglect, 21,* 1095–1107.

Barbaree, H.E., & Marshall, W.L. (1991). The role of male sexual arousal in rape: Six models. *Journal of Consulting and Clinical Psychology, 59,* 621–630.

Bargh, J.A., Raymond, P., Pryor, J.B., & Strack, F. (1995). Attractiveness of the underling: An automatic power → sex association and its consequences for sexual harassment and aggression. *Journal of Personality and Social Psychology, 68,* 768–781.

Barnett, O.W., Miller-Perrin, C.L., & Perrin, R.D. (1997). *Family violence across the lifespan.* Thousand Oaks, CA: Sage.

Baron, R.A. (1976). The reduction of human aggression: A field study of the influence of incompatible reactions. *Journal of Applied Social Psychology, 6,* 260–274.

Baron, R.A., & Bell, P.A. (1976). Aggression and heat: The influence of ambient temperature, negative affect, and a cooling drink. *Journal of Personality and Social Psychology, 33,* 245–255.

Baron, R.A., & Bell, P.A. (1977). Sexual arousal and aggression by males: Effects of type of erotic stimuli and prior aggression. *Journal of Personality and Social Psychology, 35,* 79–87.

Baron, R.A., & Byrne, D. (1991). *Social Psychology* (6th ed.). Boston: Allyn & Bacon.

Baron, R.A., & Richardson, D.R. (1994). *Human aggression* (2nd ed.). New York: Plenum Press.

Bar-Tal, D. (1990). Causes and consequences of delegitimization: Models of conflict and ethnocentrism. *Journal of Social Issues, 46,* 65–81.

Bar-Tal, D. (1997). The monopolization of patriotism. In D. Bar-Tal & E. Staub (Eds.), *Patriotism in the lives of individuals and nations* (pp. 246–270). Chicago: Nelson-Hall.

Bar-Tal, D., & Staub, E. (Eds.) (1997). *Patriotism in the lives of individuals and nations.* Chicago: Nelson-Hall.

Baumeister, R.F., & Boden, J.M. (1998). Aggression and the self: High self-esteem, low self-control, and ego-threat. In R.G. Geen & E. Donnerstein (Eds.),

Human aggression: Theories, research and implications for social policy (pp. 111–137). San Diego, CA: Academic Press.

Baumeister, R.F., Smart, L., & Boden, J.M. (1996). Relation of threatened egotism to violence and aggression: The dark side of high self-esteem. *Psychological Review, 103,* 5–33.

Bauserman, R. (1996). Sexual aggression and pornography: A review of correlational research. *Basic and Applied Social Psychology, 18,* 405–427.

Beck, R., & Fernandez, E. (1998). Cognitive-behavioral therapy in the treatment of anger: A meta-analysis. *Cognitive Therapy and Research, 22,* 63–74.

Becker-Lausen, E., Sanders, B., & Chinsky, J.M. (1995). The mediation of abusive childhood experiences: Depression, dissociation, and negative life outcomes. *American Journal of Orthopsychiatry, 65,* 560–573.

Beitchman, J.H., Zucker, K.J., Hood, J.E., daCosta, G.A., & Akman, D. (1991). A review of the short-term effects of childhood sexual abuse. *Child Abuse and Neglect, 15,* 537–556.

Beitchman, J.H., Zucker, K.J., Hood, J.E., daCosta, G.A., Akman, D., & Cassivia, E. (1992). A review of the long-term effects of child sexual abuse. *Child Abuse and Neglect, 16,* 101–118.

Belknap, J., & Erez, E. (1995). The victimization of women on college campuses: Courtship violence, date rape, and sexual harassment. In B.S. Fisher & J.J. Sloan (Eds.), *Campus crime: Legal, social, and policy perspectives* (pp. 156–178). Springfield, IL: C. Thomas.

Belknap, J., Fisher, B.S., & Cullen, F.T. (1999). The development of a comprehensive measure of sexual victimization of college women. *Violence Against Women, 5,* 185–214.

Bell, P.A. (1992). In defense of the negative affect escape model of heat and aggression. *Psychological Bulletin, 111,* 342–346.

Bendik, M.F. (1992). Reaching the breaking point: Dangers of mistreatment in elder caregiving situations. *Journal of Elder Abuse and Neglect, 4,* 39–59.

Bennett, L.W., & Williams, O.J. (1999). Men who batter. In R.L. Hampton (Ed.), *Family violence* (2nd ed., pp. 227–259). Thousand Oaks, CA: Sage.

Benton, D. (1992). Hormones and human aggression. In K. Björkqvist & P. Niemelä (Eds.), *Of mice and women: Aspects of female aggression* (pp. 37–48). San Diego, CA: Academic Press.

Bergen, R.K. (1996). *Wife rape: Understanding the responses of survivors and service providers.* Thousand Oaks, CA: Sage.

Bergen, R.K. (Ed.) (1998a). *Issues in intimate violence.* Thousand Oaks, CA: Sage.

Bergen, R.K. (1998b). The reality of wife rape. In R.K. Bergen (Ed.), *Issues in intimate violence* (pp. 237–250). Thousand Oaks, CA: Sage.

Bergner, R.M., Delgado, L.K., & Graybill, D. (1994). Finkelhor's risk factor checklist: A cross-validation study. *Child Abuse and Neglect, 18,* 331–340.

Berkowitz, L. (1962). *Aggression: A social psychological analysis.* New York: McGraw-Hill.

Berkowitz, L. (1989). Frustration–aggression hypothesis: Examination and reformulation. *Psychological Bulletin, 106,* 59–73.

Berkowitz, L. (1993). *Aggression: Its causes, consequences, and control.* Philadelphia, PA: Temple University Press.

Berkowitz, L. (1997). On the determinants and regulation of impulsive aggression. In S. Feshbach & J. Zagrodzka (Eds.), *Aggression: Biological, developmental, and social perspectives* (pp. 187–211). New York: Plenum Press.

Berkowitz, L. (1998a). Affective aggression: The role of stress, pain, and negative affect. In R.G. Geen & E. Donnerstein

(Eds.), *Human aggression: Theories, research and implications for social policy* (pp. 49–72). San Diego, CA: Academic Press.

Berkowitz, L. (1998b). Aggressive personalities. In D.F. Barone & M. Hersen (Eds.), *Advanced personality* (pp. 263–285). New York: Plenum Press.

Berkowitz, L., & LePage, A. (1967). Weapons as aggression-eliciting stimuli. *Journal of Personality and Social Psychology, 7,* 202–207.

Bernstein, J.Y., & Watson, M.W. (1997). Children who are targets of bullying. *Journal of Interpersonal Violence, 12,* 483–498.

Bettencourt, B.A., & Kernahan, C. (1997). A meta-analysis of aggression in the presence of violent cues: Effects of gender differences and aversive provocation. *Aggressive Behavior, 23,* 447–456.

Bettencourt, B.A., & Miller, N. (1996). Gender differences in aggression as a function of provocation: A meta-analysis. *Psychological Bulletin, 119,* 422–447.

Björkqvist, K., & Niemelä, P. (Eds.) (1992). *Of mice and women: Aspects of female aggression.* San Diego, CA: Academic Press.

Björkqvist, K., Österman, K., & Lagerspetz, K. (1994). Sex differences in covert aggression among adults. *Aggressive Behavior, 20,* 27–33.

Blaske, D.M., Borduin, C.M., Henggeler, S.W., & Mann, B.J. (1989). Individual, family, and peer characteristics of adolescent sex offenders and assaultive offenders. *Developmental Psychology, 25,* 846–855.

Blau, G.M., Dall, M.B., & Anderson, L.M. (1993). The assessment and treatment of violent families. In R.L. Hampton, T.P. Gulotta, G.R. Adams, E.H. Potter, & R.P. Weissberg (Eds.), *Family violence: Prevention and treatment* (pp. 198–229). Newbury Park, CA: Sage.

Blickle, G., Habasch, A., & Senft, W. (1998). Verbal aggressiveness: Conceptualization and measurement a decade later. *Psychological Reports, 82,* 287–298.

Boeringer, S.B. (1994). Pornography and sexual aggression: Associations of violent and nonviolent depictions with rape and rape proclivity. *Deviant Behavior, 15,* 289–304.

Bohner, G., Reinhard, M.A., Rutz, S., Sturm, S., Kerschbaum, B., & Effler, D. (1998). Rape myths as neutralizing cognitions: Evidence for a causal impact of anti-victim attitudes on men's self-reported likelihood of raping. *European Journal of Social Psychology, 23,* 257–268.

Bohstedt, J. (1994). The dynamics of riots: Escalation and diffusion/contagion. In M. Potegal & J.F. Knutson (Eds.), *The dynamics of aggression* (pp. 257–306). Hillsdale, NJ: Lawrence Erlbaum Associates Inc.

Bond, A.J., Lader, M.H., & Da Silveira, J.C. (1997). *Aggression: Individual differences, alcohol, and benzodiazepines.* Hove, UK: Psychology Press.

Botha, M. (1990). Stability of aggression among adolescents over time: A South African study. *Aggressive Behavior, 16,* 361–380.

Bourg, S., & Stock, H.V. (1994). A review of domestic violence arrest statistics in a police department using a pro-arrest policy: Are pro-arrest policies enough? *Journal of Family Violence, 9,* 177–192.

Bowers, L., Smith, P.K., & Binney, V. (1994). Perceived family relationships of bullies, victims and bully/victims in middle childhood. *Journal of Social and Personal Relationships, 11,* 215–232.

Bowling, B. (1993). Racial harassment and the process of victimization: Conceptual and methodological implications for the local crime survey. *British Journal of Criminology, 33,* 231–250.

Branwhite, T. (1994). Bullying and student

distress: Beneath the tip of the iceberg. *Educational Psychology, 14,* 59–71.

Breitenbecher, K.H., & Gidycz, C.A. (1998). An empirical evaluation of a program designed to reduce the risk of multiple sexual victimization. *Journal of Interpersonal Violence, 13,* 473–488.

Breitenbecher, K.H., & Scarce, M. (1999). A longitudinal evaluation of the effectiveness of a sexual assault education program. *Journal of Interpersonal Violence, 14,* 459–478.

Brener, N.D., Simon, T.R., Krug, E.G., & Lowry, R. (1999). Recent trends in violence-related behaviors among high school students in the United States. *Journal of the American Medical Association, 282,* 440–446.

Brown, J., Cohen, P., Johnson, J.G., & Salzinger, S. (1998). A longitudinal analysis of risk factors for child maltreatment: Findings of a 17-year prospective study of officially recorded and self-reported child abuse and neglect. *Child Abuse and Neglect, 22,* 1065–1078.

Browne, A., & Finkelhor, D. (1986). Impact of child sexual abuse: A review of the research. *Psychological Bulletin, 99,* 66–77.

Browne, A., Williams, K.R., & Dutton, D.G. (1999). Homicide between intimate partners. In M.D. Smith & M.A. Zahn (Eds.), *Homicide: A sourcebook of social research* (pp. 149–164). Thousand Oaks, CA: Sage.

Browne, K. (1989). The naturalistic context of family violence and child abuse. In J. Archer & K. Browne (Eds.), *Human aggression: Naturalistic approaches* (pp. 182–216). London: Routledge.

Browne, K. (1994). Child sexual abuse. In J. Archer (Ed.), *Male violence* (pp. 210–230). London: Routledge.

Bundesministerium des Inneren [Interior Ministry] (Ed.) (2000). *Polizeiliche Kriminalistatistik 1999.* Berlin: BMI.

Burgess, A.W., & Holmstrom, L.L. (1985). Rape trauma syndrome and post traumatic stress response. In A.W. Burgess (Ed.), *Rape and sexual assault: A research handbook* (Vol. I, pp. 46–60). New York: Garland.

Burke, L.K., & Follingstad, D.R. (1999). Violence in lesbian and gay relationships: Theory, prevalence, and correlational factors. *Clinical Psychology Review, 19,* 487–512.

Burks, V.S., Laird, R.D., Dodge, A., Pettit, G.S., & Bates, J.E. (1999). Knowledge structures, social information processing, and children's aggressive behavior. *Social Development, 8,* 220–236.

Burt, M.R. (1980). Cultural myths and support for rape. *Journal of Personality and Social Psychology, 38,* 217–230.

Burt, M.R., & Albin, R.S. (1981). Rape myths, rape definitions, and probability of conviction. *Journal of Applied Social Psychology, 11,* 212–230.

Bushman, B.J. (1993). Human aggression while under the influence of alcohol and other drugs: An integrative research review. *Current Directions in Psychological Science, 2,* 148–152.

Bushman, B.J. (1995). Moderating role of trait aggressiveness in the effects of violent media on aggression. *Journal of Personality and Social Psychology, 69,* 950–960.

Bushman, B.J. (1997). Effects of alcohol on human aggression: Validity of proposed explanations. In D. Fuller, R. Dietrich, & E. Gottheil (Eds.), *Recent developments in alcoholism: Alcohol and violence* (Vol. 13, pp. 227–243). New York: Plenum Press.

Bushman, B.J. (1998). Priming effects of media violence on the accessibility of aggressive constructs in memory. *Personality and Social Psychology Bulletin, 24,* 537–545.

Bushman, B.J., & Anderson, C.A. (1998). Methodology in the study of aggression: Integrating experimental and nonexperimental findings. In R.G.

Geen & E. Donnerstein (Eds.), *Human aggression: Theories, research and implications for social policy* (pp. 24–48). San Diego, CA: Academic Press.

Bushman, B.J., Baumeister, R.F., & Stack, A.D. (1999). Catharsis, aggression, and persuasive influence: Self-fulfilling or self-defeating prophecies? *Journal of Personality and Social Psychology, 76,* 367–376.

Bushman, B.J., & Cooper, H.M. (1990). Effects of alcohol on human aggression: An integrative research review. *Psychological Bulletin, 107,* 341–354.

Bushman, B.J., & Geen, R.G. (1990). Role of cognitive-emotional mediators and individual differences in the effects of media violence on aggression. *Journal of Personality and Social Psychology, 58,* 156–163.

Buss, A.H. (1961). *The psychology of aggression.* New York: Wiley.

Buss, A.H., & Perry, M. (1992). The aggression questionnaire. *Journal of Personality and Social Psychology, 63,* 452–459.

Buss, A.H., & Durkee, A. (1957). An inventory assessing different kinds of hostility. *Journal of Consulting Psychology, 21,* 343–348.

Buss, D.M., & Shakelford, T.K. (1997). Human aggression in evolutionary psychological perspective. *Clinical Psychology Review, 17,* 605–619.

Buzawa, E.S., & Buzawa, C.G. (1996). *Domestic violence: The criminal justice response.* Thousand Oaks, CA: Sage.

Byers, S., & O'Sullivan, L.F. (1998). Similar but different: Men's and women's experience of sexual coercion. In P.B. Anderson & C. Struckman-Johnson (Eds.), *Sexually aggressive women* (pp. 144–168). New York: Guilford Press.

Cahill, C., Llewlyn, S.P., & Pearson, C. (1991). Long-term effects of sexual abuse which occurred in childhood: A review. *British Journal of Clinical Psychology, 30,* 117–130.

Cairns, E., & Darby, J. (1998). The conflict in Northern Ireland. *American Psychologist, 53,* 754–760.

Cairns, R.B., Cadwallader, T.W., Estell, D., & Neckerman, H.J. (1997). Groups to gangs: Developmental and criminological perspectives and relevance for prevention. In D.M. Stoff, J. Breiling & J.D. Maser (Eds.), *Handbook of antisocial behavior* (pp. 194–204). New York: Wiley.

Cairns, R.B., & Cairns, B.D. (1994). *Lifelines and risks: Pathways of youths in our time.* Cambridge, UK: Cambridge University Press.

Calhoun, K.S., & Atkeson, B. (1991). *Treatment of rape victims: Facilitating social adjustment.* Elmsford, NY: Pergamon.

Caprara, G.V., Barbaranelli, C., & Zimbardo, P.G. (1996). Understanding the complexity of human aggression: Affective, cognitive and social dimensions of individual differences in propensity toward aggression. *European Journal of Personality, 10,* 133–155.

Caprara, G.V., Cinnani, V., D'Imperio, G., Passerini, S., Renzi, P., & Travaglia, G. (1985). Indicators of impulsive aggression: Present status of research on irritability and emotional susceptibility scales. *Personality and Individual Differences, 6,* 665–674.

Caprara, G.V., Perugini, M., & Barbaranelli, C. (1994). Studies of individual differences in aggression. In M. Potegal & J.F. Knutson (Eds.), *The dynamics of aggression* (pp. 123–153). Hillsdale, NJ: Lawrence Erlbaum Associates Inc.

Carlson, M., Marcus-Newhall, A., & Miller, N. (1989). Evidence for a general construct of aggression. *Personality and Social Psychology Bulletin, 15,* 377–389.

Carlson, M., Marcus-Newhall, A., & Miller, N. (1990). Effects of situational aggression cues: A quantitative review.

Journal of Personality and Social Psychology, 58, 622–633.

Chandy, J.M., Blum, R.W., & Resnick, M.D. (1996). Female adolescents with a history of sexual abuse. Journal of Interpersonal Violence, 11, 503–518.

Chermack, S.T., & Giancola, P.R. (1997). The relation between alcohol and aggression: An integrated biopsychosocial conceptualization. Clinical Psychology Review, 17, 621–649.

Chesney-Lind, M. (1997). The female offender: Girls, women, and crime. Thousand Oaks, CA: Sage.

Christensen, E. (1999). The prevalence and nature of abuse and neglect in children under 4: A national survey. Child Abuse Review, 8, 109–119.

Cline, V.B., Croft, R.G., & Courrier, S. (1973). Desensitization of children to television violence. Journal of Personality and Social Psychology, 27, 360–365.

Cohen, D., Nisbett, R.E., Bowdle, B.F., & Schwarz, N. (1996). Insult, aggression, and the southern culture of honor: An "experimental ethnography". Journal of Personality and Social Psychology, 70, 945–960.

Cohen, L.E., & Felson, M. (1979). Social change and crime rate trends: A routine activity approach. American Sociological Review, 44, 588–608.

Coie, J.D., & Dodge, K.A. (1998). Aggression and antisocial behavior. In W. Damon & N. Eisenberg (Eds.), Handbook of child psychology (5th ed., pp. 779–862). New York: Wiley.

Collins, K., & Bell, R. (1997). Personality and aggression: The dissipation–rumination scale. Personality and Individual Differences, 22, 751–755.

Comstock, G., Chaffee, S., Katzman, N., McCombs, M., & Roberts, D. (1978). Television and human behavior. New York: Columbia University Press.

Comstock, G., & Scharrer, E. (1999). Television. San Diego, CA: Academic Press.

Cook, P.J. (1987). Robbery violence. Journal of Criminal Law and Criminology, 78, 357–376.

Cook, P.J., & Moore, M.H. (1999). Guns, gun control, and homicide. In M.D. Smith & M.A. Zahn (Eds.), Homicide. A sourcebook of social research (pp. 277–296). Thousand Oaks, CA: Sage.

Cornell, D.G. (1993). Juvenile homicide: A growing national problem. Behavioural Sciences and the Law, 11, 389–396.

Costin, F. (1985). Beliefs about rape and women's social roles. Archives of Sexual Behavior, 4, 319–325.

Craig, M.E. (1990). Coercive sexuality in dating relationships: A situational model. Clinical Psychology Review, 10, 395–423.

Crick, N.R., & Bigbee, M.A. (1998). Relational and overt forms of peer victimization: A multiinformant approach. Journal of Consulting and Clinical Psychology, 66, 337–347.

Crick, N.R., & Grotpeter, J.K. (1995). Relational aggression, gender, and social-psychological adjustment. Child Development, 66, 710–722.

Criminal Statistics in England and Wales (1999). www.official-documents.co.uk/document/cm50/5002/5001.htm

Cross, T.P., De Vos, E., & Whitcomb, D. (1994). Prosecution of child sexual abuse: Which cases are accepted? Child Abuse and Neglect, 18, 663–677.

Currie, D.H. (1998). Violent men or violent women? Whose definition counts? In R.K. Bergen (Ed.), Issues in intimate violence (pp. 97–111). Thousand Oaks, CA: Sage.

Daly, M., & Wilson, M. (1994). Evolutionary psychology of male violence. In J. Archer (Ed.), Male violence (pp. 253–288). London: Routledge.

Darwin, C. (1859). On the origin of species. London: Murray.

Davis, R.C., Brickman, E., & Baker, T.

(1991). Supportive and unsupportive responses of others to rape victims: Effects on concurrent victim adjustment. *American Journal of Community Psychology, 19,* 443–451.

Decker, S.H., & van Winkle, B. (1996). *Life in the gang.* New York: Cambridge University Press.

Demaré, D., Briere, J., & Lips, H.M. (1988). Violent pornography and self-reported likelihood of sexual aggression. *Journal of Research in Personality, 22,* 140–153.

Department of Health (Ed.) (1999). *Children and young people on child protection registers.* London: Government Statistical Service.

Diamond, E.L. (1982). The role of anger and hostility in essential hypertension and coronary heart disease. *Psychological Bulletin, 92,* 410–433.

Diener, E. (1976). Effects of prior destructive behavior, anonymity, and group presence on deindividuation and aggression. *Journal of Personality and Social Psychology, 33,* 497–507.

Dietz, T.L. (1998). An examination of violence and gender role portrayals in video games: Implications for gender socialization and aggressive behavior. *Sex Roles, 38,* 425–442.

DiLalla, L.F., & Gottesman, I.I. (1991). Biological and genetic contributions to violence: Widom's untold tale. *Psychological Bulletin, 109,* 125–129.

Dill, K.E., Anderson, C.A., Anderson, K.B., & Deuser, W.E. (1997). Effects of aggressive personality on social expectations and social perceptions. *Journal of Research in Personality, 31,* 272–292.

Dill, K.E., & Dill, J.C. (1998). Video game violence: A review of the empirical literature. *Aggression and Violent Behavior, 3,* 407–428.

Dollard, J., Doob, L.W., Miller, N.E., Mowrer, O.H., & Sears, R.R. (1939). *Frustration and aggression.* New Haven, CT: Yale University Press.

Donnerstein, E. (1984). Pornography: Its effect on violence against women. In N.M. Malamuth & E. Donnerstein (Eds.), *Pornography and sexual aggression* (pp. 53–81). Orlando, FL: Academic Press.

Donnerstein, E., & Wilson, D.W. (1976). The effects of noise and perceived control on ongoing and subsequent aggressive behaviour. *Journal of Personality and Social Psychology, 34,* 774–781.

Donnerstein, M., & Donnerstein, E. (1978). Direct and vicarious censure in the control of interracial aggression. *Journal of Personality, 46,* 162–175.

Downs, W.R., & Miller, B.A. (1998). Relationships between experiences of parents' violence during childhood and women's psychiatric symptomatology. *Journal of Interpersonal Violence, 13,* 438–455.

Drieschner, K., & Lange, A. (1999). A review of cognitive factors in the etiology of rape. *Clinical Psychology Review, 19,* 57–77.

Duncan, R.D. (1999). Peer and sibling aggression: An investigation of intra- and extra-familial bullying. *Journal of Interpersonal Violence, 14,* 871–886.

Dunning, E., Murphy, P. & Williams, J. (1986). Spectator violence at football matches: Towards a sociological explanation. *British Journal of Sociology, 37,* 221–244.

Eagly, A.H. (1987). *Sex differences in social behavior: A social role interpretation.* Hillsdale, NJ: Lawrence Erlbaum Associates Inc.

Eagly, A.H., & Steffen, F.J. (1986). Gender and aggressive behavior: A meta-analytic review of the social psychological literature. *Psychological Bulletin, 100,* 309–330.

Eagly, A.H., & Wood, W. (1999). The origins of sex differences in human behaviour: Evolved dispositions versus social roles. *American Psychologist, 54,* 408–423.

Ellis, L. (1989). *Theories of rape: Inquiries into the causes of sexual aggression.* New York: Hemisphere.

Ellison, C.G., & Sherkat, D.E. (1993). Conservative protestantism and support for corporal punishment. *American Sociological Review, 58,* 131–144.

Englander, E.K. (1997). *Understanding violence.* Mahwah, NJ: Lawrence Erlbaum Associates Inc.

Erdley, C.A., & Asher, S.R. (1998). Linkages between children's beliefs about the legitimacy of aggression and their behavior. *Social Development, 7,* 321–339.

Eron, L.D. (1982). Parent–child interaction, television violence, and aggression in children. *American Psychologist, 37,* 197–211.

Eron, L.D. (1986). Interventions to mitigate the psychological effects of media violence on aggressive behavior. *Journal of Social Issues, 42,* 155–169.

Eron, L.D. (1987). The development of aggressive behavior from the perspective of a developing behaviorism. *American Psychologist, 42,* 435–442.

Eron, L.D. (1994). Theories of aggression: From drives to cognitions. In L.R. Huesmann (Ed.), *Aggressive behavior: Current perspectives* (pp. 3–11). New York: Plenum Press.

Eron, L.D., Huesmann, L.R., Lefkowitz, M.M., & Walder, O. (1972). Does television violence cause aggression? *American Psychologist, 27,* 253–263.

Eslea, M., & Smith, P.K. (1998). The long-term effectiveness of anti-bullying work in primary schools. *Educational Research, 40,* 203–218.

Featherstone, B. (1996). Victims or villains? Women who physically abuse their children. In B. Fawcett, B. Featherstone, J. Hearn, & C. Toft (Eds.), *Violence and gender relations* (pp. 178–189). London: Sage.

Federal Bureau of Investigation (1998). *Incidents of family violence: An analysis of 1998 NIBRS data.* www.fbi.gov/ucr/98cins.htm.

Fergusson, D.M., & Mullen, P.E. (1999). *Childhood sexual abuse.* Thousand Oaks, CA: Sage.

Feshbach, S. (1994). Nationalism, patriotism, and aggression: A clarification of functional differences. In L.R. Huesmann (Ed.), *Aggressive behavior: Current perspectives* (pp. 275–291). New York: Plenum Press.

Feshbach, S., & Zagrodzka, J. (Eds.) (1997). *Aggression: Biological, developmental, and social perspectives.* New York: Plenum Press.

Fetsch, R.J., Schultz, C.J., & Wahler, J.J. (1999). A preliminary evaluation of the Colorado rethink parenting and anger management program. *Child Abuse and Neglect, 23,* 353–360.

Finkelhor, D. (1986). *A sourcebook on child sexual abuse.* Beverly Hills, CA: Sage.

Finkelhor, D. (1994). The international epidemiology of child sexual abuse. *Child Abuse and Neglect, 18,* 409–417.

Finkelhor, D., & Browne, A. (1985). The traumatic impact of child sexual abuse: A conceptualization. *American Journal of Orthopsychiatry, 55,* 530–541.

Finkelhor, D., & Dziuba-Leatherman, J. (1995). Victimization prevention programs: A national survey of children's exposure and reactions. *Child Abuse and Neglect, 19,* 19–28.

Finkelhor, D., Moore, D., Hamby, S.L., & Straus, M.A. (1997). Sexually abused children in a national survey of parents: Methodological issues. *Child Abuse and Neglect, 21,* 1–9.

Fischhoff, B. (1992). Giving advice: Decision theory perspectives on sexual assault. *American Psychologist, 47,* 577–588.

Fitzgerald, L.F. (1993). Sexual harassment:

Violence against women in the workplace. *American Psychologist, 48,* 1070–1076.

Fitzgerald, L.F., Drasgow, F., Hulin, C.L., Gelfand, M.J., & Magley, V.J. (1997). Antecedents and consequences of sexual harassment in organizations: A test of an integrated model. *Journal of Applied Psychology, 82,* 578–589.

Fitzgerald, L.F., & Ormerod, A.J. (1993). Breaking the silence: The sexual harassment of women in the academia and the workplace. In F. Denmark & M. Paludi (Eds.), *Psychology of women: A handbook of issues and theories* (pp. 553–581). Westport, CT: Greenwood Press.

Flannery, D.J., & Williams, L. (1999). Effective youth violence prevention. In T.P. Gullotta & S.J. McElhaney (Eds.), *Violence in homes and communities: Prevention, intervention, and treatment* (pp. 207–244). Thousand Oaks, CA: Sage.

Flores, S.A., & Hartlaub, M.G. (1998). Reducing rape-myth acceptance in male college students: A meta-analysis of intervention studies. *Journal of College Student Development, 39,* 438–448.

Fortin, A., & Chamberland, C. (1995). Preventing the psychological maltreatment of children. *Journal of Interpersonal Violence, 10,* 275–295.

Frazier, P. (1990). Victim attributions and post-rape trauma. *Journal of Personality and Social Psychology, 59,* 298–304.

Freedman, J.L. (1988). Television violence and aggression: What the evidence shows. In S. Oskamp (Ed.), *Applied social psychology annual* (Vol. 8, pp. 144–162). Newbury Park, CA: Sage.

Freud, S. (1920). *Beyond the pleasure principle.* New York: Bantam Books.

Friedland, N. (1988). Political terrorism: A social psychological perspective. In W. Stroebe, A.W. Kruglanski, D. Bar-Tal, & M. Hewstone (Eds.), *The social psychology of intergroup conflict* (pp. 103–114). New York: Springer.

Friedrich, W.N., Berliner, L., Urquiza, A.J., & Beilke, R.L. (1988). Brief diagnostic group treatment of sexually abused boys. *Journal of Interpersonal Violence, 3,* 331–343.

Fritsch, E.J., Caeti, T.J., & Taylor, R.W. (1999). Gang suppression through saturation patrol, aggressive curfew and truancy enforcement: A quasi-experimental test of the Dallas anti-gang initiative. *Crime and Delinquency, 45,* 122–139.

Furby, L., Fischhoff, B., & Morgan, M. (1990). Preventing rape: How people perceive the options for assault prevention. In E. Viano (Ed.), *The victimology handbook* (pp. 227–259). New York: Garland.

Geen, R.G. (1990). *Human aggression.* Milton Keynes: Open University Press.

Geen, R.G. (1995). Violence. In A.S.R. Manstead & M. Hewstone (Eds.), *Blackwell dictionary of social psychology* (p. 669). Oxford: Blackwell.

Geen, R.G. (1998a). Aggression and antisocial behavior. In D.T. Gilbert, S.T. Fiske, & G. Lindzey (Eds.), *The handbook of social psychology* (4th ed, Vol. II, pp. 317–356). Boston, MA: McGraw-Hill.

Geen, R.G. (1998b). Processes and personal variables in affecting aggression. In R.G. Geen & E. Donnerstein (Eds.), *Human aggression: Theories, research and implications for social policy* (pp. 2–21). San Diego, CA: Academic Press.

Geen, R.G., & Bushman, B.J. (1997). Behavioral effects of observing violence. In *Encyclopedia of human biology* (Vol. 1, pp. 705–714). New York: Academic Press.

Geen, R.G., & Donnerstein, E. (Eds.) (1998). *Human aggression: Theories, research and implications for social policy.* San Diego, CA: Academic Press.

Geen, R.G., & McCown, E.J. (1984). Effects of noise and attack on aggression and physiological arousal. *Motivation and Emotion, 8*, 231–241.

Geen, R.G., & O'Neal, E.C. (1969). Activation of cue-elicited aggression by general arousal. *Journal of Personality and Social Psychology, 11*, 289–292.

Geen, R.G., & Thomas, S.L. (1986). The immediate effects of media violence on behavior. *Journal of Social Issues, 42*, 7–27.

Gelles, R.J. (1997). *Intimate violence in families* (3rd ed.). Thousand Oaks, CA: Sage.

Gelles, R.J. (2000). Estimating the incidence and prevalence of violence against women: National data systems and sources. *Violence Against Women, 6*, 784–804.

Gentry, C.S. (1991). Pornography and rape: An empirical analysis. *Deviant Behavior, 12*, 277–288.

Giancola, P.R., & Zeichner, A. (1995). An investigation of gender differences in alcohol-related aggression. *Journal of Studies on Alcohol, 56*, 573–579.

Gidycz, C.A., Coble, C.N., Latham, L., & Layman, M.J. (1993). Sexual assault experience in adulthood and prior victimization experiences. *Psychology of Women Quarterly, 17*, 151–168.

Gidycz, C.A., Hanson, K.A., & Layman, M.J. (1995). A prospective analysis of the relationships among sexual assault experiences. *Psychology of Women Quarterly, 19*, 5–29.

Glass, G.V., McGaw, B., & Smith, M.L. (1981). *Meta-analysis in social research.* Beverly Hills, CA: Sage.

Goldstein, A.P. (1994a). Delinquent gangs. In L.R. Huesmann (Ed.), *Aggressive behavior: Current perspectives* (pp. 255–273). New York: Plenum Press.

Goldstein, A.P. (1994b). *The ecology of aggression.* New York: Plenum Press.

Green, A.H. (1999). Female sex offenders. In J.A. Shaw (Ed.), *Sexual aggression* (pp. 195–210). Washington, DC: American Psychiatric Press.

Gresswell, D.M., & Hollin, C.R. (1994). Multiple murder: A review. *British Journal of Criminology, 34*, 1–14.

Griffin, L.W. (1999). Understanding elder abuse. In R.L. Hampton (Ed.), *Family violence: Prevention and treatment* (2nd ed.) (pp. 260–287). Thousand Oaks, CA: Sage.

Griffiths, M. (1997). Video games and aggression. *The Psychologist, 10*, 397–401.

Groebel, J., & Gleich, U. (1993). *Gewaltprofil des deutschen Fernsehprogramms.* Opladen: Leske & Budrich.

Gross, A.B., & Keller, H.R. (1992). Long-term consequences of childhood physical and psychological maltreatment. *Aggressive Behavior, 18*, 171–185.

Guijarro, M.L., & Hallet, A.J. (1996). A meta-analysis of research on hostility and physical health. *Psychological Bulletin, 119*, 322–348.

Gunter, B., & Harrison, J. (1998). *Violence on television.* London: Routledge.

Gustafson, R. (1994). Alcohol and aggression. *Journal of Offender Rehabilitation, 21*, 41–80.

Hall, E.R., Howard, J.A., & Boezio, S.L. (1986). Tolerance of rape: A sexist or antisocial attitude? *Psychology of Women Quarterly, 10*, 101–118.

Hall, G.C.N., & Hirschman, R. (1991). Toward a theory of sexual aggression: A quadripartite model. *Journal of Consulting and Clinical Psychology, 59*, 662–669.

Hall, G.C.N., Shondrick, D.D., & Hirschman, R. (1993). The role of sexual arousal in sexually aggressive behavior: A meta-analysis. *Journal of Consulting and Clinical Psychology, 61*, 1091–1095.

Halpern, C.T., Udry, R.J., Campbell, B., & Suchindran, C. (1993). Relationships between aggression and pubertal increases in testosterone: A panel analysis of adolescent males. *Social Biology, 40*, 8–24.

Hamberger, L.K., Lohr, J.M., Bonge, D., & Tolin, D.F. (1997). An empirical classification of motivations for domestic violence. *Violence Against Women, 3,* 401–423.

Hamilton, J.T. (1998). *Channeling violence.* Princeton, NJ: Princeton University Press.

Hamilton, M., & Yee, L. (1990). Rape knowledge and propensity to rape. *Journal of Research in Personality, 24,* 111–122.

Hampton, R.L. (Ed.) (1999). *Family violence: Prevention and treatment* (2nd ed.). Thousand Oaks, CA: Sage.

Hanson, K.A., & Gidycz, C.A. (1993). Evaluation of a sexual assault prevention program. *Journal of Consulting and Clinical Psychology, 61,* 1046–1052.

Harburg, E., Blakelock, E.H., & Roeper, P.J. (1979). Resentful and reflective coping with arbitrary authority and blood pressure: Detroit. *Psychosomatic Medicine, 41,* 189–202.

Harding, C.F. (1985). Sociobiological hypotheses about rape: A critical look at the data behind the hypotheses. In S.R. Sunday & E. Tobach (Eds.), *Violence against women: A critique of the sociobiology of rape* (pp. 23–85). New York: Gordian Press.

Harris, M.B. (1974). Mediators between frustration and aggression in a field experiment. *Journal of Experimental Social Psychology, 10,* 561–571.

Harway, M., & O'Neil, J.M. (Eds.) (1999). *What causes men's violence against women?* Thousand Oaks, CA: Sage.

Hawkins, D.F. (1999). What can we learn from data disaggregation? The case of homicide and African Americans. In M.D. Smith & M.A. Zahn (Eds.), *Homicide. A sourcebook of social research* (pp. 195–210). Thousand Oaks, CA: Sage.

Hearold, S. (1986). A synthesis of 1043 effects of television on social behavior. In G. Comstock (Ed.), *Public communication and behavior* (Vol. 1, pp. 65–133). San Diego, CA: Academic Press.

Hegar, R.L., Zuravin, S.J., & Orme, J.G. (1994). Factors predicting severity of physical child abuse injury. *Journal of Interpersonal Violence, 9,* 170–183.

Heide, K.M. (1999). Youth homicide. In M.D. Smith & M.A. Zahn (Eds.), *Homicide: A sourcebook of social research* (pp. 221–238). Thousand Oaks, CA: Sage.

Heise, L. (1998). Violence against women: An integrated, ecological framework. *Violence Against Women, 4,* 262–290.

Herman, D. (1984). The rape culture. In J. Freeman (Ed.), *Women: A feminist perspective* (3rd ed., pp. 20–38). Palo Alto, CA: Mayfield.

Hilton, N.Z., Harris, G.T., Rice, M.E., Krans, T.S., & Lavigne, S.E. (1998). Antiviolence education in high schools: Implementation and evaluation. *Journal of Interpersonal Violence, 13,* 726–742.

Himelein, M.J. (1995). Risk factors for sexual victimization in dating. *Psychology of Women Quarterly, 19,* 31–48.

Hinde, R. (1997). Is war a consequence of human aggression? In S. Feshbach & J. Zagrodzka (Eds.), *Aggression: Biological, developmental, and social perspectives* (pp. 177–183). New York: Plenum Press.

Hoel, H., Rayner, C., & Cooper, C.L. (1999). Workplace bullying. In C.L. Cooper & I.T. Robertson (Eds.), *International review of industrial and organizational psychology* (Vol. 14, pp. 195–230). New York: Wiley.

Hogben, M. (1998). Factors moderating the effect of televised aggression on viewer behavior. *Communication Research, 25,* 220–247.

Holtzworth-Munroe, A., & Stuart, G.L. (1994). Typologies of male batterers: Three subtypes and the differences among them. *Psychological Bulletin, 116,* 476–497.

Howells, K. (1989). Anger management methods in relation to the prevention of violent behaviour. In J. Archer & K. Browne (Eds.), *Human aggression: Naturalistic approaches* (pp. 153–181). London: Routledge.

Hsieh, C.C., & Pugh, M.D. (1993). Poverty, income inequality, and violent crime: A meta-analysis of recent aggregate data studies. *Criminal Justice Review, 18,* 182–202.

Huesmann, L.R. (1986). Psychological processes promoting the relation between exposure to media violence and aggressive behavior by the viewer. *Journal of Social Issues, 42,* 125–139.

Huesmann, L.R. (1988). An information processing model for the development of aggression. *Aggressive Behavior, 11,* 13–24.

Huesmann, L.R. (Ed.) (1994). *Aggressive behavior: Current perspectives.* New York: Plenum Press.

Huesmann, L.R. (1998). The role of information processing and cognitive schema in the acquisition and maintenance of habitual aggressive behavior. In R.G. Geen & E. Donnerstein (Eds.), *Human aggression: Theories, research and implications for social policy* (pp. 73–109). San Diego, CA: Academic Press.

Huesmann, L.R., & Eron, L.D. (Eds.) (1986). *Television and the aggressive child: A cross-national comparison.* Hillsdale, NJ: Lawrence Erlbaum Associates Inc.

Huesmann, L.R., Eron, L.D., Klein, A., Brice, P., & Fischer, P. (1983). Mitigating the imitation of aggressive behaviors by changing children's attitudes about media violence. *Journal of Personality and Social Psychology, 44,* 899–910.

Huesmann, L.R. & Guerra, N.G. (1997). Children's normative beliefs about aggression and aggressive behavior.

Journal of Personality and Social Psychology, 72, 408–419.

Huesmann, L.R., & Miller, L.S. (1994). Long-term effects of the repeated exposure to media violence in childhood. In L.R. Huesmann (Ed.), *Aggressive behavior: Current perspectives* (pp. 153–186). New York: Plenum Press.

Hull, J.G., Levenson, R.W., Young, R.D., & Sher, K.J. (1983). Self-awareness-reducing effects of alcohol consumption. *Journal of Personality and Social Psychology, 44,* 461–473.

Humpert, W., & Dann, H.-D. (1988). *Das Beobachtungssystem BAVIS. Ein Beobachtungsverfahren zur Analyse von aggressionsbezogenen Interaktionen im Schulunterricht.* Göttingen: Hogrefe.

Hunter, C., & McClelland, K. (1991). Honoring accounts for sexual harassment: A factorial survey analysis. *Sex Roles, 24,* 725–751.

Hyde, J.S. (1984). How large are gender differences in aggression? A developmental meta-analysis. *Developmental Psychology, 20,* 722–736.

Intons-Peterson, M.J., Roskos-Ewoldsen, B., Thomas, L., Shirley, M., & Blut, D. (1989). Will educational material reduce negative effects of exposure to sexual violence? *Journal of Social and Clinical Psychology, 8,* 256–275.

Ito, T.A., Miller, N., & Pollock, V.E. (1996). Alcohol and aggression: A meta-analysis of the moderating effects of inhibitory cues, triggering cues, and self-focused attention. *Psychological Bulletin, 120,* 60–82.

Jackson, S. (1978). The social context of rape: Sexual scripts and motivation. *Women's Studies International Quarterly, 1,* 27–38.

Jaffee, D., & Straus, M.A. (1987). Sexual climate and reported rape: A state-level analysis. *Archives of Sexual Behavior, 16,* 107–123.

Johnson, R.D., & Downing, L.L. (1979).

Deindividuation and valence of cues: Effects on prosocial and antisocial behavior. *Journal of Personality and Social Psychology, 37,* 1532–1538.

Jonas, K. (1992). Modelling and suicide: A test of the Werther effect. *British Journal of Social Psychology, 31,* 295–306.

Jones, E.D., & McCurdy, K. (1992). The links between types of maltreatment and demographic characteristics of children. *Child Abuse and Neglect, 16,* 201–215.

Jones, T.S., & Remland, M.S. (1992). Sources of variability in perceptions of and responses to sexual harassment. *Sex Roles, 27,* 358–383.

Kahn, A.S., Mathie, V.A., & Torgler, C. (1994). Rape scripts and rape acknowledgement. *Psychology of Women Quarterly, 18,* 53–66.

Kanin, E.J. (1985). Date rapists: Sexual socialization and relative deprivation. *Archives of Sexual Behaviour, 14,* 219–231.

Kazdin, A.E. (1987). Treatment of antisocial behavior in children: Current status and future directions. *Psychological Bulletin, 102,* 187–203.

Keeney, B.T., & Heide, K.M. (1994). Gender differences in serial murderers. *Journal of Interpersonal Violence, 9,* 383–398.

Kemp, A., Green, B., Hovanitz, C., & Rawlings, C. (1995). Incidence and correlates of post-traumatic stress disorder in battered women: Shelter and community samples. *Journal of Interpersonal Violence, 10,* 43–55.

Kendall-Tackett, K.A., & Marshall, R. (1998). Sexual victimization of children. In R.K. Bergen (Ed.), *Issues in intimate violence* (pp. 47–63). Thousand Oaks, CA: Sage.

Kendall-Tackett, K.A., Williams, L.M., & Finkelhor, D. (1993). Impact of sexual abuse of children: A review and synthesis of recent empirical studies. *Psychological Bulletin, 113,* 164–180.

Kent, A., & Waller, G. (1998). The impact of childhood emotional abuse: An extension of the child abuse and trauma scale. *Child Abuse and Neglect, 22,* 393–399.

Killias, M. (1993). Gun ownership, suicide, and homicide: An international perspective. In A. Del Frate, U. Zvekic, & J.J. van Dijk (Eds.), *Understanding crime: Experiences of crime and crime control* (pp. 289–302). Rome: United States Interregional Crime and Justice Research Institute.

Kilpatrick, D.G., Edmunds, C.N., & Seymour, A.K. (1992). *Rape in America: Report to the nation.* National Victim Center.

Kingston, L., & Prior, M. (1995). The development of patterns of stable, transient, and school-age onset aggressive behavior in young children. *Journal of the American Academy of Child and Adolescent Psychiatry, 34,* 348–358.

Kirby, T., & Foster, J. (1993). Video link to Bulger murder disputed. *The Independent,* 26 November 1993.

Kleck, E., & Sayles, S. (1990). Rape and resistance. *Social Problems, 37,* 149–162.

Kleck, G., & Hogan, M. (1999). National case–control study of homicide offending and gun ownership. *Social Problems, 46,* 275–293.

Kleck, G., & Patterson, E.B. (1993). The impact of gun control and gun ownership levels on violence rates. *Journal of Quantitative Criminology, 9,* 249–287.

Knight, G.P., Fabes, R.A., & Higgins, D.A. (1996). Concerns about drawing causal inferences from meta-analyses: An example in the study of gender differences in aggression. *Psychological Bulletin, 119,* 410–421.

Knudsen, D.D., & Miller, J.L. (Eds.) (1991). *Abused and battered: Social and legal responses to family violence.* New York: Aldine de Gruyter.

Kodluboy, D.W. (1997). Gang-oriented interventions. In A.P. Goldstein & J.C.

Conoly (Eds.), *School violence intervention* (pp. 189–214). New York: Guilford Press.

Koss, M.P. (1985). The hidden rape victim: Personality, attitudinal, and situational characteristics. *Psychology of Women Quarterly, 9,* 193–212.

Koss, M.P. (1992). The underdetection of rape: Methodological choices influence incidence estimates. *Journal of Social Issues, 48,* 61–75.

Koss, M.P., & Cook, S.L. (1998). Facing the facts. Date and acquaintance rape are significant problems for women. In R.K. Bergen (Ed.), *Issues in intimate violence* (pp. 147–156). Thousand Oaks, CA: Sage.

Koss, M.P., Dinero, T.E., Seibel, C.A., & Cox, S.L. (1988). Stranger and acquaintance rape. Are there differences in the victim's experience? *Psychology of Women Quarterly, 12,* 1–24.

Koss, M.P., Gidycz, C.A., & Wisniewski, N. (1987). The scope of rape: Incidence and prevalence of sexual aggression and victimization in a national sample of higher education students. *Journal of Consulting and Clinical Psychology, 55,* 162–170.

Koss, M.P., Goodman, L.A., Browne, A., Fitzgerald, L.F., Keita, G.P., & Russo, N.F. (1994). *No safe haven: Male violence against women at home, at work, and in the community.* Washington, DC: American Psychological Association.

Koss, M.P., & Harvey, M.R. (1991). *The rape victim: Clinical and community interventions.* Newbury Park, CA: Sage.

Koss, M.P., & Oros, C.J. (1982). Sexual experiences survey: A research instrument investigating sexual aggression and victimization. *Journal of Consulting and Clinical Psychology, 50,* 455–457.

Krafka, C., Linz, D., Donnerstein, E., & Penrod, S. (1997). Women's reactions to sexually aggressive mass media depictions. *Violence Against Women, 3,* 149–181.

Krahé, B. (1988). Victim and observer characteristics as determinants of responsibility attributions to victims of rape. *Journal of Applied Social Psychology, 18,* 50–58.

Krahé, B. (1991). Social psychological issues in the study of rape. In W. Stroebe & M. Hewstone (Eds.), *European review of social psychology* (Vol. 2, pp. 279–309). Chichester: Wiley.

Krahé, B. (1992). *Personality and social psychology. Towards a synthesis.* London: Sage.

Krahé, B. (1998). Sexual aggression among adolescents: Prevalence and predictors in a German sample. *Psychology of Women Quarterly, 22,* 537–554.

Krahé, B. (2000a). Childhood sexual abuse and revictimization in adolescence and adulthood. *Journal of Personal and Interpersonal Loss, 5,* 149–165.

Krahé, B. (2000b). Sexual scripts and heterosexual aggression. In T. Eckes & H.M. Trautner (Eds.), *The developmental social psychology of gender* (pp. 273–292). Mahwah, NJ: Lawrence Erlbaum Associates Inc.

Krahé, B. (2000c). *Risk markers of sexual victimization among women and (gay) men: Exploring parallels in female and male sexual victimization.* Paper presented at the XIVth World Meeting of the International Society for Research on Aggression, Valencia, Spain.

Krahé, B. (in prep.) Male victims of female sexual aggression. Manuscript in preparation.

Krahé, B., & Fenske, I. (in press). Predicting aggressive driving behaviour. The role of macho personality, age and power of car. *Aggressive Behavior.*

Krahé, B., Scheinberger-Olwig, R., & Kolpin, S. (2000). Ambiguous communication of sexual intentions as a risk marker of sexual aggression. *Sex Roles*, 42, 313–337.

Krahé, B., Scheinberger-Olwig, R., & Schütze, S. (in press). Risk factors of sexual aggression and victimization among homosexual men. *Journal of Applied Social Psychology*.

Krahé, B., Scheinberger-Olwig, R., & Waizenhöfer, E. (1999). Sexuelle Aggression zwischen Jugendlichen. [Sexual aggression among adolescents]. *Zeitschrift für Sozialpsychologie, 30*, 165–178.

Krahé, B., Scheinberger-Olwig, R., Waizenhöfer, E. & Kolpin, S. (1999). Childhood sexual abuse and revictimization in adolescence. *Child Abuse and Neglect, 23*, 383–394.

Krahé, B., Schütze, S., Fritsche, I., & Waizenhöfer, E. (2000). The prevalence of sexual aggression and victimization among homosexual men. *Journal of Sex Research, 37*, 142–150.

Krauss, H.H., & Krauss, B.J. (1995). Domestic violence and its prevention. In L.L. Adler, & F.L. Denmark (Eds.), *Violence and the prevention of violence* (pp. 129–144). Westport, CT: Praeger.

Kruttschnitt, C. (1995). Violence by and violence against women: A comparative and cross-national analysis. In B.R. Ruback, & N.A. Weiner (Eds.), *Interpersonal violent behaviors* (pp. 89–108). New York: Springer.

LaFree, G. (1999). A summary and review of cross-national comparative studies of homicide. In M.D. Smith & M.A. Zahn (Eds.), *Homicide. A sourcebook of social research* (pp. 125–145). Thousand Oaks, CA: Sage.

LaFree, G., & Drass, K.A. (1996). The effects of changes in intraracial income inequality and educational attainment on changes in arrest rates for African Americans and Whites. *American Sociological Review, 61*, 614–634.

Langley, T., O'Neal, E.C., Craig, K.M., & Yost, E.A. (1992). Aggression-consistent, -inconsistent, and -irrelevant priming effects on selective exposure to media violence. *Aggressive Behavior, 18*, 349–356.

Laplace, A., Chermack, S.T., & Taylor, S.P. (1994). Effects of alcohol and drinking experience on human physical aggression. *Personality and Social Psychology Bulletin, 20*, 439–444.

Larimer, M.E., Lydum, A.R., Anderson, B.K., & Turner, A.P. (1999). Male and female recipients of unwanted sexual contact in a college student sample: Prevalence rates, alcohol use, and depression symptoms. *Sex Roles, 40*, 295–308.

Laub, J.H., & Lauritsen, J.L. (1995). Violent criminal behavior over the life-course: A review of the longitudinal and comparative research. In B.R. Ruback & N.A. Weiner (Eds.), *Interpersonal violent behaviors* (pp. 43–61). New York: Springer.

LeBon, G. (1896). *The crowd: A study of the popular mind*. London: T. Fisher Unwin.

Lefkowitz, M.M., Eron, L.D., Walder, L.O., & Huesmann, L.R. (1977). *Growing up to be violent*. New York: Pergamon.

Leibman, M. (1970). The effects of race and sex norms on personal space. *Environment and Behavior, 2*, 208–246.

Lenington, S. (1985). Sociobiological theory and the violent abuse of women. In S.R. Sunday & E. Tobach (Eds.), *Violence against women: A critique of the sociobiology of rape* (pp. 13–22). New York: Gordian Press.

Leonard, K.E. (1989). The impact of explicit aggressive and implicit nonaggressive cues on aggression on intoxicated and sober males. *Personality and Social Psychology Bulletin, 15*, 390–400.

Leonard, K.E., & Roberts, L.J. (1996). The effects of alcohol on the marital interactions of aggressive and nonaggressive husbands and their wives. *Journal of Abnormal Psychology, 107*, 602–615.

Leymann, H. (1993). Mobbing: Psychoterror am Arbeitsplatz und wie man sich dagegen wehren kann. [Mobbing: Psychological terrorization in the work place and how to fight it.] Reinbek: Rowohlt.

Lieberman, J.D., Solomon, S., Greenberg, J., & McGregor, H.A. (1999). A hot new way to measure aggression: Hot sauce allocation. *Aggressive Behavior, 25*, 331–348.

Lightdale, J.R., & Prentice, D.A. (1994). Rethinking sex differences in aggression: Aggressive behavior in the absence of social roles. *Personality and Social Psychology Bulletin, 20*, 34–44.

Lindsay, J.A., & Anderson, C.A. (2000). From antecedent conditions to violent actions: A general affective aggression model. *Personality and Social Psychology Bulletin, 26*, 533–547.

Linz, D. (1989). Exposure to sexually explicit materials and attitudes toward rape: A comparison of study results. *Journal of Sex Research, 26*, 50–84.

Linz, D., Donnerstein, E., & Adams, S. (1989). Physiological desensitization and judgments about female victims of violence. *Human Communication Research, 15*, 509–522.

Linz, D., & Malamuth, N.M. (1993). *Pornography*. Newbury Park, CA: Sage.

Linz, D., Wilson, B.J., & Donnerstein, E. (1992). Sexual violence in the mass media: Legal solutions, warnings, and mitigation through education. *Journal of Social Issues, 48*, 145–171.

Lisak, D. (1994). Subjective assessment of relationship with parents by sexually aggressive and nonaggressive men. *Journal of Interpersonal Violence, 9*, 399–411.

Lisak, D., & Roth, S. (1990). Motives and psychodynamics of self-reported, unincarcerated rapists. *American Journal of Orthopsychiatry, 60*, 268–280.

Lochman, J.E., & Dodge, K.A. (1994). Social-cognitive processes of severely violent, moderately aggressive, and nonaggressive boys. *Journal of Consulting and Clinical Psychology, 62*, 366–374.

Loeber, R., & Hay, D. (1997). Key issues in the development of aggression from childhood to early adulthood. *Annual Review of Psychology, 48*, 371–410.

Loeber, R., & Stouthamer-Loeber, M. (1998). Development of juvenile aggression and violence: Some common misconceptions and controversies. *American Psychologist, 53*, 242–259.

Lonsway, K.A., & Fitzgerald, L.F. (1994). Rape myths. *Psychology of Women Quarterly, 18*, 133–164.

Lore, R.K., & Schultz, L.A. (1993). Control of human aggression: A comparative perspective. *American Psychologist, 48*, 16–25.

Lorenz, K. (1974). *Civilized world's eight deadly sins*. New York: Harcourt, Brace, Jovanovich.

Lubek, I. (1995). Aggression research. *Theory and Psychology, 5*, 99–129.

Maccoby, E. (1998). *The two sexes: Growing up apart, coming together*. Cambridge, MA: Belknap Press.

Malamuth, N.M. (1981). Rape proclivity among males. *Journal of Social Issues, 37*, 138–157.

Malamuth, N.M. (1998). The confluence model as an organizing framework for research on sexually aggressive men: Risk moderators, imagined aggression, and pornography consumption. In R.G. Geen & E. Donnerstein (Eds.), *Human aggression: Theories, research and implications for social policy* (pp. 229–245). San Diego, CA: Academic Press.

Malamuth, N.M., & Heilmann, M.F. (1998). Evolutionary psychology and sexual aggression. In C.H. Crawford & D.L. Krebs (Eds.), *Handbook of evolutionary psychology* (pp. 515–542). Mahwah, NJ: Lawrence Erlbaum Associates Inc.

Malamuth, N.M., Linz, D., Heavey, C.L.,

Barnes, G., & Acker, M. (1995). Using the confluence model of sexual aggression to predict men's conflict with women: A 10-year follow-up study. *Journal of Personality and Social Psychology, 69*, 353–369.

Malamuth, N.M., Sockloskie, R.J., Koss, M.P., & Tanaka, J.S. (1991). Characteristics of aggressors against women: Testing a model using a national sample of college students. *Journal of Consulting and Clinical Psychology, 59*, 670–681.

Mandoki, C.A., & Burkhart, B.R. (1989). Sexual victimization: Is there a vicious cycle? *Violence and Victims, 4*, 179–190.

Marcus-Newhall, A., Pedersen, W.C., Carlson, M., & Miller, N. (2000). Displaced aggression is alive and well: A meta-analytic review. *Journal of Personality and Social Psychology, 78*, 670–689.

Marin, A.J., & Russo, N.F. (1999). Feminist perspectives of male violence against women: Critiquing O'Neil and Harway's model. In M. Harway & J.M. O'Neil (Eds.), *What causes men's violence against women?* (pp. 18–35). Thousand Oaks, CA: Sage.

Marshall, W.L. (1989). Intimacy, loneliness and sexual offenders. *Behavior Research and Therapy, 27*, 491–503.

Martinez, R., & Lee, M.T. (1999). Extending ethnicity in homicide research. The case of Latinos. In M.D. Smith & M.A. Zahn (Eds.), *Homicide: A sourcebook of social research* (pp. 211–220). Thousand Oaks, CA: Sage.

Mattaini, M.A., McGowan, B.G., & Williams, G. (1996). Child maltreatment. In M.A. Mattaini & B.A. Thyer (Eds.), *Finding solutions to social problems* (pp. 223–266). Washington, DC: American Psychological Association.

Mattaini, M.A., Twyman, J.S., Chin, W., & Lee, K.N. (1996). Youth violence. In M.A. Mattaini & B.A. Thyer (Eds.), *Finding solutions to social problems* (pp. 75–111). Washington, DC: American Psychological Association.

Maxon, C.L. (1999). Gang homicide. In M.D. Smith & M.A. Zahn (Eds.), *Homicide: A sourcebook of social research* (pp. 239–254). Thousand Oaks, CA: Sage.

Mayall, A., & Gold, S.R. (1995). Definitional issues and mediating variables in the sexual revictimization of women sexually abused as children. *Journal of Interpersonal Violence, 10*, 26–42.

Maynard, W., & Read, T. (1997). *Policing racially motivated incidents*. London: Home Office Research Group.

Mays, V.M., Bullock, M., Rosenzweig, M.R., & Wessells, M. (1998). Ethnic conflict. *American Psychologist, 53*, 737–742.

McCurdy, K., & Daro, D. (1994). Child maltreatment: A national survey of reports and fatalities. *Journal of Interpersonal Violence, 9*, 75–94.

McDonel, E.C., & McFall, R.M. (1991). Construct validity of two heterosocial perception skill measures for assessing rape proclivity. *Violence and Victims, 6*, 17–30.

McGregor, H.A., Lieberman, J.D., Greenberg, J., Solomon, S., Arndt, J., Simon, L., & Pyszczynski, T. (1998). Terror management and aggression: Evidence that mortality salience motivates aggression against worldview-threatening others. *Journal of Personality and Social Psychology, 74*, 590–605.

McPhail, C. (1994). The dark side of purpose: Individual and collective violence in riots. *The Sociological Quarterly, 35*, 1–32.

McWhirter, B.T., & Page, G.L. (1999). Effects of anger management and goal setting group interventions on state-trait anger and self-efficacy beliefs among high risk adolescents. *Current*

Psychology: Developmental, Learning, Personality, Social, 18, 223–237.

Meichenbaum, D.H. (1975). *Stress inoculation training.* New York: Pergamon Press.

Mercy, J.A., & Hammond, W.R. (1999). In M.D. Smith & M.A. Zahn (Eds.), *Homicide: A sourcebook of social research* (pp. 297–310). Thousand Oaks, CA: Sage.

Merrill, G.S. (1998). Understanding domestic violence among gay and bisexual men. In R.K. Bergen (Ed.), *Issues in intimate violence* (pp. 129–146). Thousand Oaks, CA: Sage.

Messman, T.L., & Long, P.J. (1996). Child sexual abuse and its relationship to revictimization in adult women: A review. *Clinical Psychology Review, 16,* 397–420.

Messner, S.F., & Rosenfeld, R. (1999). Social structure and homicide: Theory and research. In M.D. Smith & M.A. Zahn (Eds.), *Homicide: A sourcebook of social research* (pp. 27–41). Thousand Oaks, CA: Sage.

Meyer, C.B., & Taylor, S.E. (1986). Adjustment to rape. *Journal of Personality and Social Psychology, 50,* 1226–1234.

Milavsky, J.R., Kessler, R., Sipp, H., & Rubens, W.S. (1982). Television and aggression: Results of a panel study. In D. Pearl, L. Bouthilet, & J. Lazar (Eds.), *Television and behavior: Ten years of scientific progress and implications for the 80s* (Vol. 2). Washington, DC: Government Printing Office.

Miles, D.R., & Carey, G. (1997). Genetic and environmental architecture of aggression. *Journal of Personality and Social Psychology, 72,* 207–217.

Milgram, S. (1974). *Obedience to authority.* New York: Harper & Row.

Miller, B.C., Monson, B.H., & Norton, M.C. (1995). The effects of forced sexual intercourse on white female adolescents. *Child Abuse and Neglect, 19,* 1289–1301.

Miller, N.E. (1941). The frustration–aggression hypothesis. *Psychological Review, 48,* 337–342.

Miller, P., & Eisenberg, N. (1988). The role of empathy to externalizing/antisocial behavior. *Psychological Bulletin, 103,* 324–344.

Miller, T.Q., Heath, L., Molcan, J.R., & Dugoni, B.L. (1991). Imitative violence in the real world: A reanalysis of homicide rates following championship prize fights. *Aggressive Behavior, 17,* 121–134.

Miller-Perrin, C.L., & Perrin, R.D. (1999). *Child maltreatment.* Thousand Oaks, CA: Sage.

Milner, J.S., & Crouch, J.L. (1999). Child physical abuse: Theory and research. In R.L. Hampton (Ed.), *Family violence: Prevention and treatment* (2nd ed., pp. 33–65). Thousand Oaks, CA: Sage.

Milner, J.S., & Wimberly, R.C. (1980). Prediction and explanation of child abuse. *Journal of Clinical Psychology, 36,* 875–884.

Mirrlees-Black, C., & Byron, C. (1999). *Domestic violence: Findings from the BCS self-completion questionnaire.* Research Findings No. 86. London: Home Office Research, Development and Statistics Directorate.

Moeller, T., Bachmann, G., & Moeller, J. (1993). The combined effect of physical, sexual, and emotional abuse during childhood: Long-term health consequences for women. *Child Abuse and Neglect, 17,* 623–640.

Moffitt, T.E., Caspi, A., Dickson, N., Silva, P., & Stanton, W. (1996). Childhood-onset vs. adolescent-onset antisocial conduct problems in males: Natural history from ages 3 to 18. *Development and Psychopathology, 8,* 399–424.

Molidor, C.E. (1996). Female gang members: A profile of aggression and victimization. *Social Work, 41,* 251–257.

Moncher, F.J. (1996). The relationship of maternal adult attachment style and risk of physical child abuse. *Journal of Interpersonal Violence, 11*, 335–350.

Mosher, D.L., & Sirkin, M. (1984). Measuring a macho personality constellation. *Journal of Research in Personality, 18*, 150–163.

Muehlenhard, C.L. (1998). The importance and danger of studying sexually aggressive women. In P.B. Anderson & C. Struckman-Johnson (Eds.), *Sexually aggressive women* (pp. 19–48). New York: Guilford Press.

Muehlenhard, C.L., & Hollabaugh, L.C. (1988). Do women sometimes say no when they mean yes? The prevalence and correlates of women's token resistance to sex. *Journal of Personality and Social Psychology, 54*, 872–879.

Muehlenhard, C.L., Powch, I.G., Phelps, J.L., & Giusti, L.M. (1992). Definitions of rape: Scientific and political implications. *Journal of Social Issues, 48*, 23–44.

Mullen, P.E., Martin, J.L., Anderson, J.C., Romans, S.E., & Herbison, G.P. (1993). Childhood sexual abuse and mental health in adult life. *British Journal of Psychiatry, 163*, 721–732.

Mullin, C.R., & Linz, D. (1995). Desensitization and resensitization to violence against women: Effects of exposure to sexually violent films on judgments of domestic violence victims. *Journal of Personality and Social Psychology, 69*, 449–459.

Mummendey, A. (1996). Aggressive behaviour. In M. Hewstone, W. Stroebe, & G.M. Stephenson (Eds.), *Introduction to social psychology* (pp. 403–435). Oxford: Blackwell.

Murdoch, D., Pihl, R.O., & Ross, D. (1990). Alcohol and crimes of violence: Present issues. *International Journal of the Addictions, 25*, 1065–1081.

Murphy, P., Williams, J., & Dunning, E. (1990). *Football on trial: Spectator violence and development in the football world*. London: Routledge.

Mynard, H., & Joseph, S. (2000). Development of a multidimensional peer-victimization scale. *Aggressive Behavior, 26*, 169–178.

National Center for Injury Prevention and Control (2000). *Youth violence in the United States.* www.cdc.gov/ncipc/dvp/fafacts.htm.

National Television Violence Study (1997). Vol. 1. Thousand Oaks, CA: Sage.

Neuman, J.H., & Baron, R.A. (1998). Workplace violence and workplace aggression: Evidence concerning specific forms, potential causes, and preferred targets. *Journal of Management, 24*, 391–419.

Nisbett, R.E. (1993). Violence and U.S. regional culture. *American Psychologist, 48*, 441–449.

Nisbett, R.E., Polly, G., & Lang, S. (1995). Homicide and U.S. regional culture. In R.B. Ruback & N.A. Weiner (Eds.), *Interpersonal violent behaviors* (pp. 135–151). New York: Springer.

Novaco, R.W. (1975). *Anger control: The development and evaluation of an experimental treatment*. Lexington, MA: D.C. Heath.

Nurius, P.S. (2000). Risk perception for acquaintance sexual aggression: A social-cognitive perspective. *Aggression and Violent Behavior, 5*, 63–78.

O'Brien, T.M. (1987). The interracial nature of violent crimes: A reexamination. *American Journal of Sociology, 92*, 817–835.

O'Donohue, W., Downs, K., & Yeater, E.A. (1998). Sexual harassment: A review of the literature. *Aggression and Violent Behavior, 3*, 111–128.

O'Hagan, K.P. (1995). Emotional and psychological abuse: Problems of definition. *Child Abuse and Neglect, 19*, 449–461.

O'Hare, E.O., & O'Donohue, W. (1998). Risk factors relating to sexual harassment: An examination of four models. *Archives of Sexual Behavior, 27,* 561–580.

O'Keefe, M. (1995). Predictors of child abuse in maritally violent families. *Journal of Interpersonal Violence, 10,* 3–25.

Olweus, D. (1979). Stability of aggressive reaction patterns in males: A review. *Psychological Bulletin, 86,* 852–875.

Olweus, D. (1991). Bully/victim problems among schoolchildren: Basic facts and effects of a school based intervention program. In D. Pepler & K. Rubin (Eds.), *The development and treatment of childhood aggression* (pp. 411–448). Hillsdale, NJ: Lawrence Erlbaum Associates Inc.

Olweus, D. (1994). Bullying at school: Long-term outcomes for the victims and an effective school-based intervention program. In L.R. Huesmann (Ed.), *Aggressive behavior: Current perspectives* (pp. 97–130). New York: Plenum Press.

Paik, H., & Comstock, G. (1994). The effects of television violence on antisocial behavior: A meta-analysis. *Communication Research, 21,* 516–546.

Painter, K., & Farrington, D.P. (1998). Marital violence in Great Britain and its relationship to marital and non-marital rape. *International Review of Victimology, 5,* 257–276.

Paludi, M.A. (Ed.). (1990). *Ivory power: Sexual harassment on campus.* Albany, NY: SUNY Press.

Pan, H.S., Neidig, P.H., & O'Leary, K.D. (1994). Predicting mild and severe husband-to-wife physical aggression. *Journal of Consulting and Clinical Psychology, 62,* 975–981.

Parker, R.N., & Auerhahn, K. (1999). Drugs, alcohol, and homicide. In M.D. Smith & M.A. Zahn (Eds.), *Homicide: A sourcebook of social research* (pp. 176–191). Thousand Oaks, CA: Sage.

Patterson, G.R., Reid, J.B., Jones, R.R., & Conger, R.E. (1975). *A social learning approach to family intervention* (Vol. 1: Families with aggressive children). Eugene, OR: Castalia.

Patterson, M.L., Mullens, S., & Romano, J. (1971). Compensatory reactions to spatial intrusion. *Sociometry, 34,* 114–121.

Perry, E.L., Schmidtke, J.M., & Kulik, C.T. (1998). Propensity to sexually harass: An exploration of gender differences. *Sex Roles, 38,* 443–460.

Pillemer, K., & Finkelhor, D. (1988). The prevalence of elder abuse: A random sample survey. *The Gerontologist, 28,* 51–57.

Pillemer, K., & Suitor, J.J. (1988). Elder abuse. In V.B. van Hasselt, R.L. Morrison, A.S. Bellack, & M. Hersen (Eds.), *Handbook of family violence* (pp. 247–270). New York: Plenum Press.

Pino, N.W., & Meier, R.F. (1999). Gender differences in rape reporting. *Sex Roles, 40,* 979–990.

Pollard, P. (1992). Judgements about victims and attackers in depicted rapes: A review. *British Journal of Social Psychology, 31,* 307–326.

Poppen, P.J., & Segal, N.J. (1988). The influence of sex and sex role orientation on sexual coercion. *Sex Roles, 19,* 689–701.

Porter, J.F., & Critelli, J.W. (1994). Self-talk and sexual arousal in sexual aggression. *Journal of Social and Clinical Psychology, 13,* 223–239.

Postmes, T., & Spears, R. (1998). Deindividuation and antinormative behavior: A meta-analysis. *Psychological Bulletin, 123,* 238–259.

Potegal, M., & Knutson, J.F. (Eds.) (1994). *The dynamics of aggression.* Hillsdale, NJ: Lawrence Erlbaum Associates Inc.

Potter, W.J. (1999). *On media violence.* Thousand Oaks, CA: Sage.

Prentky, R.A., & Knight, R.A. (1991). Identifying critical dimensions for discriminating among rapists. *Journal of*

Consulting and Clinical Psychology, *59*, 643–661.

Prino, C.T., & Peyrot, M. (1994). The effect of child physical abuse and neglect on aggressive, withdrawn, and prosocial behavior. *Child Abuse and Neglect*, *18*, 871–884.

Puzone, C.A., Saltzman, L.E., Kresnow, M.J., Thompson, M.P., & Mercy, J.A. (2000). National trends in intimate partner homicide. *Violence Against Women*, *6*, 409–426.

Randall, P. (1997). *Adult bullying*. London: Routledge.

Rayner, C. (1997). The incidence of workplace bullying. *Journal of Applied and Community Psychology*, *7*, 199–208.

Reicher, S.D. (1984). The St. Paul's riot: An explanation of the limits of crowd action in terms of a social identity model. *European Journal of Social Psychology*, *14*, 1–21.

Renfrew, J.W. (1997). *Aggression and its causes*. New York: Oxford University Press.

Renzetti, C.M. (1998). Violence and abuse in lesbian relationships. In R.K. Bergen (Ed.), *Issues in intimate violence* (pp. 117–127). Thousand Oaks, CA: Sage.

Resick, P.A., & Schnicke, M.K. (1993). *Cognitive processing therapy for rape victims: A treatment manual*. Newbury Park, CA: Sage.

Resnick, H.S., Kilpatrick, D.G., & Lipovsky, J.A. (1991). Assessment of rape-related post-traumatic stress disorder: Stressor and symptoms dimensions. *Psychological Assessment*, *3*, 561–572.

Richardson, D.R., Green, L.R., & Lago, T. (1998). The relationship between perspective-taking and nonaggressive responding in the face of an attack. *Journal of Personality*, *66*, 235–256.

Richardson, D.R., Hammock, G.S., Smith, S., Gardner, W.L., & Signo, M. (1994). Empathy as a cognitive inhibitor of interpersonal aggression. *Aggressive Behavior*, *20*, 275–289.

Riggs, D.S., O'Leary, K.D., & Breslin, F.C. (1990). Multiple predictors of physical aggression in dating couples. *Journal of Interpersonal Violence*, *5*, 61–73.

Robinson, T.W., Smith, S.W., Miller, M.D., & Brownell, M.T. (1999). Cognitive behavior modification of hyperactivity–impulsivity and aggression: A meta-analysis of school-based studies. *Journal of Educational Psychology*, *91*, 195–203.

Rosenzweig, S. (1981). The current status of the Rosenzweig Picture–Frustration Study as a measure of aggression in personality. In P.F. Brain & D. Benton (Eds.), *Multidisciplinary approaches to aggression research* (pp. 113–126). Amsterdam: Elsevier.

Rotten, J., Frey, J., Barry, T., Milligan, M., & Fitzpatrick, M. (1979). The air pollution experience and physical aggression. *Journal of Applied Social Psychology*, *9*, 397–412.

Rouhana, N.N., & Bar-Tal, D. (1998). Psychological dynamics of intractable ethnonational conflicts. The Israeli–Palestinian case. *American Psychologist*, *53*, 761–770.

Rozee, P. (1993). Forbidden or forgiven? Rape in cross-cultural perspective. *Psychology of Women Quarterly*, *17*, 499–514.

Rozee, P. (1999). Stranger rape. In M.A. Paludi (Ed.), *Sexual victimization* (pp. 97–115). Westport, CT: Greenwood Press.

Russell, D.H. (1990). *Rape in marriage*. Bloomington, IN: Indiana University Press.

Russell, D.H. (1993). *Against pornography: The evidence of harm*. Berkeley, CA: Russell Publications.

Russell, G.W. (1993). *The social psychology of sport*. New York: Springer.

Rys, G.S., & Bear, G.G. (1997). Relational aggression and peer relations: Gender and developmental issues. *Merrill-Palmer Quarterly, 43*, 87–106.

Sanday, P.R. (1981). The social cultural context of rape. *Journal of Social Issues, 37*, 5–27.

Sanders, B., & Moore, D.L. (1999). Childhood maltreatment and date rape. *Journal of Interpersonal Violence, 14*, 115–124.

Sarrel, P.M., & Masters, W.H. (1982). Sexual molestation of men by women. *Archives of Sexual Behavior, 11*, 117–131.

Schaaf, K.K. & McCanne, T.R. (1998). Relationship of childhood sexual, physical, and combined sexual and physical abuse to adult victimization and posttraumatic stress disorder. *Child Abuse and Neglect, 22*, 1119–1133.

Schachter, S. (1964). The interaction of cognitive and physiological determinants of emotional state. In L. Berkowitz (Ed.), *Advances in experimental social psychology* (Vol. 1, pp. 49–80). New York: Academic Press.

Schank, R., & Abelson, R. (1977). *Scripts, plans, goals, and understanding: An inquiry into human knowledge structures.* Hillsdale, NJ: Lawrence Erlbaum Associates Inc.

Schatz, R.T., & Staub, E. (1997). Manifestations of blind and constructive patriotism: Personality correlates and individual-group relations. In D. Bar-Tal & E. Staub (Eds.), *Patriotism in the lives of individuals and nations* (pp. 229–245). Chicago: Nelson-Hall.

Schneider, K.T., Swan, S., & Fitzgerald, L.F. (1997). Job-related and psychological effects of sexual harassment in the workplace: Empirical evidence from two organizations. *Journal of Applied Psychology, 82*, 401–415.

Schuster, B. (1996). Rejection, exclusion, and harassment at work and in schools. *European Psychologist, 1*, 293–317.

Scott, C.L. (1999). Juvenile violence. *Forensic Psychology, 22*, 71–83.

Scott, J.E., & Schwalm, L. (1988). Rape rates and the circulation rates of adult magazines. *Journal of Sex Research, 24*, 241–250.

Scottish Executive (1999). *Homicide in Scotland 1998.* www.scotland.gov.uk/library2/doc08/.

Sedlak, A.J., & Broadhurst, D.D. (1996). *Third national incidence study on child abuse and neglect.* Washington, DC: US Department of Health and Human Services.

Seligman, M.E.P. (1975). *Helplessness: On depression, development, and death.* San Francisco: Freeman.

Seto, M.C., & Barbaree, H.E. (1997). Sexual aggression as antisocial behavior: A developmental model. In D.M. Stoff, J. Breiling, & J.D. Maser (Eds.), *Handbook of antisocial behavior* (pp. 524–533). New York: Wiley.

Sheffield, C.J. (1993). The invisible intruder: Women's experiences of obscene phone calls. In P.B. Bart & E.G. Moran (Eds.), *Violence against women: The bloody footprints* (pp. 73–83). Newbury Park, CA: Sage.

Sherman, L.W., & Berk, R.A. (1984). The specific deterrent effects of arrest for domestic assault. *American Sociological Review, 49*, 261–272.

Shields, W.M., & Shields, L.M. (1983). Forcible rape: An evolutionary perspective. *Ethology and Sociobiology, 4*, 115–136.

Shotland, R.L., & Hunter, B.A. (1995). Women's "token resistant" and compliant sexual behaviors are related to uncertain sexual intentions and rape. *Personality and Social Psychology Bulletin, 21*, 226–236.

Signorelli, N. (1990). Television's mean and dangerous world: A continuation of the cultural indicators perspective. In N. Signorelli & M. Morgan (Eds.), *Cultivation analysis: New directions of media effects research* (pp. 85–106). Newbury Park, CA: Sage.

Simons, Y., & Taylor, J. (1992). A psychosocial model of fan violence in sport. *International Journal of Sports Psychology, 23*, 207–226.

Singer, J.D. (1989). The political origins of international war: A multifactorial review. In J. Groebel & R.A. Hinde (Eds.), *Aggression and war: Their biological and social bases* (pp. 202–220). Cambridge, UK: Cambridge University Press.

Smith, D.M. (1998). The psychocultural roots of genocide: Legitimacy and crisis in Rwanda. *American Psychologist, 53*, 743–753.

Smith, M.D., & Brewer, V.E. (1995). Female status and the "gender gap" in U.S. homicide victimization. *Violence Against Women, 4*, 339–350.

Smith, M.D., & Zahn, M.A. (1999). *Homicide: A sourcebook of social research.* Thousand Oaks, CA: Sage.

Smith, P.K., Morita, Y., Junger-Tas, J., Olweus, D., Catalano, R., & Slee, P. (1999). *The nature of school bullying: A cross national perspective.* London: Routledge.

Smith, S.L., & Donnerstein, E. (1998). Harmful effects of exposure to media violence: Learning of aggression, emotional desensitization, and fear. In R.G. Geen & E. Donnerstein (Eds.), *Human aggression: Theories, research and implications for social policy* (pp. 168–202). San Diego, CA: Academic Press.

Sorenson, S.B., Stein, J.A., Siegel, J.M., Golding, J.M., & Burnam, M.A. (1987). The prevalence of adult sexual assault. *American Journal of Epidemiology, 126*, 1154–1164.

Spielberger, C.D., Jacobs, G., Russell, S.F., & Crane, R.G. (1983). Assessment of anger: The state-trait anger scale. In J.N. Butcher & C.D. Spielberger (Eds.), *Advances in personality assessment* (Vol. 2, pp. 159–187). Hillsdale, NJ: Lawrence Erlbaum Associates Inc.

Sprecher, S., Hatfield, E., Cortese, A.,

Potapova, E., & Levitskaya, A. (1994). Token resistance to sexual intercourse and consent to unwanted sexual intercourse: College students' dating experiences in three countries. *Journal of Sex Research, 31*, 125–132.

St. Lawrence, J.S., Crosby, R.A., Belcher, L., Yazdani, N., & Brasfield, T.L. (1999). Sexual risk reduction and anger management interventions for incarcerated male adolescents: A randomized controlled trial of two interventions. *Journal of Sex Education and Therapy, 24*, 9–17.

Staub, E. (1989). *The roots of evil: The origins of genocide and other group violence.* New York: Cambridge University Press.

Staub, E. (1997). Blind versus constructive patriotism: Moving from embeddedness in the group to critical loyalty and action. In D. Bar-Tal & E. Staub (Eds.), *Patriotism in the lives of individuals and nations* (pp. 213–228). Chicago, IL: Nelson-Hall.

Steinmetz, S.K. (1978). Battered parents. *Society, 15*, 54–55.

Stermac, L., Du Mont, J., & Dunn, S. (1998). Violence in known-assailant sexual assaults. *Journal of Interpersonal Violence, 13*, 398–412.

Stets, J.E., & Henderson, D. (1991). Contextual factors surrounding conflict resolution while dating: Results from a national study. *Family Relations, 40*, 29–36.

Straus, M.A. (1979). Measuring intrafamily conflict and violence: The Conflict Tactics Scales. *Journal of Marriage and the Family, 41*, 75–88.

Straus, M.A., & Gelles, R.J. (1990). *Physical violence in American families: Risk factors and adaptations to violence in 8,145 families.* Brunswick, NJ: Transaction.

Straus, M.A., Hamby, S.L., Boney-McCoy, S., & Sugarman, D.B. (1996). The revised Conflict Tactics Scales (CTS2). *Journal of Family Issues, 17*, 283–316.

Straus, M.A., Hamby, S.L., Finkelhor, D.,

Moore, D.W., & Runyan, D. (1998). Identification of child maltreatment with the parent–child conflict tactics scales: Development and psychometric data for a national sample of American parents. *Child Abuse and Neglect, 22,* 249–270.

Struckman-Johnson, C. (1988). Forced sex on dates: It happens to men, too. *Journal of Sex Research, 24,* 234–241.

Struckman-Johnson, C., & Struckman-Johnson, D. (1994). Men pressured and forced into sexual experience. *Archives of Sexual Behavior, 23,* 93–114.

Sugarman, D.B., & Hotaling, G.T. (1989). Dating violence: Prevalence, contents, and risk markers. In M.A. Pirog-Good & J.E. Stets (Eds.), *Violence in dating relationships* (pp. 3–32). New York: Praeger.

Sunday, S.R., & Tobach, E. (Eds.) (1985). *Violence against women: A critique of the sociobiology of rape.* New York: Gordian Press.

Swain, J. (1998). What does bullying really mean? *Educational Research, 40,* 358–364.

Tatara, T. (1993). Understanding the nature and scope of domestic elder abuse with the use of state aggregate data: Summaries of the key findings of a national survey of state APS and aging services. *Journal of Elder Abuse and Neglect, 5,* 35–57.

Taylor, S.P. (1967). Aggressive behavior and physiological arousal as a function of provocation and the tendency to inhibit aggression. *Journal of Personality and Social Psychology, 35,* 297–310.

Taylor, S.P., & Chermack, S.T. (1993). Alcohol, drugs and human physical aggression. *Journal of Studies on Alcohol, 11,* 78–88.

Taylor, S.P., Gammon, C.B., & Capasso, D.R. (1976). Aggression as a function of the interaction of alcohol and threat. *Journal of Personality and Social Psychology, 34,* 938–941.

Tedeschi, J.T., & Felson, R.B. (1994). *Violence, aggression, and coercive actions.* Washington, DC: American Psychological Association.

Temkin, J. (1999). Reporting rape in London: A qualitative study. *The Howard Journal, 38,* 17–41.

Testa, M., & Dermen, K.H. (1999). The differential correlates of sexual coercion and rape. *Journal of Interpersonal Violence, 14,* 548–561.

Thomas, M.H., Horton, R.W., Lippencott, E.C., & Drabman, R.S. (1977). Desensitization to portrayals of real-life aggression as a function of exposure to television violence. *Journal of Personality and Social Psychology, 35,* 450–458.

Thornhill, R., & Palmer, C.T. (2000). *The natural history of rape: Biological bases of sexual coercion.* Cambridge, MA: MIT Press.

Thornhill, R., & Thornhill, N.W. (1991). Coercive sexuality of men: Is there psychological adaptation to rape? In E. Grauerholz & M.A. Koralewski (Eds.), *Sexual coercion* (pp. 91–107). Lexington, MA: Lexington Books.

Toch, H. (1993). Good violence and bad violence: Self-presentations of aggressors through accounts and war stories. In R.B. Felson & J.T. Tedeschi (Eds.), *Aggression and violence: Social interactionist perspectives* (pp. 193–206). Washington, DC: American Psychological Association.

Turner, J.C., Hogg, M.A., Oakes, P.J., Reicher, S.J., & Wetherell, M.S. (1987). *Rediscovering the social group.* Oxford: Blackwell.

Tyler, K.A., Hoyt, D.R., & Whitbeck, L.B. (1998). Coercive sexual strategies. *Violence and Victims, 13,* 47–61.

Tyler, T.R. (1980). The impact of directly and indirectly experienced events: The origins of crime-related judgments and behaviors. *Journal of Personality and Social Psychology, 39,* 13–28.

Tyson, P.D. (1998). Physiological arousal, reactive aggression, and the induction of an incompatible relaxation response. *Aggression and Violent Behavior, 3,* 143–158.

Ullman, S.E., Karabatsos, G., & Koss, M.P. (1999). Alcohol and sexual assault in a national sample of college women. *Journal of Interpersonal Violence, 4,* 603–625.

Ullman, S.E., & Knight, R.A. (1992). Fighting back: Women's resistance to rape. *Journal of Interpersonal Violence, 7,* 31–43.

Uniform Crime Reports (1999). *Crime in the United States.* Washington, DC: US Government Printing Office. www.fbi.gov/ucr

US Department of Justice (2000). *Homicide trends in the U.S.* www.ojp.usdoj.gov/bjs.

Van Hasselt, V.B., Morrison, R.L., Bellack, A.S., & Hersen, M. (Eds.) (1988). *Handbook of family violence.* New York: Plenum Press.

Veltkamp, L.J., & Miller, T.W. (1994). *Clinical handbook of child abuse and neglect.* Madison, CT: International Universities Press.

Verlinden, S., Hersen, M., & Thomas, J. (2000). Risk factors in school shootings. *Clinical Psychology Review, 20,* 3–56.

Vicary, J.R., Klingaman, L.R., & Harkness, W.L. (1995). Risk factors associated with date rape and sexual assault of adolescent girls. *Journal of Adolescence, 18,* 289–306.

Vissing, Y.M., Straus, M.A., Gelles, R.J., & Harrop, J.W. (1991). Verbal aggression by parents and psychosocial problems of children. *Child Abuse and Neglect, 15,* 223–238.

Vrij, A., van der Steen, J., & Koppelaar, L. (1994). Aggression of police officers as a function of temperature: An experiment with the fire arms training system. *Journal of Community and Applied Social Psychology, 4,* 365–370.

Waldner-Haugrud, L.K., & Magruder, B. (1995). Male and female sexual victimization in dating relationships: Gender differences in coercion techniques and outcomes. *Violence and Victims, 10,* 203–215.

Walker, L. (1984). *The battered woman syndrome.* New York: Springer.

Wann, D.L., Carlson, J.D., Holland, L.C., Jacob, B.E., Owens, D.A., & Wells, D.D. (1999). Beliefs in symbolic catharsis: The importance of involvement with aggressive sports. *Social Behavior and Personality, 27,* 155–164.

Ward, C. (1995). *Attitudes toward rape.* London: Sage.

Watt, B.D., & Howells, K. (1999). Skills training for aggression control: Evaluation of an anger management programme for violent offenders. *Legal and Criminological Psychology, 4,* 285–300.

Wehby, J.H., & Symons, F.J. (1996). Revisiting conceptual issues in the measurement of aggressive behavior. *Behavioral Disorders, 22,* 29–35.

Weise, D., & Daro, D. (1995). *Current trends on child abuse reporting and fatalities: The results of the 1994 fifty state survey.* Chicago: National Committee to Prevent Child Abuse.

Welsh, S. (2000). The multidimensional nature of sexual harassment. *Violence Against Women, 6,* 118–141.

White, J.W., & Koss, M.P. (1991). Courtship violence: Incidence in a national sample of higher education students. *Violence and Victims, 6,* 247–256.

White, J.W., & Kowalski, R.M. (1994). Deconstructing the myth of the nonaggressive woman. *Psychology of Women Quarterly, 18,* 487–508.

White, J.W., & Kowalski, R.M. (1998). Male violence toward women: An integrated perspective. In R.G. Geen & E. Donnerstein (Eds.), *Human aggression: Theories, research and implications for social policy* (pp. 203–228). San Diego, CA: Academic Press.

Widom, C.S. (1989). Does violence beget violence? A critical examination of the literature. *Psychological Bulletin, 106,* 3–28.

Wiehe, V.R. (1998). *Understanding family violence.* Thousand Oaks, CA: Sage.

Wiehe, V.R., & Richards, A.L. (1995). *Intimate betrayal.* Thousand Oaks, CA: Sage.

Williams, J.E. (1984). Secondary victimization: Confronting public attitudes. *Victimology, 9,* 66–81.

Wilson, B.J., Linz, D., Donnerstein, E., & Stipp, H. (1992). The impact of social issue television programming on attitudes toward rape. *Human Communication Research, 19,* 179–208.

Wilson, M., & Daly, M. (1985). Competitiveness, risk taking and violence: The young male syndrome. *Ethology and Sociobiology, 6,* 59–73.

Wolf, R. (1997). Elder abuse and neglect: Causes and consequences. *Journal of Geriatric Psychiatry, 30,* 153–174.

Wolfe, D.A. (1999). *Child abuse* (2nd ed.). Thousand Oaks, CA: Sage.

Wood, W., Wong, F.Y. & Chachere, J.G. (1991). Effects of media violence on viewers' aggression in unconstrained social interaction. *Psychological Bulletin, 109,* 371–383.

Wyatt, G.E., Guthrie, D., & Notgrass, C.M. (1992). Differential effects of women's child sexual abuse and subsequent sexual revictimization. *Journal of Consulting and Clinical Psychology, 60,* 167–173.

Wyatt, G.E., Newcomb, M.D., & Riederle, M.H. (1993). *Sexual abuse and consensual sex.* Newbury Park, CA: Sage.

Yeater, E.A., & O'Donohue, W. (1999). Sexual assault prevention programs. *Clinical Psychology Review, 19,* 739–771.

Younger, J.C., & Doob, A.N. (1978). Attribution and aggression: The misattribution of anger. *Journal of Research in Personality, 12,* 164–171.

Yudofsky, S.C., Silver, J.M., & Hales, R.E. (1993). Cocaine and aggressive behavior: Neurobiological and clinical perspectives. *Bulletin of the Menninger Clinic, 57,* 218–226.

Zani, B., & Kirchler, E. (1991). When violence overshadows the spirit of sporting competition: Italian football fans and their clubs. *Journal of Community and Applied Social Psychology, 1,* 5–21.

Zillmann, D. (1979). *Hostility and aggression.* Hillsdale, NJ: Lawrence Erlbaum Associates Inc.

Zillmann, D. (1994). Cognition–excitation dependencies in the escalation of anger and angry aggression. In M. Potegal & J.F. Knutson (Eds.), *The dynamics of aggression* (pp. 45–71). Hillsdale, NJ: Lawrence Erlbaum Associates Inc.

Zillmann, D. (1998). *Connections between sexuality and aggression* (2nd ed.). Mahwah, NJ: Lawrence Erlbaum Associates Inc.

Zillmann, D., Baron, R.A., & Tamborini, R. (1981). Social costs of smoking: Effects of tobacco smoke on hostile behavior. *Journal of Applied Social Psychology, 11,* 548–561.

Zimbardo, P.G. (1969). The human choice: Individuation, reason, and order versus deindividuation, impulse, and chaos. In W.J. Arnold & D. Levine (Eds.), *Nebraska symposium on motivation* (Vol. 17, pp. 273–307). Lincoln, NB: University of Nebraska Press.

Zoucha-Jensen, J.M., & Coyne, A. (1993). The effects of resistance strategies on rape. *American Journal of Public Health, 11,* 1633–1634.

Zumkley, H. (1994). The stability of aggressive behavior: A meta-analysis. *German Journal of Psychology, 18,* 273–281.

Zuravin, S., McMillen, C., DePanfilis, D., & Risley-Curtiss, C. (1996). The intergenerational cycle of child maltreatment: Continuity versus discontinuity. *Journal of Interpersonal Violence, 11,* 315–334.

Author Index

Subject Index